333 AWESOME SMALL COLLEGES
(that just might save you money!)
V. Peter Pitts, M.A.

This book has been a labor of love for all the dedicated faculty and staff who work for small private colleges. These individuals devote their lives to helping students become the best possible versions of themselves—a special thanks to the individuals who submitted essays for publication in this book.

Cover photo was provided by Monmouth College
Cover design was done by Connor Hopkins, Luther College

ACKNOWLEDGEMENTS

SO many people to thank!!!

The entire first half of this book was written by students and staff at the thirty-one colleges that are featured. It was a collaborative effort for sure! You will notice that there are distinctly different writing styles and structures, and this was intentional. I wanted the reader to get a feel for the flavor of each institution.

My thanks go out to:

Albion College: Mandy Dubiel, Vice President for Enrollment

Husson University: Eric Gordon, Executive Director of Communications; Dr. Lynne Coy-Ogan, Senior Vice President for Academic Affairs and Provost

University of La Verne: Adam Wu, Director of Undergraduate Admission; Kate Kealey, Enrollment Communications Manager

Misericordia University: Steve Secora, Director of Admissions; Samuel Jarvis, Director of Enrollment Marketing

Loyola University New Orleans: Holly Cassard, Director of Enrollment Operations; Meghan Cooley, Freelance Writer

Northland College: Alexander Patterson, Director of Admissions; Joe Cooper, Dean of Students

Saint Norbert College: Maira Rodriguez, Associate Director of Admissions; John Watters, Creative Director

Carthage College: Ashley Hanson, Vice President for Enrollment

Central College: Erin Kamp, Content Specialist — Editorial - Central College Communications Office; Sunny Eighmy, Vice President for Advancement; Chevy Freiburger, Vice President for

Enrollment Management and Dean of Admission; Steffanie Bonnstetter, Director of Communications and Marketing; Brittany Prokupek, Content Strategist — Editorial; Jeanette Budding, Content Specialist — Editorial

Hastings College: Chris Schukei - Dean of Admissions; Mike Howie - Director of Marketing; Kristin Charles - Associate Vice President of Analytic Support and Institutional Effectiveness

Gwynedd Mercy University: Lauren Yancer, Marketing & Public Relations Manager; Kelly Statmore, MEd, Vice President for Marketing and Enrollment Management; Aimee Huffstetler, MA, Assistant Vice President for Enrollment; Kirsten Swanson, MBA, Director of Marketing Communications and Social Media; Alexis Alford, B.S., Multicultural Admissions Counselor

Susquehanna University: Anna Miller, Director of Admission Communication; Aaron Martin Vice President for Marketing & Communications; DJ Menifee, Vice President for Enrollment; Jennifer Spotts, Director of Strategic Communications

Luther College: Connor Hopkins, Admissions Counselor (who not only helped with the essays about Luther, but who designed the front and back covers of this book); Matthew Beatty, Director of Admissions; Jon Lund, Director of International Admissions

Lycoming College: Mike Konopski, Senior Advisor for Enrollment Management; Lynn Zitta, Associate Director for Enrollment Marketing

Maryville College: Kelly Massenzo, Director of Undergraduate Admissions and Events; Steve Wildsmith, Assistant Director, Marketing & Communications; Karen Eldridge, Executive Director, Marketing & Communications

Holy Family University: Lauren Campbell, Director, Undergraduate Admissions; Christopher McKittrick, Marketing and Communications Director; Brittany Ballack, Admissions Counselor; Katherine Darmohray, Admissions Counselor; Sherrie Madia, Vice

President for Marketing and Communications; Edward Wright, Vice President for Enrollment Management

Edgewood College: Mara M. Springborn, Marketing Content Writer

Alverno College: Jean O'Toole, Director of Marketing and Communications; Kelly Cole, Asst. Director Marketing & Communications; Katie Kipp, Asst. Director of Admissions Graduate, Adult and Transfer; Kate Lundeen, VP for Enrollment and Marketing

Blackburn College: Kyle Lowden, Director of Marketing and Public Relations; Justin Norwood, Vice President for Inclusive Enrollment; Becky Bishop, Marketing & Public Relations Manager

Webster University: Andrew Laue, Associate Director of Undergraduate Admissions

Sweet Briar College: Claire Griffith, Senior Director of Alumnae Relations and Development

Saint Mary's University-Minnesota: Dr. Timothy Gossen, Senior Director of Admission; Ms. Nicole (Niki) Peterson, M.S., Dean of Students; Ms. Deb Nahrgang, Senior Director, Communications

Monmouth College: Stephanie Levenson, Vice President for Enrollment Management; Barry McNamara, Associate Director and Writer, Office of Communications and Marketing

Moravian University: Michael Corr, Assistant Vice President for Marketing and Communications

Springfield College: Nikki Levine, Director of Undergraduate Admissions; Christine Moauro, Associate Vice President for Marketing; Judith Kelliher, Integrated Content Writer

Mount Mercy University: J. Todd Coleman, Vice President for Enrollment & Marketing; Jamie Jones, Director of Communications and Marketing; Lauren Imhoff, '22, Recent graduate; Tiara Munoz, '23, Recent graduate

Midway University: Ellen Gregory, Vice President, Marketing & Communications

Catawba College: Jodi Bailey, Director of Marketing and Communications

Wartburg College: Tara Winter, Executive Director of Admissions; Emily Christensen,
Chief Communications Officer and Assistant Director of Marketing and Communication; Chris Knudson, Chief Marketing Officer and Director of Marketing & Communication

Florida Southern University: John Grundig, Vice President of Enrollment Management; Cassie Paizis, Assistant Vice President of Marketing

Elmhurst University: Maggie Turkovich, Data Analyst and Integration Specialist; Christine Grenier, Vice President of Admission

A special thanks to my friend Cynthia who helped with the editing and proofreading.

TABLE OF CONTENTS

Section One: Featured Colleges

SECTION ONE:
FEATURED COLLEGES

INTRODUCTION

"What makes your college special?"
"How do you make your college affordable?"
Representatives of 31 colleges answer these questions in the first section of this book.

The second section of the book is an annotated list of 333 very affordable small colleges (including the featured 31), along with some helpful lists and indexes.

I want this book to be used. After you read the paperback version, put it on your shelf next to other college reference books. Use it when developing your list of potential colleges. Go back to it often. There are some cool and unique programs at small colleges throughout the United States. If you see a college in this book that piques your interest, do a little more research and schedule a visit. It could change your life! If you are using the e-book version, you will be able to search for items, including majors that interest you, and you can click links to college websites.

All of the colleges in this book are very small (less than 3,500 undergraduate students). I chose this demographic due to the degree to which life change is inevitable and dramatic, simply due to the size of the college. It is a matter of sociometry and probability. Imagine a college with only 800 students. What is the probability of a student becoming president of the student body? Now imagine a college of 35,000 students. What is the probability of this student becoming the president of the student body? We can apply this comparison to any area (academic or extracurricular). What are the odds of a non-theatre major getting the "lead" in a play during the first year? What are the odds of being able to play a sport, be in a theatre production, or sing in the choir? What are a student's chances of being a "starter" in more than one sport, the first chair in the orchestra, and a class officer all in a student's first two years of college? What are the odds of getting a full tuition or a performing arts scholarship when competing with a dozen students instead of a hundred students? It's just math—and common sense.

Imagine an introductory psychology class. At a college of 800 students, there might be 20 to 30 students in the class. At a college of 35,000 students, 40 to 200 students might be in the class. Responding to a professor's questions, asking questions, and getting extra help—all have a higher probability of occurring at a smaller college. Classroom participation is not only possible; it is pretty much expected.

In most cases, classes at small colleges are taught by full professors instead of teaching assistants. Professors are not hired for their research and publishing potential; they are hired based on their passion for teaching students. Change at a small college is both inevitable and unavoidable. You cannot just sit in the back of the class and never talk. If you are quiet and shy going in as a first-year student, you will not be that way upon graduation. Skipping class is not only a bad idea but also potentially embarrassing (I know a professor who would take his entire class to a "repeat offender's" room to hold class). If a student has the ability to be an "A" student but is cruising through getting "Bs," professors will pull the student aside and have a one-on-one intense conversation that can, in itself, change a student's life. Many colleges in this book give a "C+" student a chance to become an "A" student. "A+" students from high school are given extra opportunities all four years of college for research, writing, and giving presentations. It is virtually impossible at a small college to go through college passively (just going to class, taking tests, and hanging out with friends).

So yes, all colleges change lives, but not all colleges change lives dynamically due to their size. Students, faculty, administration, staff, maintenance workers, cafeteria workers, and others on campus genuinely know and care for these students. There is a real "family" atmosphere in these colleges. Of course, as several people have brought to my attention, it is possible for a student at a very large university to have a "small college-type" education, but it takes special effort:

- If you have your choice of large universities (universities are made up of several colleges), consider a large university with a smaller college in your area of study.
- Go to class (every class). Don't just buy notes from students who did attend the class.
- Sit in the front of the classroom.
- Ask questions from the professor or teaching assistant (T.A.) in and out of class.
- Answer questions in class when posed by the professor or T.A.
- Talk, from time to time, with your professor or T.A. before and after class.
- Make it a goal to find and befriend some Ph.D. faculty mentors.
- Talk with your advisor early in your four years about internships and study abroad opportunities.
- Apply for, accept, and excel at internships.
- Do study abroad, even if only for a short-term trip.
- Join at least three clubs or organizations and work hard to attain leadership positions in at least one of those organizations.
- Go to orientation.
- Read all announcements. Check your emails every day.
- If you go to a university with many other students from your high school, do not room with (or near) any of them. Intentionally room and make friends with students not from your

high school, your state, your ethnicity, or your country. Make sure you have a diverse group of friends.

- Don't just sit in your room by yourself (especially on weekends). Get out and do things and make new friends.
- Get tutoring, even to boost your grade from B+ to an A, and then become a tutor when the opportunity presents itself.
- Join a study group.
- Get to know the professionals in the career planning and placement office early in your years in college (don't wait until your senior year).
- Take lots of classes that involve doing research and writing.
- Even if not required, insist on taking a speech class and a writing class, and make sure that some of your other courses involve lots of writing and speaking in class.
- Get a campus job that helps you get more involved with campus and interact with various people.
- Get to know your resident assistant on your residence hall floor, and then consider becoming an R.A. yourself when you are an upperclassman.
- Keep informed (your campus newspaper, radio, and TV will make announcements).
- Attend campus events (athletic, music, theatre, other).

These are all things that pretty much either happen, are strongly encouraged, or even required at small colleges. These are all things that will help you develop the soft skills that employers love and will give you a strong resume upon graduation. It is no accident that virtually all of the colleges in this book have more than a 95 percent placement rate within six months after graduation. Employers love to hire students who "check the most boxes" in terms of soft skills:

- Communication
- Teamwork
- Adaptability/Flexibility

- ❖ Leadership
- ❖ Organization
- ❖ Problem-solving
- ❖ Interpersonal/Social Skills (getting along with people)
- ❖ Work Ethic
- ❖ Time Management
- ❖ Critical Thinking
- ❖ Decision-making
- ❖ Stress-management
- ❖ Conflict management/resolution
- ❖ Creativity
- ❖ Positive argumentation (agreeing to disagree politely)
- ❖ Resourcefulness
- ❖ Ability to persuade
- ❖ Openness to criticism
- ❖ Ability to negotiate
- ❖ Innovation (thinking outside the box)
- ❖ Self-confidence
- ❖ Positive attitude
- ❖ Pleasant personality/friendliness
- ❖ Accountability
- ❖ Punctuality
- ❖ Ability to take initiative
- ❖ Empathy/emotional intelligence and awareness
- ❖ Tact
- ❖ Self-motivation
- ❖ Cultural fitness
- ❖ Ability to network
- ❖ Self-management
- ❖ Critical observation

These are critical skills to have in the world of work and in your day-to-day life with your significant other and your friends. A little tact and a positive attitude go a long way!

Let's hear from some of the students from colleges in this book. We asked these questions: "How has your college experience changed you?" and "What do you like most about your experiences at a small college?"

"Attending a small college rather than a university allowed me more opportunities than I could have ever imagined. First and foremost, the class sizes are much smaller which allowed me to have a better relationship with my peers and professors. You have a name, not a number, and you are part of a family, not a class. As a science major, I was in the lab using all types of laboratory equipment my very first semester. A lot of my science labs were more individualized and research based rather than following a standard protocol. In addition to my science degree, I was able to be a part of the education certification program. I was out observing in a high school my first year. I was also able to have a minor in psychology, be a tour guide, an orientation leader, and a chemistry teaching assistant, and have an internship that combined both my love for science and passion for teaching all in one. Attending a small school during the pandemic allowed me to continue to receive the education I deserved with very little online instruction, unlike some neighboring larger schools that remained remote or hybrid. Small schools have large opportunities!" —Breana McNamara, Lycoming College, Class of 2023

"College has changed my life by teaching me how to be a servant leader and allowing me to immerse myself in service. College has allowed me to meet people that have changed my life forever while being able to get the degree to advance my career for the better." —Riley Hall, Saint Mary's University of Minnesota, Class of 2024

"Albion has a way of involving students with so many amazing people that it becomes more than just going to class. It becomes a total experience. Creating a legacy is super hard to do alone, but creating a circle of friends or a community with amazing individuals who back you and support you makes it easier to leave a mark." —Anthony Neal, Albion College, Class of 2023

"Attending college has completely altered the way I look at the world. As a college athlete, student employee, and a social person on campus I found that college is where I truly belong and I know that I will remember these four years for the rest of my life." —Julia, University of La Verne, Class of 2026

"If you really want to learn something — and be able to apply what you learn to the world, this is the place for you. Nels Christensen [a well-known and popular English professor] has to be experienced. There are cool people here who teach you things. And if you want to change things, a small college is the right place to do that. This is the place to have a meaningful impact now and to learn how to have one in the future." — Liam Rappleye, Albion College, Class of 2025

"College has changed my life by giving me the space and opportunity to grow in ways that I never felt would be possible. I have met new people, joined clubs, and had new service opportunities, all while pursuing a degree that I am passionate about." —Katie Pierpont, Saint Mary's University of Minnesota, Class of 2023

"I love how small and tight-knit the community is, and I really love the

personal relationships that are made here. My professors are kind, funny, and willing to help no matter the situation. Carthage is more than just a school—it's a family. As team captain for our varsity League of Legends B Esports team, not only do I get to play a game that I love, but I also get to play with some of my closest friends—all while studying to become a pharmacist!"—Nadia Musaitef, Carthage College, Class of 2023

"Classes here are discussion-based. I learn so much when we all contribute to the learning by sharing our thoughts and theories. I love the debate and the education we provide each other. At Albion, we bring out the best in each other every day." —Jessica Harvey, Albion College, Class of 2026

"With the scholarships and grants offered by ULV, I have been able to experience a dynamic, hands-on education that has prepared me for my future. Through opportunities both in and outside the classroom, I have been able to thrive academically, socially, and professionally, while also developing the skills to continue to do so after I graduate."
—Mackay Morgan Armstrong, University of La Verne, Class of 2023

"College has changed my life by allowing me to engage in every interest I wanted to invest my time into. Whether it was sports, student government, student work, clubs, or religious activities, I have been able to investigate my individual interests better." —Sophia O'Neil Saint Mary's University of Minnesota, Class of 2023

"Carthage faculty helped me find my passions. I changed my major from

biology to communication my junior year and was still able to graduate in four years. The two internships I had taught me about cameras, deadlines, client communication, and more. I'm in Carthage Philharmonic and love being around people who enjoy music and have fun while making it. I'm also on the track and field team—they're my second family" —Edelmar Morales-Rivera, Carthage College, Class of 2023

"I toured multiple colleges that 'checked the boxes' – but I fell in love with Edgewood College and the city of Madison because it provides the best of both worlds – a small tight-knit campus where I excelled in sports and academics while living in a big city filled with opportunities." —Rachel Ehrhart, Edgewood College, Class of 2023

"At Albion, people really care about students. Professors aren't here to cash a check and move on to research. I like knowing my professors and that they know me by name. My buddies were here from another school, and we walked into a local restaurant. One of my professors was there and called me out by name. My buddies could not believe one of my professors knew me by name." —Teddy Hirschfield, Albion College, Class of 2024

"While most other schools are known for either their music or STEM programs, Carthage has great programs for both. I've found a way to follow my passion for music and engineering. My acting class has been awesome.

We all lift each other up, really making it feel like I'm working alongside everyone else—not competing against everyone. And the engineering program has already proven to be rewarding, offering clubs like the Microgravity Team that really push you to be the best you can be." —Trevor Milne, Carthage College, Class of 2026

The title of this book also contains the words "save you money." As this book is being written (2023), the most expensive colleges in the U.S. are (for tuition, housing, food, and fees) running about $84,000. The average cost for colleges in this book (sticker price, without any aid) is approximately $53,000 (ranging from $32K to $72K). However, these colleges give generous amounts of merit aid (merit aid is gift assistance, not based on family income, that never has to be paid back), so the average out-of-pocket cost (without having to take out loans) is approximately $30,000 (ranging from $10K to 35K). Some families pay a lot less, and some pay a little more, depending on family finances and academic records. Most of these colleges award scholarships to the majority, or, in some cases, all incoming freshmen, often with their admission letters. All in all, families have found that the colleges in this book have done a great job of making college more affordable. These colleges are also small enough to truly listen to and respond with empathy to a family's special or unusual family circumstances that affect their ability to pay.

In the United States, there are hundreds of small private colleges very much like the colleges in this book. They each have their distinctive flavor and offerings. My hope, as I compiled information for this book, is that I have at least piqued your interest in small colleges and that students and their parents will open their eyes to colleges that were not originally on their radar. There is no need to "follow the herd" to the most popular and populous colleges. Students should at least check out small private residential colleges. These colleges are just too good to ignore!

A few notes about the structure of this book:

In the first section of the book, chapters were written by representatives of the colleges themselves (usually by their marketing/communications and/or admissions professionals). These were assigned randomly. There is no ranking system of any kind.

In addition to the essays, you will find a list of majors, minors, and programs at their college, plus some basic statistics and contact information.

The last section of the book is a listing of 333 small private colleges that also do a great job of keeping costs at a reasonable level for families. For each college, there is a "What Caught My Eye" section gleaned from various small college websites. I am a self-proclaimed "small college website surfer." I love to read through websites for all small colleges in the U.S. looking for unique offerings and to get a feel for what makes them special. So in preparing to write this book, when I came across something unique, interesting, exceptional, or remarkable, I took notes and added these notes to the list. I also have researched colleges that offer full-tuition scholarships and/or talent/performing arts scholarships regardless of major, so I have noted this for each college. There are also helpful indexes and lists. I hope the reader finds these nuggets to be helpful as they search for their collegiate home. *Note: Information on websites sometimes changes, so I would encourage you to check with the colleges themselves to make sure the information is current. The information printed in this book was gathered in mid-2023.*

ONE: **ALBION COLLEGE**

College Name: Albion College
City, State: Albion, Michigan
Website: https://www.albion.edu
Admissions email address: admission@albion.edu
Admissions phone: 800-858-6770
Full-time undergraduate enrollment: 1,444
Number of full-time undergraduate students living on campus: 1,300
Average class size: 18
Student-faculty ratio: 12:1

Submitted by Mandy Dubiel, Vice President for Enrollment

Albion College, a small private liberal arts school that delivers big on its promises.

Victoria Fuller, a junior from Madison Heights, Michigan, went to Bishop Foley Catholic High School before deciding to study Kinesiology at Albion College. "Bigger schools actually scared me," Fuller said. "I went to a small high school and wanted the same type of experience for college. I found it at Albion. Everyone here cared and was so personable."

Fuller is a part of the Lisa and James Wilson Institute for Medicine, the president of her sorority, a First-Year Experience Mentor, a greeter at the Ludington Center, and a tour guide for Admission. She loves Albion and all the experiences she has had during her time on campus.

Like Victoria, you are going to love Albion College. Everyone does. Because here, you will join students from around the world on a historic and picturesque campus, encouraged to explore, experience, and evolve as Britons. Together, you will join a dynamic campus community that deeply values student-faculty interaction in undergraduate research and learning. Superior applied academic programs, strong campus leadership opportunities, and experiential learning opportunities define the Albion experience.

Jessica Harvey, a first-year student from Hamilton, Michigan, came to Albion with a goal in mind. And each day, she comes closer to achieving it through her educational path, her co-curricular activities with the Wilson Institute and her social activities that keep her busy with her large friend group. "Albion was the best choice I could have made. I would make it again and again. The education I am pursuing here and the way it is delivered — through small class sizes with professors who care about me and who want me to succeed holistically is something I believe I could not get anywhere else."

Our beautiful campus in southwest Michigan hums with life throughout the year, particularly while classes are in session. With 19 varsity athletic teams, more than 100 vibrant student organizations, and boundless opportunities to grow, stretch and learn, you will augment your education with many ways to develop the soft skills necessary to succeed today. And our campus is committed to celebrating the diversity of people, cultures, and ideas that make college a life-changing experience for our students.

With these values as our foundation, Albion is a college on the move, a college with a story to tell, and a college with life-changing opportunities to offer students like you. If you will bring Albion College your talents, ideas, passions, and, most of all, your commitment to working hard, we will offer you a future-proof education.

Especially through our five centers and institutes — made up of a closely knit group of highly motivated students, faculty, and staff — we provide you with an opportunity to examine your interests in a hands-on learning environment while giving you the skills, experience, and knowledge you need to do anything, go anywhere and be successful. Even to outer space with astronaut alumnus Josh Cassada, '95.

Cassada, our first Albion college graduate in space, is preparing to explore where no Brit has gone before. The former physics major, now NASA astronaut, was the pilot of the DragonX Crew-5, who recently spent 157 days aboard the International Space Station. While at Albion studying Physics, Josh made the most of the opportunities offered as part of his liberal arts education and built a solid foundation from which to launch and land among the stars.

Whether your focus is business, public policy, racial equality, medicine, or the environment, the institutes and centers give you a way to accelerate your future. Each institute and center welcomes students regardless of degree path. Gain access to assistance with career exploration, graduate school admission, and the advantage of a lifelong alumni network.

Liam Rappleye, a sophomore majoring in English with a professional writing emphasis from Grand Haven, Michigan, has certainly arrived on campus. Within six weeks of taking a staff writer position on the Pleiad, the Albion College student newspaper, he was offered a summer internship at Detroit Free Press, one of two flagship newspapers in the city of Detroit. He was named editor-in-chief of the Pleiad for the 2022-23 academic year.

"If you really want to learn something — and be able to apply what you learn to the world, this is the place for you. Nels Christensen [a well-known and popular English professor] has to be experienced. There are cool people here who teach you things."

Your education is not the prescribed, prepacked, predestined, run-of-the-mill education that follows a path, with these five classes this semester and those five classes that semester — ad infinitum. At Albion College, we'll help you deconstruct the liberal arts education so you can create the education you need to be future-proof. Here, you can be a music major who is also in the Wilson Institute for Medicine, President of the Student Senate, the starting pitcher for softball, a student advocate in the Anna Howard Shaw Center for Gender Equity, and a volunteer in the observatory. You can be any combination of parts of the liberal arts. Deconstruct our programs and construct your future.

Victoria did: "Coming into college, you have one path you think you should follow. At Albion, I started down that path but discovered quickly I was meant for another. By not following the first path, I have become such a better person and much more fulfilled."

At Albion College, you will get a solid education in the classroom from faculty who want you to learn and grow. It will be enhanced by study abroad trips to England, Vienna, and more, as well as internships at Fortune 500 companies, the 25,000-acre farm down the road, or the physician's office right across the street. You will learn in the classroom today what you will be able to use for a lifetime of tomorrows. And you will be supported and guided by staff who are invested in you, your future, and your personal goals and outcomes. Alumni will spend time with you along the way and after you graduate, helping you understand the value of your Albion degree long after you leave the Quad behind.

We invite you to visit and experience Albion for yourself. You will see what Victoria, Liam, Jessica, and Josh mean when they say there is no other place for an undergraduate degree. We'll be waiting.

Albion College invests in your academic future

Our mission is to assist students and their families in planning for and meeting their educational expenses at Albion College while supporting the College's recruitment and retention goals. We strive to provide exceptional service while ensuring that financial aid dollars are administered with the highest level of fiduciary responsibility.

Last year, we provided support to 100 percent of Albion College students.

When you apply to Albion College, we'll want to hear all about your strengths and accomplishments. Then we'll determine what types of aid you may be eligible for at Albion. That may include academic and talent-based scholarships, grants, low-interest loans, and campus work opportunities. Working together, our financial services team will help you build the most robust financial aid package possible. We will help you and your family find the resources to make an Albion education possible. And we'll help create a complex process and translate it into terms that make sense to you.

With your financial aid offer, you'll receive a guide to help you understand your offer from Albion, provide you with the starting point to developing your own personal Albion Financing Plan, and navigate you through the first steps in paying your bill. And, of course, we are always in the office, at the other end of the phone, chat, or messaging service to help.

When you apply to Albion College, you become family. Our investment in you is much more than financial; it is about your success academically, socially, spiritually, and as a human being. We care about you — the whole you.

Academic Programs

Accounting, major and minor
Actuarial Science, program
Anthropology, major and minor
Anthropology/Sociology, major and minor
Applied Mathematics, minor
Area Studies, minor
Art History, major and minor
Biochemistry, major and minor
Biology, major and minor
Business, major
Cell And Molecular Biology, minor
Chemistry, major and minor
Communication Studies, major and minor
Computer Science, major and minor
Data Analytics, minor
Earth Science, major

Economics and Management, major and minor
Economics, major and minor
Education, Elementary and Secondary/K-12, concentration
Educational Studies, minor
Engineering Dual-Degree program
English, major and minor
Environmental Biology, minor
Environmental Geology, minor
Environmental Science, concentration
Environmental Science, major
Environmental Studies, concentration
Environmental Studies, major
Ethnic Studies, major and minor
Exercise Science, major and minor
Finance, major and minor
French Language and Culture for the Professions, major and minor
French, major and minor
Gender Studies, minor
Geographic Information Systems, minor
Geology, major and minor
German Language and Culture for the Professions, major and minor
German, major and minor
Health Communication, minor
History, major and minor
Human Services, concentration
Individually Designed, major
Integrated Marketing Communication, major
International Studies, major
Law, Justice and Society, concentration
Marketing Management, major and minor
Mathematics, major and minor
Mathematics/Economics, interdepartmental major
Mathematics/Physics, interdepartmental major
Music, major
Neuroscience, concentration
Paleontology, minor
Philosophy, major and minor
Physics, major and minor
Political Science, major and minor
Post-Bacc Certificate in Premedical Studies
Predental, program
Prehealth, program

Prelaw, program
Premedical, program
Prenursing, program
Prephysical Therapy, program
Preveterinary Medicine program
Psychological Science, major and minor
Public Health, concentration
Public Policy and Service, Concentration
Public Policy, major
Religious Studies, major and minor
Sexuality Studies, minor
Sociology, major and minor
Spanish Language and Culture for the professions, major and minor
Spanish: Latin American and Latino/A Studies, major and minor
Spanish, major and minor
Sport Communication, major and minor
Statistics, minor
Studio Art, major and minor or Teaching English as a Second Language, minor
Theatre, major and minor
Transnational Studies, minor
Value Theory, minor
Women's Studies, minor
Women's, Gender and Sexuality Studies, major

TWO: HUSSON UNIVERSITY

College Name: Husson University
City, State: Bangor, ME
Website: https://www.husson.edu/
Admissions email address: admit@husson.edu
Admissions phone: 207.941.7000
Full-time undergraduate enrollment: 2,264
Number of full-time undergraduate students living on campus:
1,100-1,200
Average class size: 18
Student-faculty ratio: 16:1

Submitted by Eric Gordon, Executive Director of Communications, Husson
University

For nearly 125 years, Husson University has prepared future leaders
to handle the challenges of tomorrow through its innovative
undergraduate and graduate degrees. Central to our mission, Husson
has a longstanding commitment to providing affordable classroom,
online, and experiential learning opportunities, ensuring that higher
education is accessible to anyone, regardless of their financial
situation. Last year, the University provided students with
approximately $19 million in institutionally funded grants and
scholarships to help keep college affordable. More than 98% of
Husson students qualify to receive federal, state, community, and/or
campus-based financial aid and scholarships.

Indeed, Husson is nationally recognized for its superior value.
According to an analysis of tuition and fees by U.S. News & World
Report, Husson University is one of the most affordable private
colleges in New England.

It's no surprise, then, that Husson is Maine's leading center of business education. Four in every ten Husson students attend the College of Business, making it the largest in the state. In addition, more students choose to get their MBA from Husson University than any other college or university in Maine.

Husson University also has a strong commitment to education in healthcare-related careers. Approximately a third of Husson University students are pursuing a degree related to healthcare. Incoming students are pursuing degrees in physical therapy, exercise science, occupational therapy, nursing, pre-medicine, and pharmacy. Students are also majoring in biology, psychology, and clinical mental health counseling.

Over the past decade, Husson University has demonstrated a history of growth and success. During the past 10 years, Husson students have earned approximately 10,000 degrees and certificates. The University's graduation rate increased from a rate consistent with the national average to one that's 17% above that average. U.S. News & World Report research also shows that our graduation rate is five points higher than our profile would predict.

Students who attend Husson University like the educational experience they're receiving. Our first-year to second-year retention rate is almost 80%.

Part of the reason students prefer Husson is our faculty. Our faculty aren't just highly educated individuals with significant amounts of academic knowledge, they're also professors who have hands-on experience in the subjects they teach. At Husson, students learn from faculty who are willing to share their real-world experiences and insights with students. That helps ensure students are work ready on day one.

In addition to faculty support for our students, our campus facilities keep growing and modernizing. Husson works to provide students with educational facilities that prepare them to meet the needs of today's employers.

For example, we opened Harold Alfond Hall, a new $17 million home for our College of Business, in 2021. One year later, Husson University "cut the ribbon" on seven new science labs. Three years earlier we opened a new $3-4 million Wellness Learning Center with new facilities designed to enhance students' physical and mental health. The Marshall Road Research and Education Center opened in 2018. In addition to containing advanced research facilities for our School of Pharmacy, this facility contains advanced hands-on learning facilities for students in our physical therapy, nursing, and counseling and therapy programs.

Besides enhancing our academic learning spaces, Husson University has also upgraded our residence hall living facilities. Three new townhouse residence halls were opened in 2017 and three of the existing residence halls were completely refurbished with new rooms, bathrooms, plumbing, electricity, and internet connectivity over three years from 2017-2019.

All of this provides Husson University students with an unparalleled college experience that leads to professional success. According to a survey of recent graduates, 96% of Husson University students are employed or in graduate school within one year of graduation. More than 90% of graduates from the College of Business's hospitality, sport, and tourism management programs are employed within that time frame. Similarly, 95% of the university's occupational therapy and 100% of the nursing and physical therapy students are employed within a year of graduating. Many of these students receive full-time job offers before graduation.

This has not gone unnoticed. U.S. News & World Report has named Husson University as one of its 100 "Top Performers on Social Mobility." The colleges and universities in this elite ranking have been recognized for their service to economically disadvantaged students who are less likely than others to finish college. Husson University is more successful than other colleges and universities at advancing social mobility by enrolling and graduating large proportions of disadvantaged students who received Pell Grants. The vast majority of these federal grants are awarded to students whose adjusted gross family incomes are under $50,000.

Finally, Husson University offers students the opportunity to enjoy the perfect mix of academics and everything Maine has to offer. Students can explore Maine's pristine lakes by kayak or canoe or take a day to enjoy whitewater rafting, skiing, or snowboarding easily within reach at the nearby Sugarloaf and Sunday River ski resorts. During the fall and spring, students can hike to the summit of Mount Katahdin, the trailhead for the Appalachian Trail for hikers heading south. Acadia National Park in Bar Harbor Maine and Cadillac Mountain are both just an hour from campus.

For those who like a more urban experience, Bangor, Maine offers area residents the opportunity to enjoy local restaurants, art museums and galleries, ballets, performances by the local symphony orchestra, and nationally recognized, big-name musical acts along the Bangor Waterfront, and in the arena of the Cross Insurance Center.

In short, Husson University offers a superb education, at an affordable price, in one of the most beautiful states in New England. To find out more about Husson University, our programs and why we appeal to so many students, visit http://www.Husson.edu

How does Husson University make college affordable and a great choice financially?

Let me tell you a true story about how Husson University uses financial aid to transform student lives.

Carla Rodriguez, Class of '23, is a double major in health sciences/pre-med and psychology. When she was in high school her mom kicked her out of the house and her dad left the country to take care of her grandfather. Left alone to fend for herself, she had a part-time job and would pay as much of the rent as she could. One day, she came home from school to find an eviction notice on the front door of her apartment for not paying the rent. The money she paid the landlord from her part-time job was the only money he ever received. Her dad or mom didn't do anything to support her. She was officially homeless.

Carla was lucky. After couch-surfing for a time, the mom of one of her friends took her in. This surrogate mother taught Carla how to apply for colleges and apply for financial aid. Carla literally had nothing to her name when she applied to college, but went forward thinking she could work her way through school and somehow find the money to earn a degree.

When she applied to Husson, the University assisted her financially. She received a Women's Philanthropy Council Scholarship. Carla was also given a U & Husson Scholarship and the Provost's Academic Scholarship multiple times, along with the Husson Eagle Award and multiple grants.

Husson's generosity made Carla's education possible. Today, she has aspirations of going to med school and becoming a cardio or trauma surgeon after she graduates from the University.

And that's just one of many examples of how Husson has transformed lives through financial aid. At Husson, our friendly and knowledgeable financial aid staff are here to help students every step of the way. Financial aid offers vary depending on a student's academic standing, financial circumstances, department, and program.

Last year 98% of Husson University students qualified to receive federal, state, community, and/or campus-based financial aid and scholarships. During the 2021-2022 school year, approximately $19 million in institutionally funded grants and scholarships were awarded to Husson students.

Students are usually eligible for two types of financial aid, based on the information in their Free Application for Federal Student Aid (FAFSA®) form. This assistance consists of grants or scholarships that do not have to be repaid or self-help, like a work-study job. Students can also take out loans that will have to be repaid at a later date. Payment plans are available regardless of financial need.

Depending on a student's grades, he, she, or they may be eligible for merit scholarships. Need-based scholarships are also available to students who qualify. Both of these can help make the college experience more affordable.

If you are interested in learning more about financial aid at Husson University, visit the admissions and aid page on Husson University's website at https://Husson.edu/admissions.

Academic Programs

Accounting Major/Minor
Audio Engineering
Biology / Biochemistry Concentration
Biology Major/Minor
Biology / Environmental Science Concentration
Business Administration
Business and Professional Studies
Coaching Minor
Computer Information Systems (CIS)
Conservation Law
Criminal Justice
Criminal Justice / Psychology
Cultural and Behavioral Sciences Minor
Elementary Education
English Minor
Exercise Science
Extended Reality (XR)
Financial Planning
Forensic Science
Graphic / Visual Design
Health Sciences
Healthcare Administration and Public Health
History Minor
Hospitality and Tourism Management Major/Minor
Integrated Technology Minor
Legal Studies Pre-Law
Liberal Studies
Marketing Communications
Mathematics Minor

Military Leadership Minor
Nursing
Occupational Therapy / Healthcare Administration and Public Health
Pharmacy / Health Sciences
Physical Therapy / Health Sciences
Pre-Medicine
Professional Communications
Psychology Major/Minor
Psychology / Clinical Mental Health Counseling
Psychology / School Counseling
ROTC
Secondary Education
Software Development
Sport Management
Sports Journalism
Sustainability Minor
Tourism and Recreation Minor
Video / Film Production

Dual Undergraduate/Graduate Degree Programs:

B.S. Accounting/Master of Business Administration
B.S. Business Administration/Master of Business Administration
B.S. Criminal Justice/M.S. Criminal Justice Administration
B.S. Exercise Science/Doctor in Physical Therapy*
B.S. Financial Planning/Master of Business Administration
B.S. Healthcare Administration and Public Health/Master of Business
Administration
B.S. Healthcare Administration and Public Health/M.S. in Occupational
Therapy*
B.S. Hospitality and Tourism Management/Master of Business
Administration
B.S. Health Sciences/Doctor of Pharmacy
B.S. Integrated Technology/Master of Business Administration
B.S. Marketing Communications/Master of Business Administration
B.S. Psychology/M.S. in Clinical Mental Health Counseling
B.S. Psychology/M.S. in School Counseling
B.S. Sport Management/Master of Business Administration

Undergraduate Certificates:

3D Modeling and Motion Design

Accounting
Advanced Live Sound Production
Advanced Music Production
Advanced Post Production
Animal-Assisted Therapy
Applied Mental Health
Audio Engineering
Business Administration
Communications Technology
Competitive Intelligence
Conservation Law Enforcement
Counter Terrorism and Security
Criminal Justice
Data Analytics
Digital and Social Media Marketing
Diversity, Equity, and Inclusion
Elementary Education (Pathways II)
Entrepreneurship
Esports Management
Extended Reality
Filmmaking
Finance
Forensics
Fundamentals of Video Production
Graphic Design
Hospitality
Leadership
Marketing Communications
Paralegal Studies
Paralegal Certificate - Advanced Civil Practice
Paralegal Certificate - Advanced Criminal Practice
Pre Law Studies
Photography Certificate
Radio Broadcasting
Sales
Secondary Education (Pathways II)
Small Business
User Experience Design
Web Design
Web Media
Graduate Certificates
Business Analytics

Counter Terrorism and Security
Executive Nursing Business Management
Healthcare Management
Hospitality & Tourism Management
Human Resource Management
Innovation & Entrepreneurship
Leadership
Nursing Global Health Certificate
Risk Management

Masters Degrees:

Business
Clinical Mental Health Counseling
Criminal Justice Administration
Human Relations
Nursing
Occupational Therapy
Public Health
School Counseling
Post-Master's Certificates
Adult Gerontology Acute Care Nurse Practitioner
Counseling
Family Nurse Practitioner
Psychiatric Mental Health Nurse Practitioner
First Professional Doctorate
Pharmacy
Physical Therapy

THREE: **UNIVERSITY OF LA VERNE**

College Name: University of La Verne
City, State: La Verne, CA
Website: https://www.laverne.edu/connect
Admissions email address: admission@laverne.edu
Admissions phone: 909.448.4026
Full-time undergraduate enrollment: 2509
Number of full-time undergraduate students living on campus: 1,200
Average class size: 16
Student-faculty ratio: 14:1

Submitted by Adam Wu, Director of Undergraduate Admission, University of La Verne

The University of La Verne is a nonprofit, private university committed to supporting our students as they pursue their passions, grow personally, and prepare for a lifetime of success.

Located just 35 miles from Los Angeles, the city of La Verne offers a safe, suburban setting for studying and is a short commute to the endless recreational, cultural, and professional development opportunities of Southern California.

Across five colleges, the university's nearly 2,500 traditional-age undergraduate students make the federally designated Hispanic-Serving Institution one of the most diverse schools in the nation. About 96 percent of traditional undergraduate students receive some form of financial aid.

U.S. News & World Report ranked the University of La Verne 6th in the country for social mobility in 2022.

Outstanding Qualities
Founded in 1891, the university offers a high-quality liberal education that embraces four core values: ethical reasoning, diversity and inclusivity, lifelong learning, and civic and community engagement. Small class sizes (the average is 15) and personalized advising for every student are hallmarks of a University of La Verne education. In 2015, the University of La Verne was awarded the prestigious Carnegie Foundation Community Engagement Classification.

The university's signature academic program, the La Verne Experience, aims to educate the whole student. The program starts with the First-Year La Verne Experience, which helps students acclimate to college through learning communities. As students progress through college, the program continues with segments focusing on career preparation, community service, and goal setting. By the time students graduate, they have developed key skills and a professional resume to help them in their job search.

Students are admitted to the overall university not to a specific major, allowing them to select their own course of study or change majors if necessary. Popular majors include business administration, biology, kinesiology, psychology, criminal justice and criminology, educational studies, computer science, political science, digital media, and sociology.

Curriculum Development
The university offers 61 areas of undergraduate study for students to customize an education that fits their professional goals. The university has been working on several new academic initiatives to give our students a competitive advantage and prepare them for jobs in a variety of in-demand fields.

The Department of Computer Science and Engineering launched a certificate in cybersecurity and a concentration in artificial intelligence. In 2022, the university opened its fifth college, the College of Health and Community Well-Being, which provides a pipeline of qualified graduates to support the region's need for healthcare professionals. The college offers 10 undergraduate programs and will launch a pre-nursing program in the fall of 2023.

To give students a fast path to a career, the university created several accelerated programs that allow qualified students to complete a bachelor's degree and a graduate degree or teaching credential in five years. Programs offered include accounting, organizational management and leadership, data analytics, teaching credentials, and athletic training.

Experiential Learning
Our undergraduate curriculum focuses heavily on hands-on learning experiences and the crucial professional skills that students will need to be successful in the workplace. In our novel Integrated Business Program, business administration students use seed funds from a bank loan to create and operate their own businesses. Political science students compete against other universities in Model United Nations (MUN) to engage in diplomatic negotiations while trying to solve some of the world's most challenging problems.

Students in the early childhood education program develop professional skills by training at the local Fairplex Child Development Center in Pomona. Psychology students have a chance to participate in undergraduate research through the Anxiety and Trauma Lab and the Multicultural Cooperative Research Laboratory. The Nathan Chow Film and Television Studio allows students to train with state-of-the-art film industry equipment. Digital media and communications students also practice their skills by working on two local television stations—LVTV and KSWT—as well as the campus radio station, LeoFM.

Students immerse themselves in a new culture and ecosystem at the Bob and Mary Neher Station at Magpie Ranch, the Biology Department's summer research field station in Montana.

Career Development Services
The university's Career Center offers a robust set of digital resources, tools, career assessments, and programming to prepare current students and alumni to be competitive in the job market. Career

counseling, speaker events, workshops, job fairs, and access to the Leo Connect alumni engagement platform allow students to work on their resumes and professional network. Our career services are free and available to alumni for life.

Career development at University of La Verne is not limited to the Career Center. It is woven into the undergraduate curriculum through the La Verne Experience program. It starts with a career map developed in freshmen orientation, continues through courses in resume writing and job interview skills, and culminates in the development of a professional portfolio by graduation.

A Great Financial Choice
The University of La Verne offers competitive merit scholarships to all qualified undergraduate applicants. This practice ensures students are not competing with other students for merit funding. Merit scholarships are based on the weighted grade point average at the time of admission. No additional documentation is needed. Merit scholarship information is provided in the admission letter so students can immediately start to see how a private education can be attainable.

For financial aid consideration, La Verne only requires the FAFSA. This process simplifies the scholarship process, reducing the barriers often associated with applying for scholarships. As a result, 99% of incoming freshmen receive financial aid. For the 2021-22 year, the average scholarship package was $35,024 with merit-and need-based awards ranging as high as $47,000. As a result, over 40% of the student body are first-generation students.

Academic Programs

Accounting, BS
American Law Minor
Anthropology Minor
Anthropology, BS

Art History Minor
Art History, BA
Biology Minor
Biology, BS
Black Studies Minor
Business Administration Minor
Business Administration, BS
Business Management Minor
Chemistry Minor
Chemistry, BA
Chemistry, BS
Child Development - Integrated BS+MS
Child Development Minor
Child Development, BS
Communications, BA
Computer Science, BS
Create Your Own Major
Creative Writing Minor
Creative Writing, BA
Criminology Minor
Criminology, BS
Digital Media, BA
E-Commerce, BS
Early Childhood Special Education Added Authorization
Economics Minor
Economics, BS
Educational Studies Minor
English Minor
English, BA
Ethnic Studies Minor
Forensic Investigation and Identification Minor
French Minor
French, BA
Gender Studies Minor
History Minor
History, BA
Information Science Minor
Information Technology, BS
Interfaith Studies Minor
International Business and Language, BS
International Studies Minor
International Studies, BA

Internet Programming Minor
Japanese Minor
Journalism, BA
Kinesiology Minor
Kinesiology, BS
Latinx & Latin American Studies Minor
Legal Studies, BS
Liberal Arts, BA
Marketing Minor
Mathematics Minor
Mathematics, BS
Music Minor
Music, BA
Natural History
Organizational Management
Paralegal Studies Certificate
Philosophy Minor
Philosophy, BA
Photography Minor
Photography, BA
Physics Minor
Physics, BA
Physics, BS
Political Science Minor
Political Science, BA
Pre-Health
Pre-Nursing
Pre-Law
Psychology Minor
Psychology, BS
Public Administration, BS
Public History Minor
Religion and Philosophy, BA
Religion Minor
Religion, BA
Rhetoric and Communication Studies Minor
Rhetoric and Communication Studies, BA
Social Science, BA
Sociology Minor
Sociology, BS
Software Minor
Spanish Minor

Spanish, BA
Studio Art Minor
Studio Art, BA
Sustainability Minor
Theatre Arts, BA
Theatre Minor
Writing Program

Undergraduate certificates:

Computer Coding
Cybersecurity
Geriatric Administration
Geriatric Care Management
Health Services Financial Management
Health Services Human Resources Management
Health Services Management
Health Services Marketing and Business Development
Human Resource Management
Nonprofit Management
Organizational Leadership
Systems Engineering
Website and Internet Applications Development

Graduate Degrees:

Accounting, MS
Athletic Training, MS
Business Administration, DBA
Business Administration, MBA
Business Administration, MBA Concentrations
Business Administration, MBA for Experienced Professionals
Child and Adolescent Development, MS
Child Development - Integrated BS+MS
Child Life, MS
Clinical Psychology, PsyD
Data Analytics, MS
Educational Counseling, MS
Educational Leadership, MED
Finance, MS
Health Administration, MHA
Leadership and Management, MS

Marriage and Family Therapy, MFT
MS School Psychology and Pupil Personnel Services
Organizational Leadership, Ed.D.
Physician Assistant Practice, MS
Public Administration, DPA
Public Administration, MPA
Public Administration, MPA with Law Concentration (Dual Degree)
Special Emphasis, MED
Teaching, MA - Inclusive Education with Mild/Moderate Education
Specialist Credential
Teaching, MA - Multiple Subject Teaching Credential
Teaching, MA - Single Subject Teaching Credential

FOUR: **MISERICORDIA UNIVERSITY**

College Name: Misericordia University
City, State: Dallas, PA
Website: https://www.Misericordia.edu
Admissions email address: admiss@misericordia.edu
Admissions phone: 866-262-6363
Full-time undergraduate enrollment: 1,663
Number of full-time undergraduate students living on campus: 657
Average class size: 18
Student-faculty ratio: 10.4:1

Submitted by Steve Secora, Director of Admissions, Misericordia University

Misericordia University is a small and distinctively personal Catholic university nestled on more than 127 scenic acres in the community of Dallas, in the heart of Northeastern Pennsylvania. Founded by the Sisters of Mercy in 1924, today the university offers more than 50 academic programs (including degree programs, certificates, and related courses) in a variety of formats including in-person, online, and hybrid. The university, with a total enrollment of more than 2,200 students, also offers the lowest list tuition for a private institution in the region.

Misericordia is known for being caring, engaging, and challenging with a supportive campus environment and proven student success. Achieving national notoriety for its student retention rate, Misericordia faculty and staff engage and collaborate with students in ways that form strong bonds and lead to successful student outcomes. The university takes a purposeful approach to creating a campus community and environment where everyone is challenged to do their best and supported to do so at every step in their academic journeys.

An educational experience led by core values.
Widely known on campus, our core values of Mercy, Service, Justice, and Hospitality are evident in all our interactions with faculty, staff, and students. Misericordia University's students become professionally competent, collaborative, socially aware, and lead lives of character and impact after graduation.

Students lead lives of personal consequence guided by enduring values that forge a common bond across generations of alumni. Through Misericordia's rich heritage and an emphasis on learning through service and volunteerism, we cultivate within each student a lifelong commitment to improving the lives of others. The work we do as educators can be measured by the beneficial impact our students have during their careers and personal lives.

Small class sizes with academic programs that fulfill its mission.
Misericordia University offers 37 degree programs with new programs continuously in development. These programs are offered within the university's three academic colleges: the College of Health Science and Education, the College of Business, and the College of Arts and Sciences.

The average class size is 18 students; 18% of classes have nine or fewer students while 46% of classes have 19 or fewer students. This student-faculty ratio provides the opportunity for every faculty member to know every student.

Each year, approximately 15 undergraduate students participate in a 10-week-long summer research training program known as the Summer Undergraduate Research Fellowship (SURF) program.

As students evolve through their major programs, they have the opportunity to work closely with faculty members to expand on their classroom experience; more than 35% of seniors have worked with a faculty member on a research project. More than 70% of seniors have participated in a credited internship or field experience and almost 80% of seniors have reported that at least some courses included a community-based or service-learning project.

Our students' academic success is in the numbers.
Our annual collection of data shows that our students are well prepared to continue their educations from one year to the next at Misericordia, and are well prepared for a future beyond the Arch:
- The average GPA in the 2019-2020 academic year was 3.36.
- 84% of seniors reported they acquired job or work-related knowledge and skills while at Misericordia
- 72% of seniors have participated in an internship or field experience
- Graduation rate: 67% 4-year; 74% 6-year
- Retention rate: 80% first year to Sophomore year

Students love our supportive campus environment.
Misericordia is known for its caring, supportive campus environment.

- More than 75% of freshmen believe that Misericordia provides the support to help them succeed academically.
- 84% of freshmen and more than 75% of seniors used learning support services, such as tutors and the writing center
- More than 70% of freshmen and nearly 70% of seniors believe that Misericordia provides support for their overall well-being, including recreation, health care, and counseling

The Health and Wellness Center is under the direction of a Board-Certified Family Nurse Practitioner, providing the best possible evidence-based health care in a manner that is competent, compassionate, confidential, and timely.

The mission of the Counseling and Psychological Services Center (CAPS Center) is to foster the holistic development of student wellness, mental health, resilience, and optimal success by offering short-term clinical services, outreach and educational programming, and consultation services in a non-judgmental, inclusive environment where all are welcome.

The Office for Students with Disabilities is committed to creating an environment where all are welcome and does not discriminate in the recruitment, admissions or educational process, or treatment of students. In the spirit of hospitality and justice, we comply with Section 504 of the Rehabilitation Act of 1973 and with the Americans with Disabilities Act (ADA).

The Student Success Center enhances learning through our collaborative, compassionate, and personalized approach. We seek to empower students through the development of academic and social skills, connection to resources, and the encouragement of self-efficacy.

Around the campus.
Misericordia's students can choose from six undergraduate and four graduate student housing options.

Dining services are available at the Metz Dining Hall as well as three other locations around campus. The university also offers the popular chains Poblano's, Starbucks, and Chick-Fil-A® for student's enjoyment.

Students attain success outside the classroom.
Whether a student's interest lies in music, art, drama, journalism, broadcasting, student government, and much more, there is a club or organization they can join to explore their creativity and make long-lasting friendships. A small sampling of these clubs and organizations include:
☐ Misericordia Players
☐ MU Community Choir
☐ Multicultural Club
☐ Irish Dance Club

The Misericordia Cougars athletic program has a long history of success for its men's, women's, and co-ed teams:
☐ Athletic teams participate in the NCAA Division III Middle Atlantic Conference - MAC Freedom
☐ 27 sports for men and women, including Esports
☐ One Esports national champion

- 77 conference champions since 1990
- 42 NCAA tournament appearances
- Four individual NCAA champions
- 402 Misericordia student-athletes named to the 2021-2022 MAC Academic Honor Roll
- All athletics facilities are located on the campus
- Dedicated athletics field house and training facilities

What Makes Misericordia University Financially a Great Choice? Students and their families have a great deal to consider when selecting the best college or university as the next step in their educational journey. Aside from the academic programs, athletics, and extracurricular activities, cost plays a significant role in determining which school is right for them. Misericordia University, a private, Catholic institution founded by the Sisters of Mercy, offers its students a collaborative, hands-on learning experience at a great financial value.

Misericordia University ranks in the top tier of the Best National Universities and as a Best Value School in U.S. News and World Report's 2022 edition of Best Colleges. The Princeton Review recognizes MU as a 2022 "Best Northeastern" college, and Money Magazine includes Misericordia in its 2022-23 "Best Colleges" list.

Misericordia University's tuition for the 2022-23 academic year was $36,400, significantly less expensive than the national average cost of tuition at a private university of $41,568. Ninety-nine percent of Misericordia's full-time, first-year students receive financial aid in the form of grants or scholarships.

Part of what also makes Misericordia a smart financial choice is the low cost of living in the town of Dallas, Pa., and the surrounding Luzerne County communities. With a cost of living that is well below the national average, students will find off-campus housing, groceries, entertainment, and other essential needs to cost less than the same services in larger cities.

Misericordia is a Great Value After Graduation

The average Misericordia student graduates in 4.1 years with a median student debt of $27,000. Early career earnings reported by our graduates average $64,000 in the first year after graduation.

Individualized Support from Student Financial Services
Student Financial Services provides students and families with the information, support, and guidance needed to make the financial aid process easy and stress-free. We believe in individualized attention throughout many facets of a student's college experience, and as such, a financial aid counselor is personally assigned to each student.

Misericordia Offers Scholarships, Grants, and Need-based Aid
In addition to guiding students through the federal and state grants process and external scholarships, Misericordia offers Federal Work Study, part-time jobs, and a variety of merit scholarships and grants to qualifying students.

The Sister Mary Glennon '62 Full-Tuition Scholarship. To be considered, students must have a 3.7 GPA and be ranked in the top 5% of their class as well as take part in a rigorous essay-writing competition.

Students are automatically considered for several merit awards at the time of admission. A sample of these scholarships include:

To demonstrate its commitment to academic excellence, the university awards the Merit Scholarship to incoming freshmen who have attained outstanding academic awards. The annual scholarships are renewable until graduation, provided minimum GPAs and satisfactory academic progress are maintained. Annual award amounts range from $10,000 to $23,000.

The Misericordia Success Grant is awarded to incoming freshmen who show determination and academic promise. The annual award is renewable until graduation, providing satisfactory academic progress is maintained. The grant is awarded in the amount of $7,000.

Academic Programs

Accounting
Biochemistry
Biology
Business Administration
Chemistry
Clinical Lab. Science
Computer Science
Data Science
Diagnostic Medical Sonography
Education
English
Environmental Studies
Government, Law and National Security
Graduate Education
Health Care Management
Health Science: Exercise Science
Health Science: Medical Science Specialization
Health Science: Patient Navigation
Health Science: Surgical Technology
History
Information Technology
Mass Communications and Design
Master of Business Administration
Mathematics
Medical & Health Humanities
Medical Imaging
Nursing (Undergraduate)
Nursing (Graduate)
Occupational Therapy
Philosophy
Physical Therapy
Physician Assistant
Professional Studies
Psychology
Social Work
Speech-Language Pathology
Sport Management
Statistics

Pre-Professional Programs

Pre-Medical Health Profession
Pre-Law Specialization Program

Minors

Accounting
Addictions Counseling
Applied Economics
Biology
Chemistry
Computer Science
English
Environmental Studies
Ethics
Forensic Accounting
Gerontology
Health Care Management
History
Information Security
Management
Management Information Systems
Marketing
Mass Communications and Design
Mathematics
Medical & Health Humanities
Patient Navigation
Philosophy
Political Science
Popular Culture
Public History
Psychology
Religious Studies
Social Studies
Statistics
Studio Art
Theatre
Writing

Certificates

Addictions Counseling

Biology (Secondary Education)
Chemistry (Secondary Education)
Diagnostic Medical Sonography
Graduate Education: Reading Specialist Certificate
English (Secondary Education)
Family Nurse Practitioner (post-master's certificate)
Geriatric Care Manager (graduate certificate)
History (Citizenship Secondary Education)
Mathematics (Secondary Education)
Patient Navigation

FIVE: **LOYOLA UNIVERSITY NEW ORLEANS**

College Name: Loyola University New Orleans
City, State: New Orleans, LA
Website: www.LoyNO.edu
Admissions email address: admit@loyno.edu
Admissions phone: 504-865-3240
Full-time undergraduate enrollment: 3,369
Number of full-time undergraduate students living on campus: 2000
Average class size: 21
Student-faculty ratio: 13:1

Submitted by Holly Cassard, Director of Enrollment Operations, Loyola University, New Orleans

Find your college home: Two students tell the Loyola story:

"There are so many reasons you should go to Loyola. It has the resources of a bigger university but also a great community to support you. There are great professors who are very knowledgeable about their industry. The facilities are really good, too. It's a great place to learn your craft. You can start as an amateur and leave as a professional."

Gabe Parsons is from Pennington, New Jersey studying and working in Popular and Commercial Music. He has even more to say about Loyola:

"Every department at Loyola has hands-on learning opportunities. Loyola's programs are focused on your future: you'll learn in class and then immediately apply it to real life. For example, in my digital audio production course I learned to mix and master on pro-tools. In class, I mixed and edited records that I'm putting out now. Because I took that class, I feel like I'm competent to make the music I want.

"Classes at Loyola help me achieve my dreams. For example, I am learning how to select a manager. Another class is about designing a website and online presence. In one class, I brought a music piece I had written and my professor advised me how to write stronger lyrics and helped work on the full arrangements - drums, vocals, etc. Now, it's one of the stronger songs I've produced.

"Loyola is a Jesuit university. [Jesuits are a religious order in the Catholic Church founded by St. Ignatius.] Jesuits are about bettering yourself through the pursuit of knowledge and understanding. I took a class on Ignatius…and while it didn't bring me closer to the church, it gave me a lot to think about. One essay asked me to write about my heroes. Through the class I thought more deeply about people and places that matter.

"The welcome I received upon my arrival to Loyola was different, an example of the friendly 'neighborhood' vibe a lot of New Orleans prides itself on. I soon found the combination of people's friendliness and a scene of live music that goes toe to toe with even the biggest cities was the perfect match for me. (Having Audubon Park right at your doorstep is nice too!)

"I'll never forget walking home one Sunday past the park; seeing a wedding party with a brass band beneath the magnolias; kids running with kites; and groups of friends spread out on blankets bathed in the afternoon light, and thinking 'I've made it home.'"

Elysse June is from Slidell, Louisiana and she is studying and working in Biology/Pre-health as well as Chemistry and Spanish.

Elysse loves to share her Loyola story and doesn't think you can find a better school:

"What experience are you going to have that's going to better you for the next 4 years of your life than the one you'd get at Loyola? At another place, you're not going to meet the same kind of engaged professors, you won't get the hands-on experiences and you won't be exposed to so much. New Orleans is simply amazing. You don't have to be on Bourbon Street to enjoy so many different cultures or a melting pot of cultures. There are so many things to experience: new smells, new sounds, new places. On and off-campus professionals are here supporting, helping, and guiding you. There's no place like Loyola and no place like New Orleans.

"Within my major, there's a lot of practical application. It's very hands-on. So, as a pre-health major in my science classes, I'm not doing baking soda and vinegar experiments. It's much more advanced. Plus, you're going to understand it 100%. You get to do the work, it's not just the teacher demonstrating. Even if it is a lecture day, it's more of an open discussion with the class and further explanation of any questions.

"Loyola's pre-health advisor is amazing — constantly sending externships and internships that are an option for us. We meet four times a year to make sure we're on plan and have all we need to be successful. He organizes study groups for the MCAT, helps figure out which med school is the best fit, and coaches you through the entire process. You're not alone when figuring out your next steps after undergrad.

"Getting an internship or job experience is highly encouraged in the pre-health field especially if you want to go to medical school. I work at Children's Hospital Uptown as a tech. I work with people from so many backgrounds and races. I'm able to easily balance my shifts since it's only 4 minutes from campus. It's an amazing learning experience since I plan to be a trauma surgeon.

"I have a professor that said he wants to make sure he's teaching students to leave the world better than they found it. Because of Loyola, I think I'm going to be one of those people.

"I wasn't raised Catholic but now that I've learned about them, I love the structure of the Jesuit Values. My favorite value is having a special concern for the poor and oppressed. Being at Loyola and learning about different communities really allows students to be more empathetic and sympathetic.

"I went on a pilgrimage/mission trip to Mexico through Catholic Studies and it's one of the most important things I've done in my life so far. We spent time with the prostitute community of La Raza. We met with the women on neutral ground and spoke with them — it was very powerful. It mattered that they were seen. They wanted to learn from us and appreciate the time we had together. The entire experience had a big impact on me.

"You only do your first four years of college one time, so get involved, do as much as you can, meet friends, and be brave. Start conversations. I've had so many amazing experiences and met so many great people at Loyola and I know they will support me for years to come."

Students talk: Loyola is Affordable

"Loyola was incredibly helpful when it came to scholarships. My Loyola education's value has far exceeded its cost." - Kele Johnson from Metairie, LA. Major: Marketing

"Loyola is really good at giving scholarships to students. I don't know a single student who doesn't have some sort of scholarship. Loyola wants their students to succeed and knows how to invest in our futures. Loyola has definitely been worth the cost." - Ben Beningno from Pass Christina, MS. Major: Management and Theatre Arts

"Loyola let me file a financial aid appeal after I got my first aid package and it just wasn't enough. My financial aid counselor was very helpful in working with me and my family to make college more affordable to us." - Caroline Budd from Covington, LA. Major: Political Science

"The scholarship offered was a big part of my attending Loyola. Not having a lot of college debt was important to me." - Noel Jacquet from Shreveport, LA. Major: Biology

"Loyola is very generous when distributing scholarships as well as making information available to students about upcoming new scholarships." - Estacia Mills from Paincourtville, LA. Major: Philosophy/Pre-law

"I was blessed to get a scholarship that paid for a lot. Even if I hadn't it would have been worth it for the amazing relationships I formed with my teachers and advisors." - Catilyn Morrison from Stonewall, LA. Major: Political Science and Sociology

"Loyola offered me very generous scholarships. I totally think it is worth the price." - Jack Rossi from Cleveland, OH. Major: Finance and Economics

"The scholarships Loyola offered me have made my experience here worth it ten-fold. I know there is nowhere else I could have this all-around great experience at an accessible price." - Sasha Solano-McDaniel from Fresno, CA. Major: Sociology and Latin American Studies

A selective private education IS affordable for you at Loyola University New Orleans.
- 99% of students receive financial aid
- Impressive scholarships are offered based on academics (general merit + honors), location (both within and outside of Louisiana), and talent (athletic, music, social justice).
- Generous grants are focused across financial need levels making it truly affordable for students from various economic means.
- A financial aid counselor works with your family even before you get to campus to help determine a financial aid package you can afford, identify the smartest payment plan, and then, guide you through the details all four years.
- More than a third of students are first-generation college students and Loyola helps all families navigate the financial aid process and feel confident in their decision to attend.

New Orleans is a creative, thrilling, cultural melting pot. The music, food, and history make the location a top travel destination in the world. Loyola students make connections, gain hands-on experience in their fields, and launch their careers through relationships with more than 1500 companies and organizations and thousands of connected alumni. Loyola works hard to make these opportunities accessible to students. We want you to experience all Loyola has to offer.

Plan a Visit. Explore Loyola. Explore New Orleans.

Academic Programs

COLLEGE OF BUSINESS
Accounting
Business Analytics
Economics
Finance
Entrepreneurship
International Business
Management
Marketing
Exploratory Studies – Business
COLLEGE OF
MUSIC AND MEDIA
Music Composition
Graphic Design
Interactive Design
Digital Filmmaking
Music Industry Studies (BA, BS, BM)
Jazz Studies
Mass Communication
 Journalism
 Advertising
 Public Relations
 Visual Communications
Music Education
 Instrumental
 Vocal Performance
 Vocal with General Music
Music with Elective Studies (BAM, BM)

Instrumental
Vocal
Musical Theatre
Music Therapy
Performance – Instrumental
Guitar
Keyboard
Orchestral
Performance – Vocal
Popular and Commercial Music
Theatre Arts
Theatre Arts w/ minor in Business
Hip Hop and R&B
COLLEGE OF NURSING AND HEALTH
Pre-Nursing
COLLEGE OF ARTS AND SCIENCES
Biological Science
Ecology & Evolutionary Biology Cell & Molecular Biology Marine
Biology Pre-Health
Biophysics Pre-Health
Biochemistry Pre-Health
Chemistry (A.C.S. Certified)
Forensic Chemistry
Classical Studies
w/Latin
Computer Information Systems
Computer Science
Game Programming
Cybersecurity
Criminology and Justice
Economics
English
Film and Digital Media
Literature
Writing
Environmental Science
Biological Sciences
Environmental Studies
Humanities
Social Sciences
Exploratory Studies
French

History
 International Studies
 Pre-Law
Latin American Studies
Mathematics
Neuroscience
 Biology
 Business Administration
 Physics
 Psychology
Philosophy
 Pre-Law
Physics
 Pre-Engineering
Political Science
Psychology
 Pre-Health
Public Health (BA, BS)
Religious Studies
 Christianity World Religions
Sociology
Spanish

Accounting Minor
African and African American Studies Minor
Art History Minor
Biological Sciences Minor
Business Administration Minor
Business Analytics Minor
Catholic Studies Minor
Chemistry Minor
Classical Studies Minor
Computer Science Minor
Criminology and Justice Minor
Economics Minor
English Minor
Entrepreneurship Minor
Environmental Communication Minor
Environmental Studies Minor
Forensic Chemistry Minor
Forensic Science Minor
Graphic Design Minor

History Minor
History Pre-Law Minor
Interactive Design Minor
International Business Minor
Jazz Studies Minor
Languages and Cultures Minor
Latin American Studies Minor
Marketing Minor
Mass Communication Minor
Mass Communication Minor, Journalism
Mathematical Sciences Minor
Medieval Studies Minor
Middle East Peace Studies Minor
Music Industry Studies Minor
Music Minor
Philosophy Minor
Philosophy Pre-Law Minor
Physics Minor
Political Science Minor
Psychological Sciences Minor
Religious Studies Minor
Social Media Minor
Sociology Minor
Studio Art Minor
Theatre Arts Minor
Women's Studies Minor

SIX: NORTHLAND COLLEGE

College Name: Northland College
City, State: Ashland, WI
Website: https://www.Northland.edu
Admissions email address: admit@northland.edu
Admissions phone: 715-682-1224
Full-time undergraduate enrollment: 500
Number of full-time undergraduate students living on campus: 425
Average class size: 15
Student-faculty ratio: 10:1

Submitted by Alexander Patterson, Director of Admissions, Northland College

Northland College, located at the top of Wisconsin on the south shore of Lake Superior, prepares students to make actual change in the world. Adjacent to the Apostle Islands and nearly a million acres of national forest, Northland has an unparalleled living laboratory and natural playground just beyond our doors. We strive to offer students immersive educational opportunities in their field focused on our commitment to sustainability, environmentalism, and social justice. Students that find themselves at Northland know that they will be among the world's leaders in solving the injustices facing our planet and society every day. Students are not only in the process of picking a college, but they're also choosing a community. Where you end up will impact how you spend your free time, who your friends will be, and how you view the world after college. Northland takes that charge and makes it the center of the work we do to support our students. They will engage with dynamic research and find that they are regularly embracing the natural setting of our campus. Additionally, our location and historical dedication to our indigenous communities sets us apart for students who want a rich and vibrant dedication to culture.

Our size is also a strong part of our commitment to student excellence. You are more than a number in our community as each student finds personalized exposure to their faculty, community leaders, and partners in their field. With access to research and internships that extend both on and off campus, students can maximize their role and investment in themselves without getting lost in the process. Our career-focused, liberal arts curriculum is specially geared towards exploration. It is the culmination of the diverse expertise and life experiences of our faculty, and it's designed to help you explore your options, find your purpose, and prepare you to address the real-world problems you'll face in your personal and professional life.

Athletics at Northland allows you the flexibility to excel in the classroom while competing in your sport at a collegiate level. We support your physical and your mental life by investing in both academics and athletics.

Let's hear from one of our awesome Northland students who tells about her Northland experience:

> *"If you had asked me at any point before my senior year of high school where I hoped to go to college, I never would have seen myself at a place like Northland. For as long as I can remember, it was my desire to follow in my parents' footsteps and attend the University of Wisconsin-Madison, living in the heart of a big city, marching in the Badger Band, and doing what one does at a Big Ten school with nearly fifty thousand students. However, that all changed one day in September of my senior year when my mom got a text from my uncle asking if I had looked into Northland College as a possibility for my undergraduate studies. While I had never heard of the school, he had considered it when embarking on his college search in the 80s and, knowing my interest in the environment, thought it would be a good fit. Looking back on it now, I can honestly say that one text changed my life.*
>
> *From the first day on my freshman Outdoor Orientation trip, I could tell that I wasn't going to have a "typical" college experience. I, along with nine other incoming students and two*

upperclassmen leaders, spent six days backpacking a section of the North Country Trail. In just one short week, I abandoned my comfort zone, formed strong friendships, and established an unbreakable connection to the Northwoods. I returned to campus at the end of the week in desperate need of a shower, but already overflowing with gratitude and anticipation for what was to come.

Northern Wisconsin is my playground. I have taken full advantage of all the opportunities that Northland has to offer: biking 26.2 miles in the dark and rain along the Whistlestop Marathon route during the Starlight Ramble, getting my hands dirty with the US Forest Service while doing trail work at local recreation areas, and embarking on a variety of weekend outings offered by our Outdoor Pursuits program. I've Booked Across the Bay, skied Mount Ashwabay, biked the CAMBA trails, and canoed the Namekagon. During the week, I can be found rehearsing with the band and choir, while my weekends are spent at hootenannies, dancing the night away. Each day on campus brings something new and exciting. I am proud to call myself a Northlander knowing that I would never have these experiences anywhere else.

Northland brings its own special touch to the student experience both inside and out of the classroom. Shortly after enrolling, I discovered that my combined interests in sustainability, economics, and law would not fit into a conventional major. This led me to explore Northland's directed studies program, which allows students to craft their own major or minor, choosing classes that they believe best align with their individual interests and future career plans. I've blazed my own trail at Northland, creating a sustainable policy and economics major which I have paired with an environmental studies minor. This path allows me to enroll in courses that directly relate to my field of interest, such as Environmental Economics and Capitalism, Justice, and Sustainability, all while acquiring valuable perspectives from other fields through classes like Indigenous Environmental Justice. The directed studies program has given me the freedom to explore new interests and ideas without being confined within the constraints of a traditional major. Along the way, I have received enormous amounts of support from professors and faculty advisors, eager to see me succeed.

In addition to involving myself in campus activities and organizations, I have been able to form connections with the Northland community through my on-campus work-study job as well. I am employed in the Office of Alumni Relations as the Don Chase alumni relations intern, a position created thanks to generous gifts from alumni and friends. From managing donor data to cutting out paper snowflakes to decorate the Ponzio, I've done it all. However, when I'm not frantically driving around campus in a golf cart or chasing my boss around in a dinosaur costume, my main role in the office is centered around outreach and connection through social media. The world is changing so much, and I take great pride in being able to connect with the Northland community in this way. Watching alumni reconnect and share stories about their time at school through my posts constantly reminds me why I love being a Northland student. And, after a three-year hiatus, I was finally given an even greater chance to connect with the campus community when I helped host over two hundred alumni and friends for our first on-campus reunion since 2019. Though I had never met most of these people before, spent the weekend filled with an overwhelming sense of community that can only be found at a place as special as Northland.

It truly is the little things that make the Northland experience so unique. It's the chilly dips in Lake Superior at sunset. It's staying up until 3 a.m. hoping to catch a glimpse of the aurora borealis as it lights up the sky. It's the sound of a cheerful "weeyoo" you hear from across the mall while on your way to class. It's the Saturday morning walks down Chapple Avenue to stop at the Black Cat, bakery, and farmers' market. I cannot thank my uncle enough for the text he sent that September. If it weren't for him, I would never have found this gem of the Northwoods.

While my future is still uncertain, I can rest easy knowing that I have the support of Northland to guide me along the way. Thank you, Northland, for being the lighthouse in the middle of my Superior storm and standing with me as I find my own path at the little school on the big lake." — Alaina A. Lenz '24 (taken from an article on the Northland website)

Our students are more than a statistic that moves through our classrooms. Our faculty mentor students individually and helps them connect with resources in their field before they hit our graduation stage. Our dedicated alumni go on to careers all over the world and find fulfillment beyond the financial investment made in college. They report that they are leaving a lasting mark on the world in a life-changing way. They are remembered for their commitment to improving the world and culture they leave behind and do so as leaders in their fields. Your investment is beyond that of a college education but one of global difference.

We've been preparing students to tackle the environmental challenges of our time for decades. Whether they want to work in sustainable policy and economics or an entirely different field, sustainability is woven throughout our curriculum—offering a fresh, critical perspective on anything they do. We strive to ensure that our educational opportunities are supported by a variety of funding sources to help make college affordable.

Northland's achievement-based scholarships recognize not only your academic ability but also a wide variety of other talents and interests. Scholarship funds are generously provided by alumni gifts, Northland's endowment, and other contributions. Our goal is to ensure that students who want to make a change in the world are not restricted by the cost of a private education. All scholarships are renewable annually dependent upon meeting all continuing eligibility requirements.

Northland College is committed to social justice and inclusion while ensuring the success of our students. Every student's application is reviewed for grant eligibility. One or more of the grants listed may be included in a financial aid package. To receive financial aid from federal and state programs you must meet [certain] guidelines. We work to ensure that our international student applicants are also maximizing every opportunity afforded to them with a personal counselor who will help walk them through the financial aid process.

Academic Programs

Art
Biology
Business Management
Chemistry
Climate Change Studies*
Climate Science Directed Studies
Ecological Restoration*
Education
Engineering*
English
Environmental Education*
Environmental Humanities*
Environmental Studies*
Fisheries and Wildlife Ecology*
Forestry*
Gender and Women's Studies
Geographic Information Systems*
Geology
History
Humanities
Humanity and Nature Studies
Mathematical Sciences
Music*
Native American Studies
Natural Resources
Outdoor Education
Philosophy*
Physics*
Pre-Health Care*
Pre-Law
Pre-Ministry*
Pre-Veterinary Medicine*
Psychology
Religious Studies
Sociology and Social Justice
Spanish*
Sports Management*
Sustainable Agriculture and Food Systems*
Sustainable Community Development Water Science Writing

* Available only as a minor, emphasis, or special program.

SEVEN: **ST. NORBERT COLLEGE**

College Name: St. Norbert College
City, State: De Pere, WI
Website: https://www.snc.edu
Admissions email address: admit@snc.edu
Admissions phone: 920-403-3005
Full-time undergraduate enrollment: 1,800
Number of full-time undergraduate students living on campus: 1,600
Average class size: 18
Student-faculty ratio: 13:1

Submitted by Maira Rodriguez, Associate Director of Admissions, St. Norbert College

St. Norbert College is a small college with a big story to tell. It's a story about rigorous academics, state-of-the-art facilities, and an exceptional student experience – but also about a unique approach to educating students.

In the best liberal arts tradition, St. Norbert College encourages broad inquiry and focuses on educational experiences in every aspect of college life, both in and out of the classroom. In addition, as a Catholic, Norbertine institution – the only one in the world – it provides opportunities and encouragement for students to discern and live out their values, and to appreciate both the joys and responsibilities of being global citizens.

As a result, St. Norbert graduates are uniquely well-prepared to serve the needs of the world, and highly motivated to do so. Little wonder, then, that they are much sought-after in the workplace and by graduate programs. Those bright career prospects, coupled with generous financial aid, an excellent four-year graduation rate, and a remarkably low loan default rate among graduates, point to St. Norbert as an outstanding value.

The college offers more than 80 programs of study ranging across the natural sciences, humanities, social sciences, business, and the arts. Students are taught in small classes by professors fully dedicated to student success. The faculty-student ratio is just 13-to-1, and all classes are taught by faculty, not graduate assistants. The breadth of course offerings and the ease of exploring across disciplines make St. Norbert especially appealing for those seeking a well-rounded education, and for those who enter college undecided about their career aspirations. The college rewards and supports intellectual curiosity in other ways, as well – for instance, by offering abundant undergraduate research opportunities.

Though St. Norbert College is more than a century old, with buildings on the National Register of Historic Places, donor-funded construction has added an impressive slew of first-class facilities to the riverfront campus in just over a decade. Those include a sports stadium, a $40 million science center, a high-tech library, a beautiful dining commons, and a sports and fitness center, with more to follow.

Believing that the entirety of the student experience helps define a top-quality education, the college devotes much time and energy to enriching life on campus. About 1/3 of students participate in 23 varsity sports with an impressive tradition of winning (160-plus conference championships). Intramural sports are also very popular. Roughly 100 student organizations provide opportunities to explore myriad interests, and the college supports students interested in creating new ones. The dining program at the college is exceptional, recently rated fourth in the entire country. The surrounding De Pere/Green Bay community consistently ranks among the top places in the country to live and work. Internships are plentiful in the region's strong economy.

Four theaters and several art galleries create spaces for both student expression and the extensive roster of performers and artists invited to SNC each year. Dedicated centers on campus focus on areas integral to the college's mission, including: Peace and Justice;

Women's and Gender Studies; Norbertine History; Community Service; and International Studies. (St. Norbert's study abroad program is especially robust.)

Diversity, inclusion, dialogue, and mutual respect are at the heart of the college's mission and are reflected in day-to-day life. This has led to record enrollments of both first-generation students and students of color in recent years. A strong sense of community is palpable on campus, and a warm welcome is extended to all – a tradition of the college's founding order, the Norbertines.

St. Norbert is a place where students can learn, grow and thrive.

St. Norbert College's commitment to access and opportunity is reflected not only in its careful management of tuition, room, and board costs, but in the generous financial aid it offers to students. Merit-based scholarships range into the six figures over four years, and specialty scholarships are offered for achievements in music, multicultural leadership, faith-based activities, and more. As a result, the cost to attend St. Norbert compares favorably to most other private colleges, and many public ones, as well.

You need to look a little deeper to truly appreciate the value of a St. Norbert education, however. The college has one of the best four-year graduation rates in the Midwest; relative to the average 5 ½ years students take to graduate from other institutions, this means less tuition, room and board – and quicker entry into the workplace – for SNC students. With 96 percent of first-year graduates reporting that they're working or in grad school, St. Norbert clearly offers an impressive return on investment. One telling statistic: The loan default rate among SNC grads has fallen as low as a stunning one percent in recent years, compared to a national average that's usually around 10 percent.

Academic Programs

Accounting

American Studies
Art
Art Education
Biochemistry
Biology
Biology Education
Biomedical Science
Business Administration
Business Information Systems
Chemistry
Chemistry Education
Classical Studies
Communication
Computer Science
Creative Writing
Data Analytics
Economics
Economics Education
Elementary and Middle-Childhood Education
English
English Education
Environmental Science
Finance
Fine Art
French & Francophone Studies
French Education
General Management
Geography
Geology
German
German Education
Global Business
Graphic Design
Graphic Design & Implementation Systems
History
History Education
Human Resource Management
Human Services
Humanities
Integrative Studies
International Business & Language Area Studies
International Studies

Japanese
Latin
Leadership Studies
Marketing Business
Mathematics (Actuarial, Applied and Theoretical)
Mathematics Education
Media Studies
Music
Music Education
Natural Sciences
Nursing
Organismal Biology
Philosophy
Physics
Physics Education
Political Science
Political Science Education
Pre-Dental
Pre-Engineering
Pre-Law
Pre-Medical
Pre-Occupational Therapy
Pre-Pharmacy
Pre-Physical Therapy
Pre-Physician Assistant
Pre-Veterinary
Psychology
Psychology Education
Secondary/High School Education
Sociology
Sociology Education
Spanish
Spanish Education
Studio Art
Theatre Education
Theatre Studies
Theology and Religious Studies
Women's and Gender Studies
World Literature

EIGHT: **CARTHAGE COLLEGE**

College Name: Carthage College
City, State: Kenosha, WI
Website: https://www.carthage.edu/
Admissions email address: admissions@carthage.edu
Admissions phone: 800-351-4058
Full-time undergraduate enrollment: 2,634
Number of full-time undergraduate students living on campus: 1,844
Average class size: 17
Student-faculty ratio: 13:1

Submitted by Ashley Hanson, Vice President for Enrollment, Carthage College

Why Carthage College? Four Years. Lifetime Impact!

Carthage College emphasizes discovery and exploration. At Carthage, you will uncover new passions as you gain practical experience and marketable skills. You will study under expert faculty dedicated to your success. You will realize that there are many paths to a successful career and boundless ways that you can impact the world.

"Carthage offered a beautiful campus and a tight-knit community with an affordable price
tag. It just checked all my boxes."
– MICHAEL MALYSZEK '25

FALL IN LOVE WITH OUR LOCATION
Carthage offers students the best of both worlds: A beautiful lakeside campus near a vibrant and charming downtown, with easy access to two major metropolitan areas: Chicago and Milwaukee.

YOUR CLASSES ARE JUST THE BEGINNING
College is about more than books and exams. Be prepared to learn as much outside the classroom as you will in class. Here, you can find any activity on your bucket list. Get involved in a student organization, attend world-class concerts, cheer on national champions, sample all the drinks at Starbucks, play in the orchestra, paint Kissing Rock … the list goes on, and on, and on.

GET READY FOR WHAT'S NEXT
Your four years at Carthage will be amazing. But even as you experience all that Carthage has to offer students, you'll also be preparing for a successful career and future. Carthage has a comprehensive four-year career preparation program for all students. Learn more about The Aspire Program and begin your journey to your future.

CAREER PREPARATION STARTING DAY ONE
The Aspire Program at Carthage is a multifaceted four-year career development sequence designed exclusively for Carthage students. Identify your interests and purpose and connect the dots to potential careers. The program prepares you for a meaningful life no matter what the future holds. At Carthage, all first-year students begin career development planning from their first days on campus. Through The Aspire Program™, they develop a dynamic approach to goal-setting and life skill-building. Students will own their ability to be lifelong learners and impactful contributors in the world and to recover when plans don't go as expected. Launched in 2019, The Aspire Program builds on Carthage's strong history of providing students with the skills they need to succeed. 98%of Carthage alumni report they've secured a job or are continuing their studies six months after graduation

CLUBS AND ORGANIZATIONS
What's your passion? Chances are Carthage students have formed a club that celebrates it. There are more than 130 student organizations active on campus, with more being formed each year.

Dive in and join a group, or take the lead and create a new one. You'll make friends and have fun, all with the support of your College.

GREEK LIFE AT CARTHAGE
Carthage is home to 13 local and nationally affiliated sororities and fraternities. Carthage fraternities and sororities recruit new members every fall and spring. Fall Recruitment happens in September; Spring Recruitment happens in February. Recruitment is open to students who are second-semester freshmen or above and meet GPA requirements. Through Greek Life, you will grow as a leader, strive for academic excellence, give back to your community, and have a home away from home.

LET'S GO, FIREBIRDS!
Why sacrifice anything? At Carthage, it's possible to keep playing the sport you love and get a first-rate education at the same time. About 30 percent of the students here compete in our championship-caliber NCAA Division III athletic program.

The Firebirds pile up victories in 28 varsity sports, including 13 women's teams and a coed esports squad. Carthage student-athletes have shown it's possible to balance athletic and academic commitments, even in time-intensive majors like nursing, athletic training, and neuroscience.

#6 NATIONALLY FOR PARTICIPATION IN SHORT-TERM STUDY ABROAD
Carthage is committed to providing a strong foundation in the liberal arts for all of its students, which includes providing students with opportunities to study overseas to complement the education they receive here in Kenosha.

Spend a semester or an academic year on any continent except Antarctica. Past students have studied in locations as far-flung as Argentina, Australia, Chile, China, Costa Rica, Ecuador, Egypt, England, France, Germany, Ghana, Ireland, Italy, Japan, Mexico, Peru, Senegal, and Spain.

J-TERM (JANUARY TERM)
J-Term, or January Term, is a special month-long period of study in which Carthage students explore subjects outside their majors or minors, discover new interests, and test their creativity through classes held both on campus and around the world. It's a month to experiment, create, and dream.

FOUR-YEAR GRADUATION GUARANTEE: OUR PROMISE
While lots of schools wear the "four-year college" label, Carthage stands firmly behind it. We guarantee that any student who enters as a freshman will graduate with a bachelor's degree in four years.

Why That Matters: Besides avoiding a fifth or even sixth year of tuition, there's another big bonus to the 4-Year Graduation Guarantee: a head start in the job market. That's important to keep in mind when you're comparing colleges' value.
To fulfill this pledge, Carthage assures students that they:
WILL receive personal advising to tailor a four-year plan.
WON'T need to take on an excess course load.
WILL be able to get into the classes they need to finish in four years.
More than 90% of Carthage graduates finish in four years. Compare that to 78% at small private colleges in general, and 56% at regional public universities.

GENEROUS SCHOLARSHIPS MAKE CARTHAGE AFFORDABLE
The road map to finance the investment in a college education can be complicated. That's why we're here to help. More than 90 percent of Carthage students receive grant and scholarship assistance — the type that does not require repayment — including more than $2 million annually from competitive scholarships. And that's just the beginning.

Carthage awards automatic merit scholarships of up to $16,000 per year to qualified incoming freshmen at the time of admission. These scholarships are based on the application for admission and transcripts and are completely funded by Carthage. No additional application is required.

THE PRESIDENTIAL SCHOLARSHIP PROGRAM
(35) $27,000 to full tuition, renewable
Open to all majors and offers 35 scholarships ranging from $27,000 to full tuition per year. To compete for these scholarships, students must apply to Carthage and return the completed Presidential Scholarship Program application and required essay by December 3.

BUSINESS SCHOLARSHIPS
(2) full tuition per year, renewable
Two full-tuition per year scholarships per incorporating all Carthage assistance. To compete for these scholarships, students must apply to Carthage and return the completed Business Scholarship Program application by December 3.

MATH/SCIENCE SCHOLARSHIPS
(2) full tuition per year, renewable
Two full-tuition per year scholarships incorporating all Carthage assistance. To compete for these scholarships, students must apply to Carthage and return the completed Math/Science Scholarship Program application by December 3.

NURSING SCHOLARSHIPS
(1) full tuition per year, renewable
One full-tuition per year scholarship incorporating all Carthage assistance. To compete for this scholarship, students must apply to Carthage and return the complete Nursing Scholarship Program application by early November.

FINE ARTS SCHOLARSHIPS
$500-$13,000 per year, renewable
Carthage awards scholarships ranging from $500 to $13,000 per year to admitted students who excel in visual and performing arts. Scholarships are awarded through competitive audition and/or portfolio review. Recipients are required to participate in department activities through service and creative work. If you have an interest in the fine arts, take advantage of these scholarship opportunities by scheduling and completing an audition and/or a portfolio review by late February. (The exact date varies by program.)

MODERN LANGUAGES SCHOLARSHIPS — CHINESE, FRENCH, GERMAN, JAPANESE, AND SPANISH
Up to (10) $27,000 per year, renewable
Up to ten scholarships are awarded to students majoring or minoring in Chinese (two scholarships), French (two scholarships), German (two scholarships), Japanese (two scholarships), or majoring in Spanish (two scholarships). Each scholarship covers $27,000 per year renewable for four years and incorporates all Carthage assistance. Candidates must apply to Carthage and return the completed Modern Languages Scholarship application by December 3.

KENOSHA SCHOLARSHIPS
(8) full tuition per year, renewable
Eight full-tuition scholarships are awarded to City of Kenosha residents in recognition of the City of Kenosha's agreement to lease land to the College for residence halls and parking. These scholarships incorporate all Carthage assistance. To compete, students must apply to Carthage and return a completed Kenosha Scholarship application and essay by December 3.

DIVERSITY, EQUITY, INCLUSION, LEADERSHIP (DEIL) FELLOWS PROGRAM SCHOLARSHIPS
(15) $2,500 per year, renewable
Up to fifteen $2,500 per year scholarships are awarded to applicants who exhibit exemplary leadership qualities and potential, and commitment to actively contribute to the diversity of Carthage through participation in campus activities. These scholarships are in addition to most other Carthage assistance. To compete, students must apply to Carthage and return a completed Diversity, Equity, Inclusion, Leadership (DEIL) Fellows Program Scholarship application and essay by December 3.

TARBLE FAMILY CALIFORNIA SCHOLARSHIPS
Up to (10) scholarships up to $27,000 per year, renewable
Up to 10 scholarships ranging in value to incoming freshmen or transfer students from California. Tarble Family California Scholarships recipients will receive up to $27,000 per year in Carthage assistance. To compete, students must apply to Carthage

and return a completed Tarble Family California Scholarships application and essay by December 3.

DISCOVER YOUR CALLING
With so many big decisions to make, the college journey can seem intimidating. At Carthage, you never have to do it alone. Whether you're picking a major, exploring career fields, or searching for a deeper purpose, Carthage faculty and staff stand ready to guide you.

THE CARTHAGE ADVANTAGE:

OUT-OF-THIS-WORLD OPPORTUNITIES
From conducting NASA research in zero gravity to taking a deep dive in the ocean waters off Honduras, Carthage is all about hands-on exploration. We know students learn best by doing, and we know students find their true calling by exploring.

ROOM TO GROW
Founded in the liberal arts, Carthage College provides a motivating environment that inspires reflection and self-discovery, so you can uncover and ignite your true potential. About a third of your courses will be in your major. Another third will be core courses, common for all majors. Another third will be electives — courses you choose to enhance your major, broaden your expertise, or explore a new interest.

READY FOR ANYTHING
What are the "liberal arts"? It's simple. A liberal arts education goes beyond job skills. You'll gain an expansive cross-section of knowledge, and develop the critical thinking and communication skills you'll need to be able to adapt and thrive throughout your career and life. An education with a liberal arts foundation will make you a better physicist, designer, actor, programmer, police officer, doctor, or teacher. The essential skills you'll gain from Carthage will help you advance in any career.

VISIT
Please visit our campus. Select a day that's convenient for you, and we can build a visit that meets your needs. Visits include a meeting

with an admissions and financial aid representative. In-person visits also include a campus tour.

Academic Programs

Accounting
African Studies Minor
Allied Health Science
Art, Art Education & Art History
Asian Studies
Athletic Training Master's
Biology
Business – Design and Innovation Master's
Business Administration Minor
Chemistry
Chinese History & Culture
Climatology & Meteorology Minor
Communication
Computer Science
Game Development Emphasis
Math & Technology
Creative Writing Minor, Emphasis
Criminal Justice
Dance Minor
Data Science
Economics
Education
Music Education Emphasis
Physical Education Emphasis
Art Education Emphasis
Theatre Education Emphasis
Education
Education (M.Ed.) Master's
Engineering Dual Degree Program
English
Literature & Languages
Environmental Science
Environmental Conservation Emphasis
Environmental Analysis Emphasis

Environmental Policy Emphasis
Environment, Natural Sciences, Policy & Reform
Exercise and Sport Science
Physical Education (K-12) Emphasis
Coaching Emphasis
Adaptive Physical Education Emphasis
Health Sciences, Sports Sciences
Film & New Media Minor
Finance
French
Game Development
Geographic Information Science
Geoscience
German History & Culture
Graphic Design
History Minor
Interfaith Studies Minor
International Political Economy
Japanese
Management
Marketing
Mathematics
Music
Vocal Performance Emphasis
Instrumental Performance Emphasis
Piano Pedagogy Emphasis
Music Composition Emphasis
Education, Music & Performance
Music Theatre
Music Theatre Vocal Pedagogy (M.M.) Master's
Neuroscience
Nursing
Occupational Therapy Dual Degree Program
Paleontology
Natural Sciences Emphasis
Pharmacy Dual Degree Program
Photography
Physics
Political Science
American Government and Politics
Comparative Politics, Emphasis
International Relations Emphasis

Political Thought and Theory Emphasis
Public Law and Judicial Politics Emphasis
Politics, Policy & Reform
Pre-Health
Pre-Law
Psychology
Public Health Dual Degree Program
Public Relations Minor
Religion
Social Justice Minor
Social Work
Sociology
Spanish
Sports Management (MSc) Master's
Theatre
Theatre Performance Emphasis
Technical Direction Emphasis
Technical Costume Design Emphasis
Technical Stage Management Emphasis
Playwriting Emphasis
Music & Performance
Urban Education Minor
Women's and Gender Studies Minor

NINE: **CENTRAL COLLEGE**

College Name: Central College
City/State: Pella, Iowa
Website: https://www.Central.edu
Admissions Email Address: admission@central.edu
Admission Phone: 877-462-3687
Full-Time Undergrad Enrollment: 1,150
Number of Full-Time Undergrad Living on Campus: 1,150
Average Class Size: 18
Student to Faculty Ratio: 13:1

Submitted by Erin Kamp, Content Specialist - Editorial - Central College Communications Office

Central College is a private, four-year liberal arts college located in Pella, Iowa. A residential community of 1,150 students, the Central experience promotes lifelong connections that support open hearts and open minds. The college focuses on a rigorous undergraduate education through experiential learning. An emphasis on engaged citizenship encourages students to find their place within their communities and actively build the world they want to live in. Central aims to educate its students with a liberal arts education that prepares students for future careers.

With an average class size of 18 students and a 13:1 student-to-faculty ratio, students gain a strong mentoring environment with professors who know their names, strengths, and goals. Students have opportunities to find unique experiences in and out of the classroom. Academic programs continue to develop to ensure students are taught the most relevant, up-to-date information that prepares them for their futures. These classroom experiences are crucial to the fundamental understanding of students' career goals, but they aren't the only learning opportunities that propel Central students to success.

Central offers many opportunities outside of the classroom, including internships, off-campus study, research, and community service. More than 90% of Central students complete one or more of these experiences giving them a boost of applicable knowledge and experience. One program designed to build real-world experience is Career Kickstarter. Second-year students can register to participate in micro-internships, job shadowing, networking events, and career-building experiences during winter break. Experiences like these make all the difference, and nearly 100% of Central's graduates are employed, enrolled in graduate school ,or engaged in meaningful volunteer work within one year of graduation.

A Central student is more than a spectator. Half of Central's students participate in intercollegiate athletics. Central knows student-athletes and understands how to encourage the balance between successful athletics teams and thorough academic preparation in the classroom. Central also has multiple ensembles in the fine arts, with the Mills Gallery for artists and Kruidenier Theatre for thespians. There are more than 100 student organizations that provide opportunities for students to work in a team, lead their peers, and encourage positive change on campus. Central's dedication to volunteer work also promotes civic engagement.

Central remains closely connected with the surrounding communities of Marion County and Pella, Iowa. Volunteer opportunities are accessible through alternative days of learning like Service Day, which creates projects for students to support the community with their time. Many Central students also participate in community-based learning within their courses to engage in service and learn the importance of supporting one's community. Students often spend time around Pella supporting local organizations, nonprofits, and city properties. Thanks to strong established relationships between the college and local organizations, many students find applicable volunteer experiences, internships, and jobs that boost their résumé.

Central connections truly last for a lifetime. Students, alumni, faculty, staff, and friends of the college are connected by pride in themselves and their community. These connections grow through means of supporting one another during students' time at Central and beyond graduation.

Central College is committed to affordability and value. More than 99% of Central students are awarded financial aid. Central's commitment to students is so strong that beginning in Fall 2022, all new first-year and transfer students were awarded a $1,000 Journey Scholarship with the potential for more scholarships. The Journey Scholarship Fund is fully funded by donors who know their gifts will directly support student tuition.

Central values transparency in cost. Central was graded an "A" for top colleges in merit scholarship transparency rankings by College Aid Pro in 2022. In 2019, Central underwent major tuition changes to lower tuition and make a Central education more affordable and accessible. The college continues to earn accolades in affordability and strong academic programming. Central's tuition is comparable to state schools and is considerably less than other private colleges in Iowa.

There is no separate scholarship application for Central students. Admitted students are automatically considered for the many scholarships offered through the college. Each fall, students are invited to Scholar Days, an exclusive event for admitted students to compete for additional academic scholarships. During these scholarship events, students participate in group discussions, faculty interviews and have the opportunity to audition for music scholarships. Top scholars are selected to earn renewable scholarships up to full tuition.

A Four-Year Graduation Commitment is also made for students who meet basic criteria. Students who follow an agreed-upon academic plan and don't complete their coursework on time can attend for a ninth-semester tuition-free.

Alumni discover the value of a Central education in their careers. According to Niche.com, graduates from Central earn nearly $12,000 more than graduates of other colleges six years after graduation. And that's a worthwhile investment.

From our students:

"I love that I get to do everything that my heart desires right now. And I'm so grateful for the experiences that Central has allowed me to have and can't wait for what's to come."
— Mackenzie Biggs '24

"I ended up changing my major twice, but Central's professors are super helpful in getting your path started and identifying where your interests lie. The ability to have one-on-one conversations with faculty is crucial." — Caleb Evans '23

"My Central experience now has gotten to a point where I don't want to leave. It's not that I'm not ready to leave, it's just that I don't want to because I've really enjoyed my time here."
— Caleb Evans '23

"At Central, you can't help but get involved and form close bonds with the people around you. It's so impactful, and it absolutely sets Central apart." — Quinn Deahl '23

Academic Programs

MAJORS

Actuarial Science
Art
Biochemistry (B.A. or B.S.)
Biology
Business Management

+ Business Administration
+ Business Analytics
+ Finance
+ International Business
+ Marketing
+ Student Designed
+ Teacher Education

Chemistry (B.A. or B.S.)

Communication Studies

Computer Science
+ Data Science

Economics

Education
+ Elementary
+ Secondary

Engineering (B.S.)

English
+ Writing

Environmental and Sustainability Studies

History

Information Systems
+ Accounting Information Systems
+ Computer Information Systems
+ Management Information Systems

Kinesiology (Exercise Science)
+ Health and Exercise Science
+ Health Promotion
+ Personal Training
+ Physical Education

Mathematics
+ Data Science
+ Secondary Education

Music

Music Education
+ Instrumental

+ Vocal
Musical Theatre
    + Acting/Directing
    + Design/Tech
Natural Science
Philosophy
Physics
Political Science
Psychology
Religious Studies
    + Biblical Studies
    + Christian Studies
    + World Religions
Self-Designed Studies such as
    + Allied Health
    + American Studies
    + Arts Management
    + Food Systems
    + Gender Studies
    + Geography
    + Visual Communication
Social Science
Sociology
Spanish
Strength and Conditioning
Undecided/Exploring

MINORS

Accounting
Anthropology (Cultural)
Art
Art History
Biology
Business Management

+ Business Administration
+ Business Analytics
+ Finance
+ International Business
+ Marketing
+ Student Designed
+ Teacher Education

Chemistry (B.A. or B.S.)

Communication Studies

Computer Science
+ Data Science

Economics

English

Entrepreneurship

Environmental and Sustainability Studies

French and Francophone Studies

German Studies

Global Health

Global Sustainability

History

International and Global Studies

Kinesiology (Exercise Science)
+ Health and Exercise Science
+ Health Promotion
+ Personal Training
+ Physical Education

Mathematics
+ Data Science
+ Secondary Education

Music

Musical Theatre
+ Acting/Directing
+ Design/Tech

Not-For-Profit Management

Philosophy

Physics
Political Science
Psychology
Religious Studies
    + Biblical Studies
    + Christian Studies
    + World Religions
Self-Designed Studies such as
    + Allied Health
    + American Studies
    + Arts Management
    + Data Science
    + Food Systems
    + Gender Studies
    + Geography
    + Visual Communication
Sociology
Spanish
Writing

PRE-PROFESSIONAL PROGRAMS

Athletic Training
Chiropractic
Dentistry
Law
Medicine
Ministry
Nursing
Occupational Therapy
Optometry
Pharmacy
Physical Therapy
Physician Assistant
Podiatric Medicine

Public Health
Veterinary Medicine

TEN: **HASTINGS COLLEGE**

College Name: Hastings College
City, State: Hastings, NE
Website: https://www.hastings.edu
Admissions email address: admissions@hastings.edu
Admissions phone: 402.461.7315
Full-time undergraduate enrollment: 919
Number of full-time undergraduate students living on campus: 667
Average class size: 13
Student-faculty ratio: 12:1

Submitted by Chris Schukei, Dean of Admissions, Hastings College

Hastings College is located in the right-sized city of Hastings Nebraska, a progressive and lively community in south-central Nebraska. Its beautiful 120-acre tree-filled campus offers everything you'd expect from a private college—classic buildings like McCormick Hall, which was built in 1883 and is on the National Register of Historic Places, and modern structures like the Morrison-Reeves Science Center and Jackson Dinsdale Art Center.

As student learning and technology evolve, so has the college. It adopted a block schedule that allows students to take one or two classes at a time. This structure provides students with a more immersive and focused learning experience, allowing them to delve deeply into each subject they study. Classes meet every day, and faculty report students are more engaged in class—and students note the course structure helps reduce stress.

In addition to the block schedule, Hastings College provides all required textbooks for students. This not only helps to alleviate financial burden, but also ensures that every student has the necessary materials to succeed on the first day of class. Taking equity even further, the college provides all students with an iPad and Apple Pencil. With professors using the same technology, courses are built around the devices with many assignments being completed digitally.

Academic Excellence

Hastings College offers an impressive range of academic programs, with more than 40 majors and pre-professional tracks available. The faculty at Hastings College are experts in their fields who love to teach, and the college is renowned for its strong programs in education, business, nursing, and the arts and sciences. With a student-to-faculty ratio of 12:1, students receive personalized attention and guidance from their professors, helping them to achieve academic excellence and reach their full potential.

At Hastings, students choose a major and a minor (or second major), plus complete the Exploration and Foundation. The major gives them the expertise and depth they need, while the minor gives them additional breadth and understanding for a successful career and life.

The Foundation includes key academic skills and college life courses. It's the base students build upon for a successful college career! Exploration lets students choose courses in areas that interest them, but if they're undecided, it's a great way to help discover their passion, too.

If a student is unsure of their major, they are not alone. Our first-year program is perfect for helping them discover their path — and our Personalized Program lets students customize their experience even more.

We've found successful graduates are mentally flexible, excellent communicators, creative thinkers and able to solve problems — and the Hastings curriculum is designed to help students excel in all these areas.

Hastings College has also thought a lot about the ways students learn — and built a four-year plan to help them navigate it all — from finding their place and defining their strengths in year one, to showing the world they're ready for what's next four years later.

Active Campus Life

Hastings College offers a vibrant campus life with dozens of student organizations, including academic clubs, honor societies, service organizations, and social clubs. The college encourages student involvement and leadership through these organizations, providing students with opportunities to explore their interests, develop their skills and make lasting connections with their peers.

Personalized Support

Hastings College is committed to providing personalized support to all students, offering a range of services to help them succeed academically and personally. The college's tutoring center provides one-on-one and group tutoring services to students in a variety of subjects, while academic advisors work with students to create academic plans that will help them achieve their goals. The college's career services office offers career counseling, job search assistance, and networking opportunities to help students prepare for their post-graduation careers.

Performance Opportunities

Through a variety of performance activities ,Hastings College lets its students shine. Choir, Band, Theatrical productions, competitive speech, visual arts, media opportunities (including live streaming, student news, and website management), and Esports all have scholarships connected to those programs. Additionally, students with interests in religion/spirituality, creative writing, and Model United Nations will find faculty and other interested students ready to help you thrive in those areas.

Athletics and Wellness

Hastings College is home to 25 athletics teams, including baseball, basketball, football, soccer, softball, track and field, and volleyball. In the school colors of crimson and white, the Broncos participate in the Great Plains Athletic Conference (GPAC) and the National Association of Intercollegiate Athletics (NAIA). The college's athletic programs are highly-regarded and offer students the opportunity to compete at a high level while receiving a quality education. In addition, the college provides a comprehensive wellness program, including fitness classes, intramural sports, and access to a state-of-the-art fitness center.

The Sports Management Internship Program at Hastings College is ideal for students looking to be involved in athletics and work directly with student athletes on holistic development. Participants gain experience and grow leadership skills as they develop the expertise that supports all facets of a healthy athletic department — from managing athletic events to coaching drills.

Community Engagement
Hastings College is dedicated to community engagement and service, providing students with opportunities to make a positive impact in the world. The college offers a range of service opportunities, including service-learning courses, volunteer opportunities ,and community service projects. Through these activities, students develop their leadership skills, learn about the needs of their communities and make a difference in the world.

International Programs
Hastings College provides students with opportunities to become global citizens and learn about other cultures. The college offers a range of international programs, including a variety of study abroad programs, from two-week travel programs to a seven-week Irish Fellows experience to a full semester abroad. These programs allow students to gain a global perspective, develop their language skills, and become more culturally aware.

As an excellent institution that provides students with a unique, immersive learning experience through its block schedule, strong academic programs, active campus life, athletics and wellness opportunities, and personalized support, Hastings College is a top choice for students seeking an exceptional education and college experience.

Hastings College recognizes college is an investment — but it's the type of investment that pays dividends the rest of your life. The

Hastings College experience and comprehensive education prepares students perfectly for a changing world where careers shift and a broad understanding puts them in a position to succeed.

While some believe "private college" means "out of reach," Hastings College has learned that its scholarship and financial aid program levels the playing field for many families. Hastings College students received more than $21 million in scholarships and grants in 2022 — and every student received aid.

Add in all the financial aid possibilities — plus the fact that Hastings provides all required textbooks plus an iPad and Apple Pencil — and Hastings College is a great option.

The outstanding academics provided by professors who care and get to know you; opportunities to be involved and have an active life; and successful internship, job, and volunteer programs set you up to land that first job and get your career off to a great start.

It's a complete package and an advantage Hastings offers.

Hastings College academic scholarships are test blind and awarded based on a student's grade point average. Since students provide this information on their admissions application, there is no separate form to fill out.

Our grid of academic scholarships can be found here:

Scholarship Name	GPA	Scholarship
Crimson	4.0 and above	$18,000
Ambassador	3.75-3.999	$16,000
Ringland	3.20-3.749	$14,000
Pro Rege	2.65-3.199	$12,000
Student Success	<2.64	$10,000

In addition to academic scholarships, Hastings College students can also earn additional talent scholarships.

These scholarships recognize a student's ability, potential ,and willingness to share with the Hastings College campus community. This is a great way to help pay for college while having a fulfilling college experience and doing something students enjoy!

High-achieving academic students can participate in Bronco Scholars Day. The event, held in February, is a chance to celebrate academic excellence and compete for additional scholarships to attend Hastings College — including being named a Scott Scholar, which covers full tuition, fees, and room and board!

Scott Scholars Program
The Hastings College Scott Scholars Program, funded in partnership with the Suzanne and Walter Scott Foundation of Omaha, targets seven high-achieving students per year to participate in an exclusive experiential learning program and to receive a renewable scholarship covering 100 percent of tuition and fees, plus room and board, and $2,000 in annual educational and experiential enrichment funding.

To be considered for the Scott Scholars Program, students must major or double major in Biology, Chemistry, Physics, Business/Economics or Math/Computer Science and have an ACT of 26+ or SAT of 1230+.

Transfer information
Through the Bronco Transfer Program at Hastings College, students maximize their transfer credits, and receive significant academic scholarships – plus are eligible for talent and need-based scholarships and grants. Community College graduates may qualify for the Bachelor Bound Grant worth 50% of tuition costs.

Academic Programs

Majors

Actuarial Science (pre-professional track)

Accounting
Art
Art Therapy (pre-professional track)
Biochemistry
Biology
Business Administration
Chemistry
Chiropractic (pre-professional track)
Communication Studies
Community Health & Wellness
Computer Science
Criminology
Dentistry (pre-professional track)
Economics
Education (Elementary, Secondary)
Education – Masters Program
Engineering (pre-professional track)
English
Exercise Science
Finance
History
History & Philosophy
Law (pre-professional track)
Library Science (pre-professional track)
Marketing
Mathematics
Medicine (pre-professional track)
Music
Music Education
Nursing (Health Systems)
Occupational Therapy (pre-professional track)
Pharmacy (pre-professional track)
Philosophy and Religion
Physical Education
Physical Therapy (pre-professional track)
Physician Assistant (pre-professional track)
Physics
Political Science
Psychology
Radiography (Health Technology)
Sociology
Spanish

Special Education
Theatre
Theology (pre-professional track)
Unsure / Still Deciding
Veterinary Medicine (pre-professional track)
Wildlife Biology

Minors

Accounting
Advanced Manufacturing Design Technology
Agri-Business
Art
Art History
Biology
Chemistry
Communication Studies
Computer Science
Construction Technology
Drafting and Design Technology
Economics
Electrical Technology
Energy Technology
English
Entrepreneurship & Small Business Management
Environmental Studies
Hospitality Management and Culinary Arts
Human Resource Management
Information Technology & Systems
Mathematics
Marketing
Media Arts (allows specialization in broadcasting, graphic arts, photography and video production)
Music
Music Performance
Musical Theatre
Philosophy
Political Science
Physics
Precision Agriculture
Psychology

Public Service
Religion
Science – General
Sociology
Sports Media
Spanish
Strength and Conditioning
Theatre
Welding Technology
Writing

ELEVEN: **GWYNEDD MERCY UNIVERSITY**

College Name: Gwynedd Mercy University (GMercyU)
City, State: Gwynedd Valley, PA
Website: https://www.gmercyu.edu/
Admissions email address: admissions@gmercyu.edu
Admissions phone: 215.641.5510
Full-time undergraduate enrollment: 1,412
Number of full-time undergraduate students living on campus: 231
Average class size: 16
Student-faculty ratio: 10:1

Submitted by Lauren Yancer, Marketing & PR Manager, Gwynedd Mercy University

At Gwynedd Mercy University, you will see and be seen, hear and be heard, know and be known. That's because GMercyU is large enough to offer the academic, athletic, and real-world learning opportunities you're looking for, but small enough that your professors know you by name.

Everything we do is inspired by our Mercy mission – it's our middle name, after all! –along with our Core Values of integrity, respect, service, and social justice. These values are integrated into every one of our 40+ undergraduate majors so that our graduates are ready to do well and do good as professional and global citizens.

While our community is comprised of people of all backgrounds and beliefs, we all share a common goal — making a difference, for ourselves and for others.

Location, Location, Location

Gwynedd Mercy University is a private, Catholic university nestled on 160 acres in Gwynedd Valley, Pa. Our park-like campus offers the best of both worlds – an oasis from the city where you can enjoy nature but close enough to take advantage of all the excitement the city has to offer.

Just 30 minutes from one of the country's best cities – Philadelphia – you can intern at top companies, eat at 5-star restaurants, take in the music and theater scene, or cheer on a local sports team and still make your 8 a.m. class the next day.

GMercyU is also just a short drive or train ride away from popular attractions like the King of Prussia Mall, Hershey Park, Jersey Shore, and other major cities like New York or D.C. As a GMercyU Griffin, you'll have access to discounted tickets and a complimentary shuttle to and from the local train station. All students, even freshmen, can have a car on campus.

The Griffin Edge

Built on the 5 E's: Excellence, Engagement, Experience, Empathy, and Encouragement, the Griffin Edge is designed to help you customize your education so you have an intentional, reflective, and proactive college journey.

Throughout your time here, you'll be challenged in the classroom academically, but you'll also take part in real-world experiences and service opportunities. In fact, 100% of first-time, full-time students participate in service, research, internships, and other real-world experiences to put their knowledge to the test. You might sharpen your leadership skills as part of our Griffin Student Leadership Institute (GSLI), or build your teamwork skills as a student-athlete in one of our 17 NCAA Division III athletic teams or as part of one of our many clubs and organizations.

Through it all, you'll continue to document and reflect on your GMercyU experiences in an e-portfolio — and ultimately learn how to share your personal story in a way that will resonate with future employers and set you apart.

"From day one, The Griffin Edge helped me design a rigorous course schedule to achieve academic excellence, engage in clubs and organizations across campus, and gain real-world experience through internships on and off campus. Faculty and staff are encouraging of every student. Particularly, my academic advisor served as my biggest supporter and contributed to my success at GMercyU," said Lauren '21, Marketing.

Mercy Makes the Difference

Gwynedd Mercy University was founded in 1948 by the Sisters of Mercy. If you're not familiar with the Sisters of Mercy, the best way to describe them is that they "get stuff done" — always with a focus on staying true to their mission and core values. They have been meeting the needs of the underserved and underrepresented since 1831 when Catherine McAuley, the founder of the Sisters of Mercy, opened up her house on Baggot Street in Ireland. The Sisters of Mercy don't wait for anything or anybody; when they see a need, they look for solutions and take action immediately.

This vision – and approach – continues today.

GMercyU carries forth this mission by preparing students to have a successful career and lead a meaningful life.

"We are told that our service is meant to plant seeds of Mercy. We may not see them grow, but we lay the foundation, and that's what matters most," —Justin '25, Social Work major.

We bring Mercy to life starting on your first day on campus. During orientation, you will engage in a service project with classmates to see first-hand how Mercy makes a difference – for yourself and your community. Students have the opportunity to attend Alternative Break trips, mission trips with their major, and the Dublin pilgrimage to dedicate time to serving communities in need across the country and the globe.

Now is the Time

It is such an exciting time to become a Griffin. In Fall 2023, GMercyU will be celebrating its 75th anniversary. While we are celebrating our history and all of the University's many accomplishments, we are also progressing ahead to the future, as the Sisters of Mercy have always done.

GMercyU is undergoing transformational enhancements. Renovations to our baseball and softball fields and enhancements to Loyola Hall, one of our residence halls for first-year students, will be completed in Fall 2023.

In Fall 2023, construction for the new Frances M. Maguire Healthcare Innovation Center will begin. This future state-of-the-art hub of healthcare innovation will address the healthcare needs of today and tomorrow, to improve access and equity for all. Here, healthcare majors will collaborate with Social Work, Psychology, Computer Information Science, and other majors to advocate for the "whole" patient.

This opportunity to work in interprofessional teams is one of the things that makes a GMercyU education unique – and it's part of the reason why our graduates are so successful when they leave here.

It's why 96% of recent graduates were employed or in graduate school within 6 months of graduating (2022 survey). And, it's a huge part of why for the first time, U.S. News & World Report now ranks GMercyU among the top universities nationwide in their annual Best Colleges Rankings.

But, it's our commitment to infusing Mercy values into everything we do that will help you become your best self.

What our students say about GMercyU:

"Attending college changed my life a lot, being a first generation who is attending college and it feels like a huge responsibility that I want to make my family proud. Also, being a student requires me

to be more independent and be aware of your time management."
—Shah, a sophomore Nursing student

"College has changed my life for the better. I am learning so much about myself and other people. I am glad that I chose Gwynedd Mercy as my college, and I have been gifted with many special privileges that I couldn't find at other schools. Don't get me wrong, I am still working on a few things and have many struggles and challenges to overcome, but I belong at GMercyU."—Alex, a freshman Occupational Science student

"Attending college changed my life by helping me find more of a sense of myself and being passionate about what I want to do. I came in as a nursing major. Although it is a great major it was not for me. Then, I ended up switching to respiratory therapy which I feel was the true nature of what I always wanted to do. All of this has made me better understand the growth and value of myself and others. I have grown a lot in finding my likes and dislikes." — Jackie, a junior Respiratory Care student

"Attending Gwynedd Mercy University has changed my life by helping me build the confidence to be a part of many different clubs and be in different leadership positions on campus. And these positions have helped me advocate for the student body as well for myself." —Ijahnae, a sophomore Public Health student

"Attending college has changed my life because it has opened so many doors for me to gain leadership opportunities. These leadership skills and positions developed at Gwynedd Mercy will follow me throughout the rest of my collegiate and future nursing career."—Alyssa, a junior Nursing student with a Psychology minor

Making any kind of investment, whether it's buying a car or going to college, is a big decision. Unlike buying a car, however, where your investment decreases as soon as you drive off the lot, a college degree increases in value over an entire lifetime. When you decide to invest in your education, you not only learn the skills needed for your chosen career, but you also build a network, expand your opportunities, and figure out how you want to live your life.

Figuring out how to pay for college, though, can feel overwhelming. Through our distinct financial aid strategy, along with our unique scholarships and grants, we provide numerous funding opportunities to make a GMercyU education more affordable.

In fact, 100% of first-time, full-time students receive some form of financial aid, including generous scholarships.

Together, our Financial Aid and Admissions teams work with students and their families to guide them through the entire financial aid process. We help students complete the Free Application for Federal Student Aid (FAFSA), talk families through their financial aid package to break down the costs, explain the difference between various types of awards, and answer any questions they may have.

We understand that each student and family is unique, and we work with them to find solutions. In addition to GMercyU's merit-based scholarships, we also offer funding options based on financial need and other factors. For example, you may earn an additional grant if you attend a partner high school, if your sibling attends GMercyU, or if you are a member of a Transfer Honors Society, to name a few. We even offer an additional scholarship if you plan to live on campus. In addition to scholarships and grants, which don't need to be paid back after graduation, many students also take advantage of work-study positions and loans. Work study positions are a fantastic opportunity to help cover college expenses, all while gaining work experience and building your real-world skill set. GMercyU has many work-study positions available so you can choose the ones that make the most sense for you.

The idea of taking on loans can be scary, but remember our example of buying a car? When done responsibly, taking out a loan can be beneficial. From building credit to investing in your future, loans can be an important tool in your kit, as long as you make the decision carefully. At GMercyU, we know students and families are looking for value. They want a great education that will prepare them for success throughout their careers. It's why 96% of 2022 graduates were employed or in graduate school within six months. It's also why so many of our graduates go on to make such a huge difference in their careers and communities. Few investments have such a significant impact on your ability to live the life you've always envisioned for yourself. We look forward to supporting you — academically, socially, and financially — in achieving your goals.

Academic Programs

Accounting/Accounting CPA option (4+1 MBA option)
Biological Sciences Minor
Biology
Business Administration with Health Care Administration (Non-Term)
Business Administration with Organizational Management (Non-Term)
Chemistry Minor
Computer Information Science (Artificial Intelligence, Cybersecurity, and Web Design)
Computer Information Science Minor
Counseling and Interpersonal Relations Minor
Criminal Justice
Criminal Justice Minor
Digital Communication
Digital Communication Minor
Early Education PreK-4
Early Education/Special Education (PreK- 4/SPE PreK-12)
Education Studies
Finance (4+1 MBA option)
Health Administration Minor
History
History Minor
History w/Secondary Education
Management (4+1 MBA option)
Marketing (4+1 MBA option)
Mathematics Minor
Medical Laboratory Science
Microbiology Minor
Music Minor

Nursing
Occupational Science (3+2 Occupational Therapy option)
Philosophy
Philosophy Minor
Psychology
Psychology Minor
Public Health
Radiation Therapy
Radiologic Technology
Religious Studies Minor
Respiratory Care
Social Work
Sports Management (4+1 MBA option)

TWELVE: SUSQUEHANNA UNIVERSITY

College Name: Susquehanna University
City, State: Selinsgrove, PA
Website: https://www.susqu.edu
Admissions email address: suadmiss@susqu.edu
Admissions phone: 570.372.4260
Full-time undergraduate enrollment: 2,200
Number of full-time undergraduate students living on campus: 2,068
Average class size: 18
Student-faculty ratio: 12:1

Submitted by Anna Miller, Director of Admission Communication, Susquehanna University

Susquehanna University is the future-ready institution for today that prepares students to create their own paths and maximize their unique potential. Invested in cultivating intellectual grounding, active learning, and global citizenship for all students, Susquehanna empowers each graduate to lead a successful and meaningful life.

With over 100 majors and minors, a solid liberal arts foundation, and guaranteed opportunities for students with varying interests, Susquehanna is a place where academic innovation thrives. The newly established innovation center has already launched three academic programs that marry the interests of future students with workforce demands. SU's latest majors include criminal justice, entrepreneurship & corporate innovation, and real estate.

Susquehanna has a rich history of distinctive programs and interdisciplinary learning within its schools of the arts, business, humanities, and natural & social sciences, and is keen on identifying new and emerging areas of study. Studying exceptional programs like creative writing, publishing & editing, luxury brand marketing & management, and sports media, students cultivate their creative passions into practiced and precise skills — often pairing two (or more) majors or minors to tailor coursework specific to their interests.

Where nobody goes unnoticed and everyone stands out, Susquehanna is committed to being an engaged, culturally inclusive, anti-racist campus that provides a sense of belonging for all individuals and groups. With academic excellence at the forefront of its living and learning environment, Susquehanna's diverse community improves educational experiences and opportunities. Furthering its commitment to diversity, equity, inclusion, and justice, Susquehanna's efforts are comprised of establishing the Division of Inclusive Excellence, adding Building Inclusive Excellence Curriculum for faculty and staff, and diversifying its Board of Trustees and Senior Leadership Team by adding more women, individuals of color and openly LGBTQ+ members.

The contagious Susquehanna spirit inspires the community to take risks, build resilience and focus on their collective well-being. We do this on an intimate scale in the restorative environment in which our campus is nestled, near the Susquehanna River, the university's namesake. With a strong commitment to sustainability, evidenced by a solar array that powers 30% of campus operations, Susquehanna is one of the nation's most environmentally responsible colleges (The Princeton Review Guide to Green Colleges, 2022).

Susquehanna's required and award-winning Global Opportunities program deepens global perspective and cultural competence. This guaranteed experience for all SU students differentiates Susquehanna in the marketplace. Through the GO program, students study away from campus in a cross-cultural setting during a semester-long, study-abroad program or a two-week experience during summer or winter break. They gain knowledge while embracing global citizenship and understanding that practical application is paramount. Ninety percent of the student body completes an internship, research, or practicum before graduation, with more than half of students amassing two, and many adding international internships to their portfolios, which are guaranteed for students studying business.

Susquehanna is an invested institution. Its commitment to access is backed by financial, academic and social assistance that spans the core of campus. In fact, SU is recognized for socioeconomic diversity and social mobility (Washington Monthly, 2022) annually. Staff at the Center for Academic Success, Campus Safety, Counseling & Psychological Services, Geisinger-Susquehanna Student Health Center, Inclusive Excellence, Leadership & Engagement, Student Financial Services, TRiO Support Services, and beyond, are dedicated to supporting students as they navigate their Susquehanna journey. Annually, the career center partners with SU's robust alumni network to host Break Through, an on-campus professional conference open to all students. Events like Break Through, Women's Leadership Symposium, and career fairs, coupled with strong faculty advising and mentorship, place 96% of Susquehanna graduates in full-time employment or have them pursuing advanced degrees within six months of commencement.

Opportunities abound on Susquehanna's breathtaking residential campus. Students can get involved in the existing 150+ clubs and organizations or they can create their own. Susquehanna sponsors 23 NCAA Division III sports as a member of the Landmark Conference, as well as varsity cheerleading and club and intramural sports. The River Hawks are competitive on the field, court, course, and in the pool, as well as in the classroom. In 2021–22, varsity student-athletes earned a cumulative GPA of 3.43 and bested conference opponents to claim the Landmark Conference Presidents' Trophy for a league-best fifth time. In doing so, the Orange & Maroon tallied six conference championship titles, saw seven student-athletes earn All-America honors and picked up eight Coaching Staff of the Year honors.

Guided by a mission of educating students for productive, creative and reflective lives of achievement, leadership and service in a diverse, dynamic and interdependent world, Susquehanna stands out.

"Susquehanna University has opened doors for me that have fostered substantial personal growth and have positively enriched my life." – Samantha '23

"Susquehanna University has provided me with so many experiences professionally, academically and in athletics. These experiences have prepared me for life after college." – Gerrit '24

When students and families choose to invest their time, talents and resources in Susquehanna University, their Susquehanna experience continually demonstrates a significant return on their educational investment. Susquehanna's combined quality and affordability earns it annual recognition on The Best Colleges in America, Ranked by Value list (Money.com, 2022).

Affordability is foundational at Susquehanna. Students pay an average annual cost of $25,396 (collegescorecard.ed.gov, 2023) to attend SU. For 2023–24, Susquehanna offered generous academic merit scholarships of up to $42,000 based on an assessment of academic achievement. Additionally, need-based awards — contingent on students filing the FAFSA — result in 99% of first-year students receiving financial aid.

Susquehanna ensures opportunity. A member of The American Talent Initiative, an alliance to substantially expand the number of talented, low- and moderate-income students at America's undergraduate institutions with the highest graduation rates, Susquehanna is consistently ranked for social mobility (U.S. News & World Report, 2023).

"Susquehanna's history of providing a transformative, world-class education to meritorious students with modest financial resources is a point of pride for me and remains one of our most important aspirations," says University President Jonathan D. Green. "We are committed to supporting these students socially, academically, and financially, from before they arrive on campus to graduation and beyond."

With a six-year graduation rate that exceeds the national average by more than 20% and retention performance amongst the highest 10% of higher education, the data is unwavering. Susquehanna students persist and graduate, and many do so by earning more than one degree — at no extra cost.

Susquehanna forges success. Continued high achievement of alumni ranks Susquehanna in the top 11% nationally for graduate earnings (Georgetown University Center on Education and the Workforce, 2022). Specifically, the report found that by the end of their careers, Susquehanna graduates could expect to earn an additional $1 million in today's dollars than if they had not gone to college.

Susquehanna inspires excellence. The university continually renews its investment in our campus community — from the people to the place — and beyond, as students venture the world to engage in global opportunities. Susquehanna ensures a superior environment for learning, practice, interaction, and invigoration.

Supportive and understanding of the varying pressures — regardless of financial circumstances — facing students as they finalize their college decision, Susquehanna partners with students throughout the process. Admission staff and Student Financial Services experts help families explore and coordinate all available options, from scholarships and grants to loans and student employment opportunities.

If you want to change the world, start with a school that opens the world to you — like Susquehanna University — an invested institution.

Now, see for yourself! Visit Susquehanna's must-see campus, where you can find your people and your passion while immersing yourself in the calm expanse of the university community. www.susqu.edu/visit

Academic Programs

Majors & Minors (*minor program only)

SCHOOL OF THE ARTS

Art History
Arts Administration*
Graphic Design
Music
• Church Music*
• Composition
• Education
• Music (B.A.)
• Performance
• Technology*
• Theory & Literature*
Studio Art
• Painting & Drawing
• Photography
Theatre
• Performance
• Production & Design
• Theatre Studies

SCHOOL OF HUMANITIES

Africana Studies*
Applied Linguistics*
Asian Studies*
Communications
• Advertising & Public Relations
• Broadcasting
• Communication Arts
• Communication Studies
• Journalism & Digital Content
• Sports Media
Creative Writing
Education
• Early Childhood Education, PreK–4
• English as a Second Language (ESL) certification
• Secondary certification (7–12 available in many disciplines)
• Special Education, PreK–12
English
• Literature

- Professional & Civic Writing*
- Publishing & Editing
Film Studies*
French
German
History
Italian*
Jewish & Israel Studies*
Leadership*
Philosophy
Religious Studies
Spanish
Women & Gender Studies*

SCHOOL OF NATURAL & SOCIAL SCIENCES
Actuarial Science*
Anthropology
Biochemistry
Biology
Biomedical Sciences
Chemical Physics
Chemistry
Computer Science
Criminal Justice
Data Science & Analytics*
Diversity Studies*
Earth & Environmental Sciences
Ecology
Environmental Studies
Health Care Studies*
International Relations*
International Studies
- Comparative Cultures
- Diplomacy
- Trade & Development
Legal Studies
Mathematics
Museum Studies*
Neuroscience
Physics
Political Science
Psychology

Public Policy
Sociology

SIGMUND WEIS SCHOOL OF BUSINESS
Accounting
Business Data Science
Economics
• Financial Economics
• General Economics
• Global Economy & Financial Markets
Entrepreneurship & Corporate Innovation
Finance
International Business
Luxury Brand Marketing & Management
Management
Marketing
Professional Accounting*
Professional Sales*
Real Estate
Sustainability Management*

PRE-PROFESSIONAL
Health Care Careers
Pre-law
Pre-ministry
Strategic Studies*
Military Science/Army ROTC*

THIRTEEN: **LUTHER COLLEGE**

College Name: Luther College
City, State: Decorah, IA
Website: https://www.Luther.edu/
Admissions email address: admissions@luther.edu
Admissions phone: 563.387.1287
Full-time undergraduate enrollment: 1,600
Number of full-time undergraduate students living on campus: 1,600
Average class size: 16
Student-faculty ratio: 10:1

Submitted by Connor Hopkins, Admissions Counselor, Luther College

Founded in 1861 where river, woodland, and prairie meet, Luther College is a private liberal arts college located in Decorah, Iowa. Luther's mission statement reads: "As people of all backgrounds, we embrace diversity and challenge one another to learn in community, to discern our callings, and to serve with distinction for the common good." Grounded by its unique geographic location, shaped by diverse expressions, and globally focused by its curriculum, Luther College is an exceptional community committed to the liberal arts and sciences.

Luther College, which is home to nearly 1,600 students and 200 faculty members, is located in the Driftless region of Iowa, an area known for its unique geology and natural beauty. The region is characterized by its rolling hills, rugged bluffs, and winding rivers, providing ample opportunities for outdoor recreation, exploration, and research. Nestled in the Oneota River Valley alongside the Upper Iowa River, Luther's location is something that provides awe-inspiring beauty with each passing season and has for over 160 years.

Today, Luther College continues to uphold its mission by providing over 60 academic programs. These programs include majors in areas such as business, biology, global health, music, and education, among others. The college also offers a range of pre-professional programs, including pre-law, pre-engineering, and pre-health, to help students prepare for careers in these fields. The college's curriculum is designed to provide students with a well-rounded education, including courses in the humanities, social sciences, and natural sciences. This approach ensures that students are exposed to a wide range of perspectives, ideas, and approaches, helping them develop critical thinking, communication, and problem-solving skills.

Beginning in Fall 2023, Luther faculty inaugurated a new curriculum, one that not only provides a breadth and depth of study but is also more in touch with the realities of today's students. A Luther education is designed to be flexible, experiential in nature, grounded in place, global in engagement, and tailored to the individual needs of each student.

One of the key aspects of Luther's educational approach is its emphasis on faculty involvement. The college's faculty members are highly engaged in the academic and personal development of their students, providing them with mentorship, guidance, and support throughout their college careers. This involvement is reflected in the small class sizes at Luther, which allow for more personalized attention and meaningful interactions between students and faculty members. With an average class size of 16 and a student-to-faculty ratio of 10:1, individualized attention is the norm on Luther College's campus. In fact, it isn't uncommon for students to develop strong relationships with their professors, to the point that students are often invited over to their mentors' homes for dinner, or asked to babysit professors' children. For many Luther College students, these close relationships are what help them to not only thrive in college but to go far beyond their wildest expectations.

In addition to its academic programs, Luther College is also known for its commitment to sustainability. In 2004, the college implemented a range of initiatives to reduce its environmental impact, including a campus-wide recycling program, a renewable energy plan, and sustainable building practices. Luther's sustainability efforts are rooted in a sense of stewardship and of place. The College has reduced its greenhouse gas emissions by more than 72% since 2003 – and is on track to achieve carbon neutrality by 2030.

Some of the sustainable practices on campus include the installation of a wind turbine (which students have named "Darryl" for over a decade now), the construction of a solar farm, the use of geothermal power, locally sourcing food for the cafeteria, composting, and a litany of other programs. It's no wonder that Luther is #4 among baccalaureate institutions nationally on the Sustainable Campus Index (AASHE 2022 Sustainable Campus Index).

While Luther College is strongly committed to excellence in the Northeast corner of Iowa, there is a commitment to global engagement as well. Ranked #2 nationally for Most Students Studying Abroad, Luther College also has a strong focus on global education with study-away programs being a central component of the college's educational philosophy. Ninety percent of Luther students study away during their time on campus, and two-thirds of the student population at Luther will study abroad in that time, with many of those students studying abroad more than once. With those study abroad experiences, students also have the option to choose programs that range between three weeks and a year long, depending on what their preferences and desires are. Current students have the opportunity to study in more than 70 different countries around the world, allowing them to gain a deeper understanding of different cultures, languages, and ways of life. This global outlook is essential for preparing students to become responsible global citizens and leaders in their communities.

Our campus is currently home to students from 44 states and 60 different countries. Of those approximately 1,600 students, 22% of them are first-generation college students. It's no wonder why we are considered a top performer for social mobility, as 95% of graduates are employed, in grad school, or doing service work within eight months of graduation (on average for the past 25 years). The

Luther experience truly is not only shaped by you but is built on bigger dreams as well.

Despite its many accolades and achievements, Luther College remains somewhat of a "hidden gem" in the world of higher education. Luther is consistently ranked as one of the top hidden gem schools not only in the state of Iowa but in the entire country. However, if you were to ask any Luther alum what makes this place special, they will commonly cite the place, the strong sense of community, the vibrant campus life, as well as everything in between. With a rich history, the college has developed a strong reputation for academic excellence, a commitment to sustainability, and a dedication to creating responsible global citizens.

Many students are often surprised at how affordable Luther College can be. In looking at the sticker price, shock tends to set in rapidly. However, the number that is most important when considering financial aid at Luther is the number of students that receive aid from the college–100%. Every student at Luther receives something, with the average aid package for the incoming class of 2026 being $46,775. This brings the average remaining cost of attendance for those students down to $9,055. But how does this break down? At Luther, we offer gift assistance in the form of scholarships, grants, and work-study.

There is a plethora of institutional scholarships available at Luther, but the biggest among them are our academic scholarships. These range between $18,000-28,000 a year, renewable all four years. These scholarships are based on GPA at the time of application and will be among the first scholarships awarded for accepted students. On top of those "counselor applied" scholarships, we offer scholarships for diversity, All-State music, distinction schools, Lutheran Summer Music, and legacy students. All of these awards are based on the applicant and do not require any additional work.

From there, Luther does offer a few other scholarships that require extra steps from the student, like our talent scholarships. Ranging between $3,000-7,000, these scholarships are available to students who audition in vocal and instrumental music, theatre, dance, and art.

Once a student is accepted to Luther, they are then welcome to audition for any of those scholarships (provided it's something they are interested in pursuing academically or as a co-curricular at Luther).Additionally, Luther offers scholarships for sustainability, nursing, history, and several other departments.

Additionally, Luther has a few extra incentives and grants for students to make some quick, easy cash. Our Future Norse Referral Program is an online form for Luther alumni to refer prospective students, and once filled out, the student will receive a $4,000 award over four years. Besides that, our FAFSA Filing Grant is another incentive, wherein students place Luther on their list of schools to submit the FAFSA to by our given deadline, and they receive $1,000 each year they do it. Luther is also fortunate to have an incredibly strong and generous alumni network, who give back to the college each year, allowing us to fund our Luther Grant, which is given to students based on their demonstrated need.

As if that isn't enough, Luther's work-study program also allows students to either work to pay their tuition or keep that money for themselves. Luther Works positions are offered to virtually every full-time student who applies for one and can earn $1,500-2,500 per year by working six to ten hours a week. Not only will students make money, but they will gain valuable work experience–often in their career fields of interest–that will prepare them for employment in future years.

At the end of their four years in Decorah, the average Luther student will graduate with about half the national average amount of student loan debt–truly a testament to how affordable Luther College can be. To see what scholarships, grants, and awards are available, please visit luther.edu/admission-aid/cost-financial-aid for more information.

Academic Programs

Accounting MAJOR
Africana Studies MINOR
Anthropology MAJOR | MINOR
Applied Leadership Studies MINOR
Art MAJOR | MINOR
Art History MINOR
Biology MAJOR | MINOR
Chemistry MAJOR | MINOR
Classical Studies MINOR
Communication Studies MAJOR | MINOR
Computer Science MAJOR | MINOR
Counseling MINOR
Dance MINOR
Data Science MAJOR | MINOR
Economics MAJOR | MINOR
Education MAJOR | MINOR
English MAJOR | MINOR
Engineering Science MAJOR (new!)
Environmental Studies MAJOR | MINOR
Exercise Science MAJOR | MINOR
French MAJOR | MINOR
German MAJOR | MINOR
Global Health MAJOR
History MAJOR | MINOR
Identity Studies MAJOR | MINOR
Individualized Interdisciplinary MAJOR
International Business MINOR
International Studies MAJOR | MINOR
Journalism MINOR
Law and Values MAJOR
Management MAJOR | MINOR
Mathematics MAJOR | MINOR
Mathematics/Statistics MAJOR
Museum Studies MINOR
Music MAJOR | MINOR
Music Education MAJOR
Musical Theatre MINOR
Neuroscience MAJOR
Nordic Studies MAJOR | MINOR
Nursing MAJOR
Philosophy MINOR
Physics MAJOR | MINOR

Political Science MAJOR
Pre-Engineering PRE-PROFESSIONAL
Pre-Health PRE-PROFESSIONAL
Pre-Law PRE-PROFESSIONAL
Pre-Ministry PRE-PROFESSIONAL
Psychology MAJOR | MINOR
Religion MAJOR | MINOR
Social Welfare MINOR
Social Work MAJOR
Sociology MAJOR | MINOR
Spanish MAJOR | MINOR
Theatre MAJOR | MINOR
Visual Communication MAJOR | MINOR

FOURTEEN: **LYCOMING COLLEGE**

College Name: Lycoming College
City, State: Williamsport, PA
Website: https://www.Lycoming.edu/
Admissions email address: admissions@lycoming.edu
Admissions phone: 800.345.3920
Full-time undergraduate enrollment: 1,200
Number of full-time undergraduate students living on campus: 1,020
Average class size: 16
Student-faculty ratio: 11:1

Submitted by Mike Konopski, Senior Advisor for Enrollment Management, Lycoming College

Lycoming College is a place where students are confident in their pursuit of knowledge and bold in its application. They immerse themselves in high-impact experiences and reap the rewards. They see beyond their history and culture to become citizens of the world. They prepare for reality but adapt as life evolves. They form enduring friendships, gain mentors, discover talents, and build platforms that launch them into careers of significance and lives of meaning. They know the future is limitless because they THINK DEEPLY and ACT BOLDLY.

A 21st-Century Academic Offering
Founded in 1812, Lycoming College is among the nation's oldest liberal arts and sciences institutions, but its cutting-edge programs, experiential learning, and faculty mentors create a distinctive, 21st-century education. The College offers 44 majors and 64 minors but encourages students to craft cross-disciplinary and market-driven programs tailored to their interests and career goals. Additionally,

Lycoming has made investments in programs exploring the century's most important topics, such as neuroscience, biochemistry, computer science, entrepreneurship, and astrophysics. An innovative yet rigorous curriculum instills graduates with the deepened intellectual curiosity, expanded worldview, and critical thinking skills employers are looking for.

High-Impact Experiences

Unique to Lycoming is the Center for Enhanced Academic Experiences (CEAE), which takes a revolutionary approach to career advising and applied learning. The CEAE fosters partnerships with faculty, alumni, and organizations to connect students with hands-on learning experiences locally, nationally, and internationally. Through individualized guidance from career advisors specializing in distinct academic areas, students have studied reliable drinking water and sustainable coffee farming in the Dominican Republic; translated poetry with faculty; interned at the Smithsonian National Museum of Natural History; explored the history of mathematics in Italy and Greece; and completed research for NASA. In fact, 100% of Lycoming students participate in at least one enhanced academic experience, such as student-faculty research, internships, fieldwork, or global study.

The Center's collaboration with faculty enables course assignments and class projects to be designed to deepen understanding of academic content while making purposeful connections with career aspirations. The CEAE also facilitates workshops and individual support for resumes and cover letters, graduate school search strategies, mock interviews, networking, and business dinner etiquette. As a result, Lycoming students engage in career preparation activities at twice the rate of other college seniors (NSSE 2021).

An Active, Supportive Community

As a solely undergraduate institution serving just 1200, Lycoming College can provide every student with an individualized, supportive experience. Classes aren't just about lecturing and listening; they're opportunities for discussing, debating, workshopping, translating, exhibiting, and experimenting. They go beyond the four walls of a classroom—modeling the Euclidean Algorithm with frisbees on the Quad or studying water quality with Eastern hellbenders in Loyalsock Creek. With an 11:1 student-to-faculty ratio, professors are more than just instructors—they become mentors and friends for life. They frequently include students in personal research and publications and even invite students to their homes for dinner. As a result of this mentorship, two out of every three Lycoming seniors have discussed their career interests and goals with a faculty member, compared to just 44% of seniors at peer institutions (NSSE 2021).

With 85% of students living on campus, Lycoming is an active, diverse community where students can uncover the best version of themselves. Thirty-seven percent of students at Lycoming are domestic students of color or international and several on-campus organizations are supporting and strengthening that cross-cultural exchange. One-third of students participate in the 19 NCAA Division III intercollegiate sports teams on campus. Lycoming also has more than 60 student-run clubs and organizations, plentiful opportunities for service, and affinity housing communities.

A hallmark of Lycoming's student life is its Outdoor Leadership & Education (OLE) program. Open to any student, OLE designs adventures that develop leadership skills, perseverance, and independence. OLE hosts around 100 events every year, from climbing the campus rock wall and day trips to hiking or biking nearby trails to larger-scale spring break excursions to the Grand Canyon, Shenandoah National Park, and the Bahamas. Students can even train to become paid OLE instructors.

City Excitement. Outdoor Paradise.
Lycoming College is located in Williamsport, Pennsylvania. The site of a world-class healthcare system, modern manufacturing, federal offices and county seat, energy and natural gas resources, and the Little League World Series, Williamsport is a regional leader and gateway to the world. This affords Lycoming students ample opportunities to gain experience volunteering, interning, teaching, and working in nearly every industry.

Lycoming is just a five-minute walk from a thriving business and arts district with many dining and entertainment options such as art galleries, boutiques, a performance center, and more. Situated in the heart of the Susquehanna River Valley, the area is also a rich, natural landscape, offering lots of opportunities for outdoor activities like cycling, skiing, hiking, rock climbing, and kayaking.

Williamsport is less than four hours from five major cities (Philadelphia, Pittsburgh, Baltimore, New York City, and Washington, D.C.), and the College often hosts complimentary trips to explore metropolitan areas with no fixed agenda. Lycoming is proof that you don't need to be in a major city to build a national— and even international—reputation.

Extraordinary Outcomes
The breadth and depth of a Lycoming College education enables extraordinary outcomes. Look no further than Lycoming's 16,000 alumni, who have found success across all industries: executives of Fortune 500 companies; public servants; Pulitzer, Oscar, and Emmy Award winners; doctors; lawyers; and teachers. But graduates don't need to wait years to find that success. In fact, 99 percent of the Class of 2021 was employed or in a graduate program within 6-12 months after graduation. Because of the built-in opportunities for research and hands-on learning, Lycoming students have a high rate of success getting into graduate, law, and medical schools. Young alumni and current students are no strangers to receiving awards as prominent as the Fulbright and Goldwater scholarships. Lycoming College is committed to preparing graduates not only for their first job but for a lifetime of professional growth and personal fulfillment.

Lycoming College is committed to providing a top-tier liberal arts and sciences education at an affordable price. Its comprehensive aid program ensures that financing an education this valuable isn't a pain point, but a pride point. Focused on recognizing outstanding academic accomplishments and providing a variety of resources to help bridge the gap between family resources and educational costs, Lycoming can award more than $34M in financial aid annually. Eighty-five percent of Lycoming students receive need-based financial aid, and all accepted first-year applicants are automatically considered for merit scholarships. Lycoming also offers a handful of talent scholarships for students interested in studying or participating in art, creative writing, film and video arts, music, or theatre. For Lycoming's highest achievers, several scholars programs offer up to $5,000 that may be used to support an enhanced academic experience during the student's sophomore, junior, or senior year, including but not limited to study abroad programs and research experiences. More than twenty-two percent of Lycoming alumni aid in the mission of providing a first-rate education for students—a significantly higher participation rate than many of its peer institutions. This consistent generosity ensures that even as students progress in their education at Lycoming, funding is available for both experiential and critical needs.

With an endowment of $190M, ranking among the highest per student in the country, Lycoming offers more resources for every student and creates the added value families should expect. From academic, experiential, and leadership opportunities to premier facilities, advanced equipment, accomplished faculty, and world-renowned visiting scholars, Lycoming students have access to life-changing resources from day one.

Lycoming's academic quality, career services, outcomes, graduation rates, affordability/aid, and alumni satisfaction have received top marks by numerous third-party publications, most notably U.S. News & World Report, The Princeton Review, and Money Magazine. Lycoming College surged to its highest-ever ranking in U.S. News & World Report's "Best Colleges" ranking in 2022, leaping 13 spots to land at No. 111. In addition, it rose to No. 11 in the publication's Social Mobility ranking, which measures graduation rates of Pell-awarded students. Lycoming is recognized alongside only seven percent of the nation's four-year undergraduate institutions in The Princeton Review's 2022 "Best Value Colleges" list, earning one of the country's highest ROI (Return on Investment) rankings. Money Magazine agrees, having also named Lycoming a "Best Value College" and ranking it #46 among the 236 private colleges under 2500 students on their list.

Many of the jobs that will exist in the future haven't been invented yet. To succeed, students need to be creative, adaptable, and well-informed—not narrowly trained for a specific job or industry. At Lycoming, students gain a depth of knowledge in their field and so much more. By providing an accessible and affordable education comprised of rigorous academics and abundant resources, a Lycoming College education is one of the most valuable educations you can earn.

"Attending a small college rather than a university allowed me more opportunities than I could have ever imagined. First and foremost, the class sizes are much smaller which allowed me to have a better relationship with my peers and professors. You have a name, not a number, and you are part of a family, not a class. As a science major, I was in the lab using all types of laboratory equipment my very first semester. A lot of my science labs were more individualized and research based rather than following a standard protocol. In addition to my science degree, I was able to be a part of the education certification program. I was out observing in a high school my first year. I was also able to have a minor in psychology, be a tour guide, an orientation leader, a chemistry teaching assistant, and have an internship that combined both my love for science and passion for teaching all in one. Attending a small school during the pandemic allowed me to continue to receive the education I deserved with very little online instruction, unlike some neighboring larger schools that remained remote or hybrid. Small schools have large opportunities!" —
Breana McNamara Class of 2023

Academic Programs

Majors
Accounting
Actuarial Science
American Studies

Anthropology
Archaeology
Art History
Astronomy
Astrophysics
Biochemistry
Biology, BA
Biology, BS
Business Administration
Chemistry, BA
Chemistry, BS
Computational Physics
Computer Science
Corporate Communication
Creative Writing
Criminal Justice
Criminology
Economics
Engineering Physics
English (Literature)
Film & Video Arts
French
Gender, Sexuality, & Womens Studies
German
History
International Studies
Mathematics
Medieval Studies
Music
Neuroscience
Philosophy
Physics, BA
Physics, BS
Political Science
Psychology, BA
Psychology, BS
Religion
Sociology
Spanish
Studio Art
Theatre

Minors

2D Animation
Accounting
American History
American Politics
American Studies
Anthropology
Archaeology
Art History
Astronomy
Biblical Languages
Biblical Studies
Biology
Business Administration
Chemistry
Classical Studies
Computational Science
Computer Science
Corporate Communication
Criminal Justice
Design/Tech
Domestic Public Policy
Economics
Energy Studies
Entrepreneurship
Environmental Science
Ethics and Political Philosophy
European History
Film & Video Arts
Film Studies
Financial Analysis
French
Gender, Sexuality and Women's Studies
German
Global History
Graphic Design
History
History of Philosophy
Human Services
International Public Policy
Latin American Studies
Legal Studies

Literature
Mathematics
Medieval Studies
Multiculturalism
Music
Neuroscience
Painting
Performance
Philosophy
Philosophy and Law
Philosophy and Science
Photography
Physics
Political Science
Psychology
Quantitative Economics
Religion
Sculpture
Social and Economic Justice
Sociology
Spanish
World Politics
Writing

Programs/Certificates
Early Childhood Ed
Secondary Ed
K-12
Special Ed PK-12
Clinical Lab
Engineering 3-2
MBA 4-1
Pre-Dentistry
Pre-Engineering
Pre-Health
Pre-Law
Pre-Med
Pre-Min
Pre-Optometry
Pre-Pharm
Pre-PT
Pre-Vet

FIFTEEN: **MARYVILLE COLLEGE**

College Name: Maryville College
City, State: Maryville, TN
Website: https://www.maryvillecollege.edu/
Admissions email address: admissions@maryvillecollege.edu
Admissions phone: 865.981.8092
Full-time undergraduate enrollment: 1,065
Number of full-time undergraduate students living on campus: 720
Average class size: 17
Student-faculty ratio: 12:1

Submitted by Kelly Massenzo, Director of Undergraduate Admissions, Maryville College

For 200 years, Maryville College has stood proud in the shadow of the Great Smoky Mountains, turning out graduates who carry with them the admonition of our founder, the Rev. Isaac Anderson, who called on us to "Do good on the largest possible scale."

Our approach to higher education is designed to give our students programs of study that challenge them not just in the acquisition of knowledge, but in the ways they apply that knowledge to life outside of their respective fields. We like to say that we encourage our undergraduates to study everything so that they're prepared for anything, and with more than 70 majors and pre-professional tracks, there's ample opportunity for them to do so.

We offer Bachelor of Science and Bachelor of Arts degrees in classics of the liberal arts paradigm like English, History, and Philosophy, of course. We also offer a Bachelor of Music degree for those interested in performance and teaching, as well as a Master of Arts in Teaching Secondary STEM. In addition, we provide opportunities you'd be hard-pressed to find anywhere else. Our

American Sign Language and Deaf Studies or American Sign Language-English Interpreting programs are some of the oldest in the country in those particular fields; our Fine Arts degrees in Theatre Studies, Music, Design, and Art are full of immersive experiential learning opportunities; and our Division of Natural Sciences takes full advantage of our proximity to the Great Smoky Mountains National Park, the most visited and biodiverse in the National Parks System and a perfect learning laboratory for students majoring in Biology, Environmental Studies and more.

At Maryville College, we're always looking for ways to combine the needs of tomorrow's workforce with the education of today's students. As a result, we've continued to grow our curriculum, adding such majors as Hospitality and Regional Identity — designed to capitalize on our allegiance to the Southern Appalachian region we call home — and minors such as Fermentation Science, built around the American craft beer boom and the demand for scientific know-how, economic savviness, and business acumen required to succeed in such a field.

Students at Maryville College pursue such degrees on a historic campus just a stone's throw from the site where Rev. Anderson founded it in 1819 in downtown Maryville, Tennessee, a bedroom community to Knoxville, the state's third-largest city. In 1867, stewards of Maryville College purchased the land upon which it currently sits. Those original 60 acres have grown into 263, which includes 140 acres of urban forest known as the Maryville College Woods, an apropos addition to a campus that's also home to an outdoor adventure partner (Mountain Challenge) that doubles as a nonprofit advocating health, wellness and outdoor activities (Fit.Green.Happy.®). The institution's oldest building, Anderson Hall, was constructed in 1870, and today its distinctive bell tower is part of the college's logo. It's serendipitous, almost, that across from Anderson sits the Clayton Center for the Arts — a world-class fine arts complex consisting of three theaters, art studios, galleries, and more that was built in 2010.

Today, a student population made up of native East Tennesseans and individuals from across the country draw inspiration from the historic figures whose names are a part of the Maryville College legacy: women like Mary Wilson, who was the first woman to earn a bachelor's degree from a Tennessee college in 1875; and men like Kin Takahashi, a graduate of 1895, who helped raise money for Bartlett Hall and turned clay dug from the very ground upon which it sits into bricks used in its construction.

Over the decades, so many Maryville College Scots — a mascot chosen for its connection to the Scots-Irish heritage so pervasive to Southern Appalachia — left the school with legacies that survive to the present day and beyond. Austin Coleman "Cole" Piper, for example, graduated in 1968 and died unexpectedly in 2021, but his devotion to his alma mater led to the construction in 2022 of a $3 million track and field complex that's a crown jewel of the Collegiate Conference of the South, to which we belong. Such devotion is a hallmark of those who learn and grow here, and every summer alumni of all ages return to campus to give back in sweat equity what the college gave them: not just opportunities to better themselves, but to improve the lives and communities they encounter after they leave us.

Such goals may seem lofty, but for those who consider themselves Scots, they're written into our DNA. Maryville College admitted minority students long before many schools in the United States began integrating; in 1880, William Henderson Franklin, born to parents who were slaves, became what's believed to be the first Black graduate of a predominantly white college in Tennessee.

It's little wonder, then, that Maryville College has long been a destination for students not just from the United States, but from around the world. Today, international undergraduates make up roughly 5% of the MC student population. The International House and the MC Center for Global Engagement provide them with auxiliary support, and as part of the Scots community, they enjoy all the benefits of a small college where the ratio of students to professors is roughly 12:1.

Whether they're taking part in on-stage theatrical productions or choir performances, or competing as members of one of our 16

NCAA Division III varsity teams, our students are given numerous opportunities to flourish academically, socially, culturally, and more. At the same time, through financial aid packages that require service commitments to the wider community or involvement in aspects of campus spiritual life directly related to our Presbyterian roots, we continue to advocate for doing good on the largest possible scale.

At Maryville College, we pride ourselves on so many things, from our history to our community of origin … from the top-tier academics to the top-notch athletics … from the student organizations on campus to student involvement in off-campus internships and job studies. That we can offer so much to so many, and that we've done so for more than two centuries, is an honor we don't take lightly.

Sticker shock is par for the course with major purchases, and a college education is no different … but at Maryville College, we work to ensure that a comprehensive and time-tested curriculum offered at a nationally ranked institution of higher education is not the exclusive domain of the financially well-to-do.

As of this writing (2023), 100% of Maryville College students receive some form of financial aid, be it scholarships of merit for academic or personal achievement or needs-based grants that allow those with big dreams but limited resources to join what they discover is a vibrant community open and welcoming to all.

The goal of our enthusiastic and capable Admissions team is the same, regardless of the applicant: To help every potential student regardless of background find the means to become a Maryville College Scot. Our Enrollment Counselors will assist students and families throughout the financial aid process, and they work diligently to ensure all students and their families get the most financial relief possible.

Since we were first established by the Rev. Isaac Anderson in 1819, our goal has been to make an education at Maryville College available to all who seek it, and to honor that mission, we offer each student a chance to apply for the Scots Legacy Award. Every admitted undergraduate is eligible for the $20,000 scholarship simply by committing to live on campus, and that's just the start of the financial aid packages offered to both incoming high school graduates and nontraditional students.

Our message to all who apply is that your passions, your abilities, and your backgrounds can and should be honored through various aid packages designed to best meet your needs. From scholarships for marginalized communities like the Equal Chance for Education Scholarship to the financial awards for students from diverse cultural and ethnic backgrounds ... from aid to first-generation students to the state-provided TN Hope Scholarship ... from full-tuition McGill Scholarships to Church and College fellowships intertwined with our Presbyterian roots ... from need-based service awards like the Bonner Scholarship to aid for veterans and military dependents ... from packages awarding individual talent in STEM and fine arts to fellowships through our outdoor adventure partner Mountain Challenge ... the number of aid packages is vast in number and broad in scope, so that all those who wish to become a part of the Maryville College community may do so.

Most importantly: Navigating those financial intricacies is made less complicated thanks to the ease of a process we've perfected over decades. From initial admission, students will be awarded a merit scholarship, regardless of test scores, and from there, our financial aid team will assist all students and their families in getting the most benefits possible.

Why? Because our founder believed that a higher education should be affordable to all, and for more than 200 years, we've held true to that mission. At Maryville College, we'll help you explore all options, so that the process of getting that education is never outweighed by the burden of paying for it.

Academic Programs

GRADUATE DEGREE
Master of Arts in Teaching (M.A.T.) Secondary STEM
UNDERGRADUATE DEGREES
(* Exclusively a minor or certification)
DIVISION OF BEHAVIORAL SCIENCES
American Sign Language & Deaf Studies
American Sign Language - English Interpreting
Counseling
Developmental Psychology
Neuroscience
Psychology
DIVISION OF EDUCATION
Teacher Education:
Elementary Education (K-5)
Educator Preparation (PK-12)(K-12)(6-12)
Licensure Programs:
Biology
Chemistry
English
Foreign Languages
History
Mathematics
Music
Physical Education/Health
Theatre
DIVISION OF FINE ARTS
Art
Design
Music - Instrumental Programs / Vocal Programs
Theatre
DIVISION OF HEALTH SCIENCES & OUTDOOR STUDIES
Exercise Science
Health & Wellness Promotion
Nursing / Healthcare
Outdoor Studies & Tourism
Physical Education/Health for K-12 Teacher Licensure
Pre-Physical Therapy
DIVISION OF HUMANITIES
American Studies*
Appalachian Studies*
History
Medieval Studies*

Ministry & Church Leadership Certification*
Philosophy
Pre-Law
Pre-Seminary
Religion

DIVISION OF LANGUAGES & LITERATURE
English/Literature
English as a Second Language - Teaching
Foreign Language Minors*
Medieval Studies*
Spanish
Pre-Law
Writing Communication
DIVISION OF MATH & COMPUTER SCIENCES
Analytics*
Business Analytics
Computer Science
Data Analysis*
Engineering
Mathematics
Statistics*
DIVISION OF NATURAL SCIENCES
Biochemistry
Biology
Biopharmaceutical Sciences/Pharmacy
Chemistry
Environmental Science
Pre-Dentistry
Pre-Med
Pre-Physician Assistant
Pre-Vet/D.V.M.
DIVISION OF SOCIAL SCIENCES
Accounting*
Business*
Criminal Justice
Economics
Environmental Studies
Finance/Accounting
Gender & Women's Studies*
Hospitality & Regional Identity
Human Resource Management

International Business
International Studies
Management
Marketing
Nonprofit Leadership Certification*
Political Science
Pre-Law
Sociology
Sustainability Studies*

Minors:

Accounting
American Studies
Analytics
Appalachian Studies
Art
ASL & Deaf Studies
Biology
Business
Chemistry
Child Trauma and Resilience
Community Psychology
Computer Science
Criminal Justice
Data Analysis
Design
Developmental Psychology
Economics
Educational Studies
English
Environmental Science
Fermentation Sciences (new!)
Foreign Languages
Gender and Women's Studies
German
Health and Wellness Promotion
History
Hospitality and Regional Identity
International Studies
Japanese
Management

Marketing
Mathematics
Medieval Studies
Music
Outdoor Studies and Tourism
Philosophy
Political Science
Psychology
Relationships and Sexual Health
Religion
Sociology
Spanish
Statistics
Sustainability Studies
Theatre Studies
Writing / Communication

SIXTEEN: **HOLY FAMILY UNIVERSITY**

College Name: Holy Family University
City, State: Philadelphia, PA
Website: https://www.holyfamily.edu/
Admissions email address: admissions@holyfamily.edu
Admissions phone: 215.637.3050
Full-time undergraduate enrollment: 1,842
Number of full-time undergraduate students living on campus: 261
Average class size: 17
Student-faculty ratio: 13:1

Submitted by Lauren Campbell, Director, Undergraduate Admissions, Holy Family University

Holy Family University is a selective, private Catholic institution with campus locations in Pennsylvania in Northeast Philadelphia and Newtown, Bucks County. Founded in 1954 by the Sisters of the Holy Family of Nazareth, Holy Family was established with a foundational mission that is informed by its core values of family, respect, integrity, service and responsibility, learning, and vision. At Holy Family, we see how education transforms the lives of students – and also transforms their families, their communities, and ultimately, society.

Holy Family offers graduate, undergraduate, and non-degree programs in four academic schools led by faculty who are experts in their fields. We pride ourselves on offering a wide array of programs at an affordable cost. Holy Family is ranked Top 10 by University HQ for the Best Bachelor's Degree in Pennsylvania and has been recognized as a College of Distinction in nine categories: 2022-23 Colleges of Distinction, Pennsylvania, Catholic, Affordable, Career

Development, Equity & Inclusion, Business, Education, and Nursing.

The Philadelphia campus offers the advantages of a quiet residential neighborhood that is just minutes from the excitement of Center City and all of the cultural and historic happenings that are a hallmark of Philadelphia. In Bucks County, the Newtown campus includes the same resources, amenities, and top-tier programs that students experience on the Philadelphia campus.

Holy Family prides itself on being rated in the annual Clery Report as one of the safest campus environments in the region. Niche, a college ranking site, ranked Holy Family as the safest campus in Philadelphia and one of the Top 10 safest campuses in Pennsylvania. The Department of Public Safety is resolutely focused on maintaining a safe and secure environment for students, faculty, staff, and visitors.

With each incoming class, Holy Family sets out to develop first-rate learning opportunities, including hands-on experiences in the field. We proudly place 100 percent of students in internships for their programs of study to help them assess their career interests, open doors to permanent employment, and inform their academic experiences so they are applying their knowledge. Holy Family's Career Development team begins working with students to offer them real-world experiences in their very first year to help them develop the skills needed to become successful in the job market after graduation. Holy Family is committed and dedicated to the success of their students, so much so that approximately 92 percent of recent graduates are working or attending graduate school within a year of graduation. Students receive individualized career guidance in formulating and pursuing their career goals. From self-assessment, through career exploration, to devising the tools for an effective job search, personalized service helps meet the needs of each student.

Holy Family's alumni stay connected and create a powerful network that students can rely on – for networking, friendship, and career advice. Holy Family graduates are leaders across industries, including CEOs in business, Department heads in healthcare, educators, and clinical psychologists. Their impact is felt across all sectors of Philadelphia and beyond.

The University's core curriculum offers students the opportunity to choose courses across all four years that can help guide them in finding and following their authentic path. These courses are intended to orient students to their strengths, connect them to their community, and guide them toward their vocation through an individualized pathway.

At Holy Family, faculty and staff get to know students because we understand that each student's experience will be a singular journey. Holy Family University faculty are renowned for their teaching, research, and practice. In addition to their expertise, they are experts in ensuring that students succeed by creating an open and caring learning environment. Educational excellence is paired with a philosophy that each student arrives with a unique learning style. Students consistently report that the dedication of our faculty is what makes a Holy Family education not only valuable but also truly distinct.

To ensure student success, we invest in robust academic support services, including the Center for Teaching & Learning, which was built with the help of a $2 million grant from the Department of Education. This is a resource hub for students to ensure that they have every available tool for learning — from tutoring to group projects to space for commuter and resident students alike to relax and socialize between classes.

Holy Family's Athletics programs are also premier. The University has 18 NCAA Division II teams, and the University's athletes are true competitors and student-athletes. Holy Family's Academic Success Rate, which is the percentage of student-athletes who graduate within six years of enrollment, is 92 percent compared to the national average of 76 percent. The newest Athletics programs include Esports, which is supported by a cutting-edge, dynamic Esports facility.

Holy Family offers an active student life that provides vast opportunities for both resident and commuter students. Residence halls offer suite-style dorms as well as independent apartments and single-room options, complete with amenities to ensure a comfortable living experience on campus.

We offer residents and commuters opportunities to be adventurous, grow, have fun, and forge lasting relationships with classmates and faculty. There are plenty of opportunities for student involvement ranging from student government, clubs related to academics, honor societies, study abroad programs, and community service. Nearly all first-year students participate in service opportunities on campus and with local community organizations, including Holy Family's Habitat for Humanity chapter.

We also know that college is a critical journey of enlightenment and self-discovery. Holy Family is a community where each student feels valued in an inclusive and inviting campus environment. We encourage students to try new things, learn new perspectives, and give back to the community, and we provide countless opportunities for students to explore — from activities and intriguing discussions to experiences with different cultures and perspectives so that students can learn about others and themselves. Holy Family University realizes that we are not just offering education — we are providing a transformative path designed to create a holistic experience so that students will be prepared to do well and do good for life.

Holy Family University is committed to ensuring students achieve the goal of a first-rate private university education at an affordable price. We understand that cost and value are critical factors when it comes to a student's college selection. At Holy Family University, we take pride in ensuring that students' dollars go further with our values-based, student-centered approach.

Holy Family is the most affordable, values-focused university in Philadelphia. Holy Family is the lowest net cost of any private university in Philadelphia as well as one of the lowest net cost private universities in Pennsylvania, according to the National

Center for Education Statistics. The University has also been recognized by PhillyMag.com as one of "The 10 Best Philly Colleges for The Money" and by Colleges of Distinction as an Affordable College of Distinction for being one of the most cost-effective institutions nationally.

Improving one's life generally requires work and financial investment. For eligible students, Holy Family University offers several financial aid and assistance options. Scholarships, grants, loans, and work-study programs are among them. Close to 100 percent of Holy Family undergraduates receive some form of financial aid. Through federal, state, institutional, and private sources, the Financial Aid Office is committed to helping families find the resources to help meet the cost of higher education.

We believe that rewarding students' hard work will help develop them to be great professionals in the future. All new undergraduate students applying to Holy Family for their first bachelor's degree who are accepted receive a scholarship or merit award. Amounts vary depending on the GPA. Along with scholarships, the University also offers generous financial aid packages.

Financing a college education can seem complex, so our Financial Aid counselors are dedicated to becoming partners in explaining available options, helping students and families navigate each step, and making the process seamless and easy in making education affordable for students and their families.

The affordability of Holy Family extends to long-term financial growth. Students who earn a four-year degree from Holy Family in one of our career-ready majors have higher average salaries than graduates from other Pennsylvania colleges. Holy Family graduates succeed in the workforce with our unique job market tools and Fortune 500 internship opportunities.

Academic Programs

Holy Family University Majors

Accounting
Applied Computer Science
Art
Art - Graphic Design
Art - Pre-Art Therapy
Art-Secondary Education
Biochemistry
Biology
Biology - Pre-Med Track
Biology - Pre-Physical Therapy
Biology - Pre-Physician's Assistant
Biology - Secondary Education
Business Analytics
Computer Information Systems (CIS)
Criminal Justice
Cybersecurity Administration
Cybersecurity and IT Management
Education: Early Childhood Pre K-4
Education: Early Childhood Pre K-4/Special Education Pre K-12
Education: Special Education Pre K-12
English
English - Secondary Education
Healthcare Administration and Management
Health Promotion and Wellness
History
History/Social Studies - Secondary Education
Interdisciplinary Humanities
Management-Marketing
Mathematics
Mathematics - Secondary Education
Medical Laboratory Science
Neuroscience
Nursing
Psychology
Radiologic Science (A.S.)
Radiologic Science (BSRS-General)
Radiologic Science (BSRS-Computed Tomography)Radiologic Science
(BSRS-Magnetic Resonance)
Radiologic Science (BSRS-Vascular Interventional)
Religious Studies

Sport Marketing-Management
Undecided

Holy Family University Minors
Actuarial Sciences
American Studies
Applied Behavior Analysis
Art-Studio
Business Administration
Business Analytics
Chemistry
Childhood Studies
Computer Information Systems
Creative Writing
Criminal Justice
Cybersecurity Administration
Digital Marketing
Education
Environmental Science
Esports and Gaming Administration
Forensic Science
Gerontology
History
Literature
Management-Marketing
Mathematics
Mental Health Services
Natural Sciences
Neuroscience
Philosophy
Political Science
Pre-Law
Psychology
Religious Studies
Sociology
Spanish
Writing

SEVENTEEN: **EDGEWOOD COLLEGE**

College Name: Edgewood College
City, State: Madison, WI
Website: www.edgewood.edu
Admissions email address: admissions@edgewood.edu
Admissions phone: 608.663.2294
Full-time undergraduate enrollment: 1,194
Number of full-time undergraduate students living on campus: 483
Average class size: 15
Student-faculty ratio: 12:1

Submitted by Mara M Springborn, Marketing Content Writer, Edgewood College

Edgewood College is a liberal arts Catholic institution, deeply rooted in the Dominican Catholic traditions. Conveniently located in Madison, Wisconsin, students have all the benefits of a capital city on a friendly and diverse campus. Serving approximately 2,000 undergraduate and graduate students during the academic year, more than 40 academic undergraduate programs are available.

At the heart of Edgewood College is the belief in fostering and engaging students within a community of learners committed to building a just, compassionate, and sustainable world. "Cor ad Cor Loquitur" is a Latin phrase embraced by the institution and it means "Heart Speaks to Heart." This means a feeling – a connection – that resides within the heart and is felt at the first moment on our campus. It is a professor, coach, mentor, friend, or teammate, who believes in you – your potential, your friendship, and your capabilities.

The Heart of Learning

Students have been transforming their lives on the sacred grounds of Edgewood College since 1927. Campus visitors will discover an inclusive community with full-time undergraduate students, adult students completing their degrees, and graduate students enjoying challenging and engaging educational experiences. New academic programs are frequently introduced and help prepare students for an increasingly dynamic world. Hybrid and online programs are available that maintain quality and enhance the learning experience.

Education is the pulse of Edgewood College. With an average class size of 15 students, the student-to-teacher ratio is 12:1. Students can expect to receive a personalized approach to learning, will benefit from being able to interact one-on-one with teachers, and can participate in hands-on learning from practicing professors with applicable experience.

100% of incoming students receive GRANTS or SCHOLARSHIPS. Students admitted to Edgewood College have a variety of scholarships available to help make their education affordable.

When seeking Financial Aid, students should first complete the Free Application for Federal Student Aid (FAFSA). The FAFSA allows students to be considered for Federal, State, and Institutional need-based grants as well as loans and student employment opportunities.

Talent Scholarships: Awards are available for talented freshman and transfer students who have a strong interest in art, music, or theatre.

Academic Scholarships: Students admitted to Edgewood College are automatically considered for several renewable, academic scholarships. No additional application is required. Scholarship level is based on cumulative high school GPA.

Transfer Scholarships: Students admitted to Edgewood College are automatically considered for merit-based transfer scholarships. No additional application is required to receive these scholarships. Students must have 12 or more credits from an accredited institution. Continuous, full-time enrollment is required.

Specialty Award Scholarships: Students admitted to Edgewood College are invited to apply for additional competitive merit and need-based awards. Students are selected for these awards based on their demonstrated interests and experiences. Completion of the Free Application for Federal Student Aid (FAFSA) or the DACA/Dreamer Student Financial Aid Application is encouraged. Applications are reviewed as funding is available. Limited awards are available.

Additional Outside Scholarship Opportunities: Edgewood College strives to provide all possible options to aid students in making their education possible. They provide additional information about outside scholarship opportunities that are administered by third party organizations.

For specific details, scholarship amounts, and steps to maximize eligibility, visit the Tuition & Financial Aid web page at https://www.edgewood.edu/admissions/tuition-and-financial-aid . The Edgewood College Net Price Calculator is available to help students learn more about individual financial aid options and what to expect for the bottom line.

Exploring Campus & Greater Madison
Nestled in the heart of Madison, college students get the best of both worlds – an open community where they are known that is within a capital city full of potential for a successful academic experience. Students can explore the quaint campus which is located in a beautiful residential neighborhood along the peaceful backdrop of Lake Wingra.

The city of Madison offers countless academic, cultural, and recreational opportunities. Just a few blocks from all the major resources of a big city, students can explore live music, a vibrant arts scene, a farmer's market, theatres, museums, and large sporting events. They will find coffee shops, restaurants, and biking trails that are within walking distance or a short drive from campus.

Community & Connection

Meet lifelong friends as you participate in career-building internship experiences, pursue a major that paves the path toward your career, and attend campus and student-organized events. Discover more than 25 student-led social, educational, professional, and service organizations. Edgewood College is that feeling students get when they make real connections with people. It's an environment where everyone can express their individuality and participate in activities, organizations, events, experiences, and opportunities where they grow, reach, and expand. Students can expect to find ways to lead on-campus; student ambassadors, student-athletes, student leaders in organizations, resident assistants, orientation leaders, etc.

Edgewood College offers a vibrant athletic community – including its Esports Teams. Participating together as a team, coaches, and student-athletes strive to foster healthy competition, cooperation, and an understanding of every individual's value while maintaining a commitment to academic and athletic excellence. For students that don't wish to participate, there are always opportunities to support their competing Eagles. It is through this participation that we develop an awareness of our responsibility to a greater community – seeking truth, compassion, justice, and partnership.

The Heart of Our History
For almost a century, Edgewood College has been putting students first in everything we do. Students have enjoyed this comfortable and friendly campus, the relationships created here, and the academic experiences that will continue to open doors for years to come. With a foundation in the Dominican tradition, Edgewood College is committed above all to the lifelong search for truth. Each person — students, faculty, and staff of all nationalities and backgrounds, regardless of their personal spiritual beliefs — are partners in the pursuit of a just and compassionate world.

We recognize the sacred land upon which Edgewood College exists. Our Dominican heritage, educational mission, and core values call us to be stewards of this land and the Native mounds located throughout our campus. We respectfully acknowledge our local First Nation, the Ho-Chunk, and the additional 11 Indigenous Nations of

Wisconsin that have shaped our state's history and our local community.

Our mission and vision make the college experience unique because identity and core values guide the leadership and that positively impacts the student experience. But most importantly, Edgewood College is special because of our people – students, faculty, staff, administration, and their Trustees. We remain steadfast and committed to creating a learning environment where students from all walks of life are embraced and feel welcome. We believe students deserve a home away from home where they are comfortable expressing themselves in the pursuit of a fuller life.

Words from our students:

"My connections have expanded beyond what I imagined they could. Professors who bring in high profile people in their field for us to meet, volunteer to help us with career aspirations and ideas, and want the best for you." —Alexis Vogt

"At Edgewood College, I've been able to explore and participate in opportunities that inspire my creative thinking because of my close contact with faculty and staff. Each interaction provides the support of my ideas to make progress in achieving my goals through meaningful experiences." —Miguel Meza

"I toured multiple colleges that 'checked the boxes' – but I fell in love with Edgewood College and the city of Madison because it provides the best of both worlds – a small tight-knit campus where I excelled in sports and academics while living in a big city filled with opportunities." —Rachel Ehrhart

"As a commuter student, I find there is something going on that expanded my interests. I was able to find people and passion and community at Edgewood College. My goal was to find a school where I could have more experience to be successful while in college and post-graduation. Here, professors support your whole

person, not just the academic part of your experience. "—Belle
Foley

*"Here is a place in which I can be a change-leader through the
opportunities and experiences that are not just presented to me, but
that I am an active and involved member in. Within a short time I
have excelled academically and personally from the vested interest
and support I have received from faculty and my peers – which has
been a transformational experience, and I am looking forward to
the 'what's next?' with my time at Edgewood College.* "—Ezekiel
Brown

Academic Programs

Accounting
Art
Art and Design Teaching
Art History Minor
Art Therapy
Bilingual Education Minor
Biology
Broad Field Natural Science
Broad Field Social Studies
Business
Business - Accelerated
Chemistry
Child Life
Communication Studies
Computer Information Systems
Computer Science Minor
Criminal Justice
Cytotechnology
Economics
Education
Elementary Education (Grades 1-8)
English
English as a Second Language (ESL) Minor
Entrepreneurship Minor

Environmental Science
Environmental Studies
Ethnic Studies
Exercise Science
Film Studies Minor
Geoscience
Global Studies Minor
Graphic Design
Health Sciences
History
Human Services
Individualized Studies
Latin American Studies Minor
Mathematics
Music
Music Media and Production
Music Promotion and Industry
Neuroscience
Nursing
Organizational Leadership
Philosophy Minor
Photography
Physics
Political Science
Pre-Engineering
Psychology
Religious Studies
Secondary Education (Grades 6-12)
Sociology
Special Education Minor
Studies in Education
Theatre Arts
Web Design and Development
Women's and Gender Studies Minor

EIGHTEEN: **ALVERNO COLLEGE**

College Name: Alverno College
City, State: Milwaukee, WI
Website: https://www.alverno.edu/
Admissions email address: Admissions@Alverno.edu
Admissions phone: 414.382.6100
Full-time undergraduate enrollment: 864
Number of full-time undergraduate students living on campus: 200
Average class size: 15
Student-faculty ratio: 7:1

Submitted by Jean O'Toole, Director of Marketing and Communications, Alverno College

No matter where you're headed, Alverno College will get you ready for what's next. Since our founding in 1887 by the School Sisters of St. Francis, Alverno has taken a bold, results-oriented approach to education by preparing students for personal and professional growth. As one of the largest Catholic women's colleges in the nation, our students experience a collaborative learning environment in which they grow as leaders. Our community is here to welcome you and empower you to achieve your full potential. Every class you take at Alverno requires you to demonstrate competency in our Eight Abilities – skills that are essential to succeed both on the job and in life. Our students stand out because they've mastered these abilities, many of them landing jobs before graduation. Located on a 46-acre campus in a residential Milwaukee neighborhood, Alverno offers a close-knit community with big-city access.

A leader in higher education innovation, Alverno has earned international accolades for its highly effective ability-based, assessment-as-learning approach to education, which emphasizes hands-on experience and develops in-demand skills. The college,

Wisconsin's first Hispanic-Serving Institution, consistently ranks among the top schools in the Midwest for its commitment to undergraduate teaching and innovation by U.S. News & World Report.

We offer students several distinctive opportunities to flourish, including:

- The Thea Bowman Institute for Excellence and Leadership, a cohort-model, full-tuition scholarship program for Black undergraduates who have a strong desire to serve as leaders.
- The Center for Academic Excellence, which provides opportunities for all students to develop academic excellence by extending their learning beyond the classroom, working collaboratively with supportive peers, faculty, staff, and the professional and greater community.
- The Research Center for Women and Girls, a center devoted to taking scholarly research that applies to the real world where it can inspire, transform and support initiatives that improve the lives of women and girls in Wisconsin and beyond.
- The Alverno Greenhouse, a state-of-the-art aquaponics facility that sustainably grows plants, vegetables, and perch, offering students an opportunity to engage in hands-on learning, participate in research projects, and explore new career paths in food, urban agriculture, water research, conservation, and human services industries.

The College intentionally creates an inclusive community that engages students in active and collaborative learning and fosters academic excellence. Expanding its mission through graduate and other programs that are open to both men and women, nearly 74% of incoming students are the first in their families to attend college. Nearly 100% of Alverno's undergraduate full-time students who apply for financial aid receive assistance from the College's financial aid program. Alverno is an international leader in teaching and assessment innovations, with colleagues and institutions around the globe admiring and emulating its methods.

The College's full-time faculty hold the highest degree in their respective fields. They instruct students in 60-plus undergraduate program areas reflecting majors, minors, and adult and degree completion programs. They are contained within four schools:

☐ School of Professional Studies (including the Business and Education divisions)
☐ JoAnn McGrath School of Nursing and Health Professions
☐ School of Arts and Sciences
☐ School of Adult Learning and New Initiatives

Within the School of Arts and Sciences are the divisions of Arts; Behavioral Sciences; Humanities; and Natural Sciences, Mathematics, and Technology. The School of Adult Learning and New Initiatives reimagines traditional education, offering accelerated degrees, certificates, and micro-credential programs for women and men.

Our graduate programs, open to women and men, include an Educational Specialist in School Psychology; a Master of Arts in Education for teachers; a Master of Science in Nursing with eight tracks; a Direct Entry Master of Science in Nursing offered in both Milwaukee and Mesa, Arizona; a Master of Business Administration; a Master of Music Therapy; a Master of Science in Community Psychology; a Master of Arts in Music and Liturgy; a Doctor of Nursing Practice; and a Doctorate in Education.

Since 1973, Alverno's ability-based curriculum has been described as innovative and revolutionary. We believe the real benefit of knowledge is knowing how to apply it, which is why we integrate eight core abilities into our curriculum. The Eight Abilities are the foundation of the Alverno experience, and students practice these essential skills throughout their educational journey, working toward mastery. Ultimately, the Eight Abilities are what give our students and alumni the power to stand apart from the crowd and to succeed both personally and professionally. The Eight Abilities are:
● Communication: Makes meaning of the world by connecting people, ideas, books, media, and technology.
● Analysis: Develops critical and independent thinking.

- Problem Solving: Helps define problems and integrate resources to reach decisions, make recommendations, or implement action plans.
- Valuing in Decision Making: Approaches moral issues by understanding the dimensions of personal decisions and accepting responsibility for consequences.
- Social Interaction: Facilitates results in group efforts by eliciting the views of others to help formulate conclusions.
- Developing a Global Perspective: Requires the understanding of — and respect for — the economic, social, and biological interdependence of global life.
- Effective Citizenship: Involves making informed choices and developing strategies for collaborative involvement in community issues.
- Aesthetic Engagement: Integrates the intuitive dimensions of participation in the arts with broader social, cultural, and theoretical frameworks.

Alverno's 46-acre campus is located in a safe, residential area in Milwaukee's Jackson Park neighborhood, and includes walking paths, picnic tables, and places for socializing, studying, and reflection. The college is just 15 minutes from downtown Milwaukee, home to the lakefront, many trendy restaurants, galleries, and festivals. We offer a diverse, welcoming community of students and faculty, plus opportunities to learn, lead, explore and give back, and have fun. Some of the ways students get involved outside of the classroom include:

☐Athletics: We offer eight NCAA Division III sports including basketball, cross country, golf, soccer, softball, tennis, track & field, and volleyball.
☐Campus Ministry: Inclusive programming for students from a wide range of faith traditions as well as volunteer opportunities in Milwaukee and beyond.
☐Student Activities and Leadership: With 30+ student organizations and numerous leadership opportunities, it's easy for students to find their fit and enhance their resume.

An Alverno education will get you ready for your future. It has the power to transform your life as well as the lives of your family members and your community. That's why we don't want anything to stand in your way. The Alverno Financial Aid team is here to help you, from putting together your initial financial aid package to helping you manage the cost of your education. And we'll help you make sure that when you leave here, you do so on solid ground.

Alverno offers a variety of merit-based and need-based scholarships to help support your education, along with grants, student loans, and student employment. We are happy to help you search for and identify scholarship opportunities from organizations outside of Alverno as well as to assist you with your scholarship applications.

Currently (2023), incoming freshmen receive anywhere between $14,000 and $20,000 per year, based on cumulative HS GPA. In addition to merit-based scholarships, Alverno offers first-year undergraduate students additional opportunities to receive competitive merit scholarships ranging from an additional $2,000 up to full tuition.

Academic Programs

Accounting   major
Adult Education   minor
Art /Art Studies emphasis
Art Education   emphasis
Art Therapy   major
Biologymajor
Biology Broad Field   major
Biomedical Sciences   major
Business Analytics   minor
Business Management   major
Chemistry   major
Communication/Communication Studies   major
Computer Science   major
Creative Arts   minor

Creative Media Design major
Dance minor
Data Analytics minor
Data Science major
Early Childhood Education emphasis
Elementary Education emphasis
English emphasis
Environmental Science major
Environmental Water Science major
Film Studies minor
Global Studies major
Health Education major
History major
Human Biology major
International Business & Language Area Studies major
Kinesiology - Pre-Physical Therapy major
Kinesiology - Sport Management major
Liberal Studies/Elective Studies minor
Mathematics emphasis
Mathematics/Computer Science major
Media Design minor
Mega Broad Field Business major
Molecular, Cellular & Integrative Biology major
Music minor
Music Therapy major
Nursing major
Nursing, Accelerated Second Degree major
Pharmaceutical Science major
Philosophy major
Political Science minor
Politics &/or Government minor
Psychology major
Public Health major
Religion/Religious Studies major
Religious Studies major
RN to BSN Completion major
Secondary Education emphasis
Social Studies/Sciences Broad Field emphasis
Social Work major
Sociology major
Spanish for the Professional major
Spanish/English Healthcare Interpretation minor

Special Education   minor
Studio Art/Integrated Studio Arts   major
Technical Theater   major
Women's &/or Gender Studies   major
Writing, Creative or Professional   minor

NINETEEN: **BLACKBURN COLLEGE**

College Name: Blackburn College
City, State: Carlinville, IL
Website: https://www.blackburn.edu/
Admissions email address: admissions@blackburn.edu
Admissions phone: 217.854.5517
Full-time undergraduate enrollment: 350
Number of full-time undergraduate students living on campus: 270
Average class size: 12
Student-faculty ratio: 11:1

Submitted by Kyle Lowden, Director of Marketing and Public Relations, Blackburn College

There is no other college in the United States quite like Blackburn College.

Established in 1837, Blackburn was founded with the notion that the ideal student would be intelligent, forward-thinking, and forward-looking. For almost 200 years, this has been a place where students can excel academically and also excel in preparation for real-world career success.

Located in the heart of the Midwest, Blackburn offers a traditional college experience and so much more. The campus is a unique living laboratory, where we meld a rigorous liberal arts curriculum with our nationally acclaimed Work Program. Students get all the exploration, engaged academics, and community along with real-life, ready-for-the-workforce skills. These leadership skills immediately apply to nearly every job situation, giving graduates the running start to their futures.

While there are ten recognized Work Colleges in the country, Blackburn has the only program exclusively managed by students, adding a whole new dimension to the college experience. The College relies on students to help run the campus. Students manage and coach their peers in the program, serve on critical planning committees, and help facilitate day-to-day operations—fully recognizing that their success and the college's success go hand-in-hand.

Over the years, our students have built Blackburn brick by brick. In fact, Blackburn enjoys the distinction of being the only college campus in the United States to have been largely built by its students. Today Blackburn students carry on this tradition by staffing mission-critical jobs as administrators, plumbers, carpenters, landscapers, cooks, servers, graphic artists, campus safety officers, tutors, and teaching assistants.

Blackburn's Work Program also helps make a Blackburn education attainable for many, like offsetting tuition costs at one of the already lowest-cost private four-year colleges in Illinois, making the dream of a college education affordable for thousands of first-generation and underserved students.

As a small, four-year liberal arts college, Blackburn fosters close, meaningful relationships between faculty, staff, and students. That sort of true collaboration shapes the academic culture and the campus community. Students come from diverse social, economic, and cultural backgrounds, including many from underrepresented populations. Coming to campus as curious learners, they find a welcoming and inclusive environment that allows students to grow, build essential life and work skills, and forge friendships that last a lifetime.

Student life at Blackburn is as multidimensional and diverse as our student population. There are countless ways to share your creativity—in performance spaces, art galleries, and literary publications. Bothwell Auditorium features state-of-the-art light and sound systems, and Blackburn is an official All-Steinway school, joining the Oberlin Conservatory and Yale School of Music ranks.

Blackburn Beavers are kind community leaders but fiercely competitive when the games begin. The school offers 15 NCAA Division III teams where athletes train with seasoned coaches to sharpen their skills. As the championship banners in Dawes Gymnasium reveal, athletes channel the trademark Blackburn work ethic, collaboration, and leadership into consistent success.

Blackburn is the only college in downstate Illinois to be honored as a Tree Campus USA and Bee Campus USA. Blackburn has been certified as pollinator-friendly, maintaining nearly 20 beehives, producing honey, and supporting campus bee and bat initiatives. The College also has an eight-acre solar farm, one of the largest projects of its kind in Illinois, which provides 80% of Blackburn's energy needs.

This College is more than just another four-year institution; it's a head start on everything else that follows. From academics to campus life to friends and community—our purpose is to help you prepare for life after college. Blackburn College is here to provide an extraordinary head start and help the next generation of leaders, problem-solvers, and creative thinkers rise to meet their purpose.

You can't afford to risk your future on a degree that doesn't work. And with Blackburn College's tuition already among the lowest of all private, four-year, residential colleges in Illinois, you won't. When you add in our unique Work Program providing tuition credit, you get a degree you actually can afford and the future you've earned.

The transformative Blackburn experience begins the day you enter campus. You'll become a valued leader in creating the Blackburn culture while developing invaluable professional skills and enjoying a rich and joyful college life. And, it's not because you're paying the highest tuition and fees. It's because we believe a good college education should be attainable for anyone who aspires to pursue it.

We firmly believe that a rich, diverse student population is the lifeblood of our school. Our nationally acclaimed Work Program plays a vital role in bringing a socially, culturally, and economically diverse and inclusive population to our campus each year.

Blackburn's approach has also helped make a college education affordable to thousands of first-generation students and working-class families. U.S. News & World Report has not only ranked Blackburn as one of the best colleges and universities in the Midwest, but the publication also recognizes Blackburn as a top performer for social mobility. Blackburn has a unique ability to serve low-income and underrepresented populations, a testament to its deep commitment to ensure that access to higher education is more inclusive.

The reality of college tuition can be challenging. Our faculty and staff work incredibly hard to ensure that your time and your money are well spent. By integrating learning, work, and service, we're able to align your work duties with your academic goals. This creates as efficient a learning and skill-gathering college experience as possible. This is your head start.

Combining our personalized approach to academics and the hands-on experience in our nationally-recognized Work Program, Blackburn is an incredible investment into your personal and professional future. Blackburn's Financial Aid team works tirelessly to find the optimal tuition arrangement for your unique situation. We work with students, families, the state of Illinois, the federal government, private sources, and endowments to uncover merit and need-based financial solutions.

Blackburn has long been invested in identifying and eliminating barriers to accessing higher education. A student's performance in the classroom over their entire high school career is a better indicator of future academic success—so the school removed testing requirements from its admissions process. Blackburn also doesn't charge a fee to apply, removing unnecessary obstacles to ensure students and families from all socioeconomic backgrounds can take advantage of earning a transformational Blackburn degree.

Hear from two of our students:

"Blackburn has truly been life-changing for me, and I will never forget all of the awesome experiences, people, and events I have encountered along the way. It is forever a part of my identity and it has shaped me as an individual in many positive ways. I love it and will always be grateful for what it has given me!" —Emily Fleck, '22

"The Work Program has already helped me launch my career - even before graduation. My experience working in the Marketing & Public Relations office, the effort founding Blackburn's bat research initiative, and the leadership skills I gained as a department manager all combined to help me to secure social media and event planning roles that will allow me to hit the ground running after earning my degree. Blackburn College lit a fire in me to get involved, and it burns brightly still today." —Lexi Hoffman, '23

Academic Programs

Majors

Art
Graphic Design
Biology
Biology - Environmental Track
Biology - General Track
Biology - Molecular Biology Track
Biology - Pre-med & Other Health Prof. Track
Medical Laboratory Science
Secondary Science Education: Biology)9-12)
Business Administration and Economics
Accounting
Business Administration

Business Management
Human Resource Management
Marketing
Chemistry and Physics
Computer Science
Computer Science - Cybersecurity Track
Computer Science - Game Design Track
Computer Science - General Track
Justice Administration
Justice Administration
Education
Early Childhood Education
Elementary Education (K-9)
Foreign Language: Spanish (K-12) Education
Middle Grades Education
Physical Education (K-12)
Secondary English Education (9-12)
Secondary Mathematics Education (9-12)
Secondary Science Education: Biology (9-12)
Secondary Social Science Education: History (9-12)
Special Education (LBS I)
Educational Studies
 Educational Studies–Educ. Paraprofessional Track
English & Communications
 Communications
Creative Writing
English
Secondary English Education (9-12)
History
History
Secondary Social Science Educ: History (9-12)
Leadership, Law, and Public Service
Political Science–General Track
Political Science–Law Track
Organizational Leadership
Mathematics
Mathematics–Finance Track
Mathematics–General Track
Secondary Mathematics Education (9-12)
Modern Languages
Foreign Language: Spanish (K-12) Education
Spanish

Music & Theatre
Music–Piano Performance
Music–Voice Performance
Theatre
Philosophy & Religion
Physical Education
Physical Education (K-12)
Sport Management
Psychology
Psychology

Minors

Art History
Graphic Design
Studio Art
Biology
Accounting
Business Administration
Business Management
Economics
Human Resource Management
Marketing Communications
Chemistry
Computer Science
Information Systems
Justice Administration
Business Communications
Communications
Creative Writing
English
Gender and Sexuality Studies
Sports Communication
History
Leadership
Liberal Arts and the Law
Political Science
Mathematics
Spanish
Music
Theatre
Philosophy

Religious Studies
Coaching
Exercise Science
Physical Education
Psychology

TWENTY: **WEBSTER UNIVERSITY**

College Name: Webster University
City, State: St. Louis, MO
Website: https://www.webster.edu/
Admissions email address: admit@webster.edu
Admissions phone: 314.246.7800
Full-time undergraduate enrollment: 2,000
Number of full-time undergraduate students living on campus: 750
Average class size: 20-25
Student-faculty ratio: 12:1

Submitted by Andrew Laue, Associate Director of Undergraduate Admissions, Webster University

Located in the beautiful St. Louis suburb of Webster Groves, Missouri, Webster University offers the best of both worlds: The advantages of a comprehensive university near a major metropolitan area, and the benefits and personalized attention of a small college.

Students who attend Webster do so because they want an experience that is different from a traditional large university. At Webster, students are comfortable knowing they can be themselves, participate in student organizations open to everybody, explore multiple academic areas, engage in hands-on learning early and often, and enjoy a culture that celebrates diversity and inclusion.

Creativity is a central theme to the Webster experience, and this is reflected in some of the academic programs offered. These include Animation, Filmmaking, Music, Dance, Illustration, Creative Writing, Music Production, Songwriting, Theatre, Video Game Design, Music Direction for Musical Theatre, Scriptwriting, Graphic Design, and Photography. Freshmen students enter these majors right away and will typically take multiple classes related to their academic discipline during their first year. For example, Filmmaking majors check out digital cameras and shoot video around campus; Graphic Design students explore traditional and digital artistic formats; and those in the Conservatory of Theatre Arts become immersed in a professional training experience from day one.

In addition, Webster offers traditional liberal arts programs in Business, Humanities, Sciences, and Education. Within these departments, there are some unique majors offered such as Human Rights, Sports and Entertainment Management, and Cybersecurity. Regardless of which academic area a student chooses to pursue, they will benefit from real-world learning and instruction from faculty who are experts in their field.

"The academic environment at Webster emphasizes the importance of student advising and made sure I was on my best-fit path as a student, which was of utmost importance to me so I could attain my goals post-graduation. I also found Webster's small class sizes beneficial because they facilitate discussion among students and the professor, allowing you to look at any subject more critically."
—Sara McMullin, BA Psychology

Outside of the classroom, students will find NCAA Division III athletics, over 70 student clubs and organizations, and opportunities for leadership development.

Another critical element to the Webster experience is internationalism and global citizenship. Webster is an international university with campuses located across the world. As such, there are opportunities for study abroad that can be as short as one week, or as long as one year. Students may study abroad as early as the second semester of their freshman year, and the University provides airfare assistance. All students will complete the Global Citizenship Program requirement, which is the core coursework that makes up the foundation of the Webster academic experience. This program is flexible and students are in control of how they want to satisfy their requirements. Students spread out the GCP requirements over four years, which allows them to become involved in their major area right away, and/or sample multiple academic areas during their first two years.

"Studying abroad at Webster Geneva gave me what was missing at my large university campus. I found the space to take initiative by contributing to organizations, and had access to resources at the United Nations as a place for study and networking, especially at the conferences and events."—Alexandra Belize, Webster Geneva study abroad student

The Academic Resource Center caters to those students who have differentiated learning abilities, or perhaps need additional support to fully realize their academic potential. The learning environment at Webster promotes success for all, and faculty are always willing to meet students where they are and help them develop a plan for achievement. All academic support services are offered free of charge. Opportunities for individual excellence exist both in and out of the classroom, and a formal leadership development program is an option for all students.

If students have earned college credit while in high school, Webster will accept those credits if certain criteria are met. This typically means an AP test score of 3 or higher; a dual credit grade of C or higher; completion of the International Baccalaureate Diploma (separate IB subject scores can be evaluated on an individual basis).

Financial Aid and scholarships are widely available. Merit-based awards are offered up to full tuition, and other programs provide assistance for room and board costs. In addition, there is no difference in tuition for out-of-state students and talent scholarships are offered for certain majors.

The Webster University experience is special. Students will find an environment that is comfortable and judgment-free. The approach to academics ensures that all students are given the best chance possible to succeed, transforming them into global citizens who will impact the world for future generations.

Academic Program

Accounting
Acting
Advertising and Marketing Communications
Animation
Anthropology and Sociology
Art
Business Administration
Chemistry
Computer Science
Costume Construction
Costume Design
Creative Writing
Criminology and Criminal Justice
Cybersecurity
Dance
Directing
Economics
Education
Education Studies
English
Exercise Science
Film Studies
Film, Television and Video Production
Finance
French
Games and Game Design
General Studies
German
Global Studies
Graphic Design
History
Illustration
Interactive Digital Media
International Business
International Human Rights

International Relations
Journalism
Legal Studies
Lighting Design
Management
Management Information Systems
Marketing
Mathematics
Media Studies
Media Production
Music
Music Composition with an Emphasis in Concert Music
Music Composition with an Emphasis in Songwriting
Music Direction for Musical Theatre
Music Performance with an Emphasis in Jazz
Music Performance with an Emphasis in Orchestral Instruments
Music Performance with an Emphasis in Piano
Music Performance with an Emphasis in Voice
Music Education
Musical Theatre
Nursing (2+2 program)
Philosophy
Photography
Political Science
Pre-Dentistry
Pre-Engineering
Pre-Medicine
Pre-Pharmacy
Psychology
Public Relations
Scene Design
Scene Painting
Scriptwriting
Sound Design
Sound Recording and Engineering
Spanish
Sports Communication
Sports and Entertainment Management
Stage Management
Strategic Communication
Technical Direction
Wig and Makeup Design

Women, Gender, and Sexuality Studies

TWENTY-ONE: **SWEET BRIAR COLLEGE**

College Name: Sweet Briar College
City, State: Sweet Briar, VA
Website: https://www.sbc.edu/
Admissions email address: admissions@sbc.edu
Admissions phone: 434.381.6142
Full-time undergraduate enrollment: 460
Number of full-time undergraduate students living on campus: 428
Average class size: 16
Student-faculty ratio: 8:1

Submitted by Claire Griffith, Senior Director of Alumnae Relations and Development, Sweet Briar College

Since 1901, women have arrived at Sweet Briar with different dreams and goals, but each one graduates ready to fulfill those goals and be successful in their careers and life. At Sweet Briar, young women become active problem-solvers, decision-makers, and collaborators. Your classmates, in addition to your professors and staff across campus, will support and strengthen you. Sweet Briar women know that success derives from hard work, a strong will, and a supportive network. Here, you will find a community of driven intellectuals supporting and encouraging you to succeed in any chosen area. You will be surrounded by brilliant professors who engage you in hands-on learning experiences and become mentors for life.

A Sweet Briar education is more affordable than you might think — *all* students admitted to Sweet Briar are considered to receive merit-based scholarships. We offer a transparent tuition model to make it easy to calculate your costs since investing in your education is the most important investment you will ever make. We will share in that investment by administering a personalized financial aid program tailored to your needs.

At Sweet Briar, you will be respected, you will be heard, you will be pushed, and you will succeed. We believe in women's leadership so strongly that we've built it directly into our curriculum. In our women's leadership core, you will learn practical skills such as collaborative change-making, preparing you for every role leaders take on—from a champion of accountability to a financial strategist. Our women's leadership core curriculum consists of 10 courses over four years designed to teach you how to harness your natural leadership abilities. You'll be ready to lead regardless of your chosen life path.

Throughout your four years at Sweet Briar, you'll develop communication skills, learn to sift through evidence, and gain an understanding of diverse cultural and academic perspectives. You'll look squarely upon our world's problems and become empowered to craft solutions. **With more than 20 programs of study, there are infinite ways to craft an educational path that suits you and your interests.** We have strong liberal arts and STEM curricula, with programs from engineering science to creative writing and archaeology to pre-law. In fact, many students pursue multiple areas of study or create their own major entirely.

We know that each woman's path is unique, and we will help and support you no matter where you want to go from here. **Hands-on learning is a critical part of all academic programs at Sweet Briar.** After all, talking about a subject is an excellent skill, but the ability to put your newfound knowledge to work is crucial. Professors and alumnae alike will help you connect with employers and established professionals so you can get practical work experience through internships during college and pursue desirable jobs after graduation. Of course, hands-on learning doesn't have to happen off campus. Here, award-winning authors mentor budding creative writers, and business executives inspire future entrepreneurs. **Nearly 60% of our students do in-depth research with a professor over the summer or as a research assistant during the academic year. You can also apply for one of our Grants for Engaged Learning—which provides up to $2,000 to**

experience the learning you just can't get in a classroom, such as a study abroad trip or an internship that needs to be supplemented. Whatever your passion, you can pursue it at Sweet Briar College.

In three of the last four years, *U.S. News and World Report* named Sweet Briar to the Most Innovative Schools list. We're proud to be recognized for our academic and institutional innovations. Our ABET-accredited engineering program is hands-on, project-based, and focused on solving complex problems. Graduates become engineers and succeed at top companies and grad schools where big-picture thinkers stand out in the crowd.

We are gaining national attention for our sustainability and conservation initiatives, where our students are directly involved in our greenhouse and other agricultural operations. Our 2,847-acre campus is an experiential learning laboratory comprising farmlands, vineyards, forests, wetlands, and meadows. Plus, relationships with state and federal partners create opportunities to help you become a leader in the future of agriculture and sustainability.

Sweet Briar's nationally-ranked equestrian program and facilities stand out as some of the best in the country. Our NCEA team won the 2021 Single-Discipline National Championship, and our ODAC team won the conference championship for the sixth time in 2021. Thanks to a generous donor, our stables were renovated in 2020—undoubtedly a critical element of our teams' excellence. Our future is bright as a longstanding destination for the nation's top hunter-jumper equestrians.

Sweet Briar College has launched the careers of alumnae in just about every field you can imagine. **Our alumnae have pursued graduate study at some of the best colleges and universities in the world, and in the last ten years, our vet school placement is 100 percent!** Our most recent graduating class features young women working at NASA, Boeing, the Navy, and more. Others are attending graduate school at Columbia, Duke, Georgetown, Ohio State, Vanderbilt, Virginia Tech, University of Virginia, the University of St Andrews in Scotland, and others.

Sweet Briar women are strong, determined, and tenacious. You'll leave here empowered and ready to be a leader regardless of field or endeavor. Our alumnae are civic leaders, scientists, doctors, authors, entrepreneurs, educators, engineers, change-makers—and so much more. We have a passion for helping women become leaders. And just like the 80% of our students who have taken on at least one leadership role on campus, you'll have a chance to put everything you learn into practice.

Some people see a beautiful landscape. We see a natural training ground for leaders. Our 2,847 acres of diverse landscape and historic buildings will become your classrooms, laboratories, and studios. Sweet Briar will inspire, center, and ground you—preparing you for a life dedicated to sustainability, innovation, entrepreneurship, and leadership. Among the busiest places at Sweet Briar are the pollinator habitat and apiary, just a short walk from the heart of campus. They're buzzing with butterflies, hummingbirds, honey bees, and all the other creatures that ensure our food sources, habitats, and ecosystems flourish. These are fine places for you to grow, too. Learn insect biology up close in the pollinator habitat. Join our Audubon Campus Conservation Chapter, one of the first of its kind in the nation. In our 20-hive apiary, build beekeeping skills and learn about bee biology and the environment supporting pollinators, like our campus wildflower meadow. Collaborate with local growers on social entrepreneurship and economic development projects. Our campus becomes your vantage point to explore all the issues driving sustainability and the global food economy. If you're interested in sustainability, we're a natural fit!

Most students are actively involved in at least one (but more often, three or four!) extracurricular activity—from being an athlete on one of our eight varsity athletic teams to participating in (and in many cases leading) one of our many clubs and organizations. You'll find a robust outdoor program and active student government here. You'll swim, work out and cheer on your friends at our Fitness and Athletic Center. You'll have dinner at the professors' houses. You'll spend time in our Quad, with the traditions near and dear to every Sweet Briar student's heart: from the Daisy Ceremony in your first week to Lantern Bearing and

Commencement in your last. These traditions will create memories that will stay with you long after you graduate, connecting you in powerful ways to the alumnae who have gone before and the generations of Sweet Briar women who will come after.

See what Sweet Briar has to offer for you! We will even help you come to campus for a visit!

Academic Programs

Undergraduate Majors and/or Minors

- Ancient Studies *(Minor)*
- Archaeology *(Minor)*
- Archaeology and Ancient Studies [Tracks: Ancient Studies, Archaeology] *(B.A.)*
- Art History *(B.A.)*
- Biology *(B.S. | Minor)*
- Business *(B.A. | Minor)*
- Chemistry *(B.S. | Minor)*
- Dance [Options: Performance, Teaching] *(Minor)*
- Economics *(B.A. | Minor)*
- Elementary Education and Teaching *(B.A.)*
- Engineering Science *(B.S. | Minor)*
- English and Creative Writing *(B.A. | Minor)*
- Environmental Science *(B.S. | Minor)*
- History *(B.A. | Minor)*
- Interdisciplinary Studies [Self-designed major] *(B.A.)*
- Mathematics *(B.A. | Minor)*
- Music *(Minor)*
- Musical Theatre *(Minor)*
- Performing Arts [Tracks: Dance, Music, Theatre] *(B.A.)*
- Philosophy *(B.A. | Minor)*
- Political Science *(B.A. | Minor)*
- Psychology *(B.A. | Minor)*
- Studio Art *(B.A. | Minor)*
- Teacher Licensure

- <u>Theatre</u> (Minor)

Certificate Programs

- <u>Arts Management</u>
- <u>Equine Studies</u> [Concentrations: Management, Teaching and Schooling]
- <u>Leadership in Sustainable Agriculture and Food Systems</u>

Teacher Licensure

- <u>Biology</u> *(6-12)*
- <u>Chemistry</u> *(6-12)*
- <u>Dance Arts</u> *(PreK-12)*
- <u>Elementary Education</u> *(PreK-6)*
- <u>English</u> *(6-12)*
- <u>History and Social Science</u> *(6-12)*
- <u>Mathematics</u> *(6-12)*
- <u>Special Education General Curriculum</u> *(K-12, add-on endorsement)*
- <u>Theatre Arts</u> *(PreK-12)*
- <u>Visual Arts</u> *(PreK-12)*

Pre-professional and Programs of Interest

- <u>Pre-law</u>

- <u>Pre-medicine</u>

- <u>Pre-veterinary</u>

- Self-designed study of foreign languages

Graduate

- <u>Master of Arts in Teaching</u> *(M.A.T.)*

TWENTY-TWO: SAINT MARY'S UNIVERSITY OF MINNESOTA

College Name: Saint Mary's University of Minnesota
City, State: Winona, MN
Website: www.smumn.edu
Admissions email address: admission@smumn.edu
Admissions phone: 507.457.1700
Full-time undergraduate enrollment: 950
Number of full-time undergraduate students living on campus: 850
Average class size: 16
Student-faculty ratio: 13:1

Submitted by Dr. Timothy Gossen, Senior Director of Admission, Saint Mary's University of Minnesota

Saint Mary's University of Minnesota is a special place with a long history of educating students. The Lasallian Catholic heritage was bestowed on us by the De La Salle Christian Brothers, many of whom still are connected with the institution. Our Lasallian Catholic values respect the individuality of all persons, meet them where they are, and make education accessible to all students. Thanks to the De La Salle Christian Brothers, students experience faith, service, and community throughout their educational experience. This work is accomplished daily on our beautiful Winona, Minnesota, campus in a caring community. Students surround themselves on campus with nature, good people, and lots to do—both on campus and around Winona.

Saint Mary's has been ranked in the top 30 of the most beautiful college campuses by College Consensus. The beauty and recreational opportunities are unrivaled. Our beautiful 450-acre campus, nestled in the bluffs, offers a scenic disc golf course and trout stream. We also have 15 kilometers of groomed cross-country running and cross-country ski trails. We even make our own snow!

Off-campus, you can paddle the backwaters of the Mississippi River, eat the best donuts in the state, hike SugarLoaf, or hammock by Lake Winona. If you are looking for an inner-city experience, this campus is not for you.

U.S. News & World Report ranked Saint Mary's #3 Best Value in Regional Universities Midwest and #1 Best Value in Minnesota (2022). Niche also ranked our dorms as #2 in the state of Minnesota.

Students tell us they choose Saint Mary's because of its real value. Value goes beyond the cost of your education to your total experience and return on investment. Students are treated with respect, taught with humanity, and supported on their journey—it is all about you. The campus is full of energy, with lots to do—from student organizations to residence life programming to cheering on the 15 NCAA Division III Teams. There is always something to do.

We strongly believe participating in social, educational, and service programs provides you with the opportunity to have fun and become involved on campus. Programs are created by our Residence Life team to maintain a strong and active residential experience. The 11 residence halls are your home away from home. You will enjoy living with peers and energetic professional residence life staff who care about your overall well-being, safety, and engaging student experience.

Within the classrooms, all students can expect hands-on experiential learning, practical knowledge, and developing skills that prepare students for today and tomorrow. Students say they learn how to go from making a living to making a life. The well-rounded educational approach will help build skills that are sought-after by employers.

At Saint Mary's you'll find that faculty and staff at all levels care about each student as an individual, not just as a name on the roster. Our faculty are here to help you find your place in the world—and go out and make it better. They will help you find your sense of purpose, land a meaningful career, and lead a thriving life. Faculty will help develop skills like communication, empathy, adaptability, creative thinking, networking, critical thinking, public speaking, authenticity, and enthusiasm. We believe you will be ready for your career and we make it a top priority for you to be real-world ready.

Students will use the skills they learn at Saint Mary's daily. The education you receive will prepare you for graduate school and your professional career. Not only will this education provide you with a foundation of knowledge, but it also will introduce you to a network of alumni who will provide support and help as you move through your educational journey.

Saint Mary's will provide an environment that builds a sense of community. Students consistently tell us the environment on campus reflects our Cardinal spirit that is inclusive and engaging. Students are empowered to develop character, virtue, a sense of individual responsibility, and self-discipline. Students form lasting interpersonal relationships and build connections with peers and mentors. Each student is supported and respected as they navigate their educational journey.

For those students who want the benefit of a Lasallian Catholic experience, the heritage can offer a great deal because of a network of schools all with the same mission. A student at Saint Mary's is a member of the great international Lasallian Catholic network of 1000+ educational ministries, of which 60+ are high educational institutions, within 80 countries worldwide. This group of educational institutions distributed around the world is dedicated to quality student-centered education and learning in the Lasallian Catholic tradition.

We also have outstanding opportunities that await you in Winona. It has a diverse economic base with multiple international business corporations, including Fastenal, RTP Company, Fanatics, and Watkins. We are also located near world-class healthcare organizations such as the Mayo Clinic. Know that you will have many opportunities for internship experiences here. The city also has a vibrant arts culture, serving as the home of the Great River Shakespeare Festival, the Minnesota Beethoven Festival, the Frozen

River Film Festival, and the Sandbar Storytelling Festival, just to name a few.

Students have many opportunities both on and off campus to learn. It does not matter what your academic interest is. Our faculty and staff will be ready to help you be successful in the areas you wish to focus on.

We invite all to visit this special beautiful place. It is the best way to experience Saint Mary's—being here in person.

It is our mission to make education accessible to as many students as possible and that means financial accessibility as well. We strongly believe education is an investment in yourself that will return lifelong dividends. We understand families have invested in you and we hope that will continue. Our staff is here to assist you with explaining how the financial aid process works at Saint Mary's University of Minnesota.

Our dedicated admission counselors are committed to making this quality education available to you. The university strives to keep our tuition low in comparison to our peer institutions without compromising the outstanding quality of our academic and co-curricular programs. 100% of our first-year students receive financial aid assistance. It is core to who we are and our foundation of being a Lasallian Catholic institution is built on a centuries-old tradition of access to the best education for all.

We offer generous merit-based, visit, and distance scholarships. Scholarships for attending a Catholic high school and being a child or grandchild of an alum from Saint Mary's or the College of St. Theresa is available. All of which are stackable and renewable as long as the student stays in good academic standing.

Transfer and international students also receive similar scholarships.

Each student who files a FAFSA will sit down with an admission counselor one on one to discuss the investment needed to attend Saint Mary's.

181

We also offer the Cardinal Promise scholarship for Pell-eligible Minnesota and Wisconsin students. This generous scholarship, to qualifying students, will cover 100% of the tuition for these students. Annually, we offer benefactor-funded first-generation scholarships (full tuition, room, board, and fees) for students who have parents that never had an opportunity to attend a four-year college experience. All students are encouraged to apply for local scholarships and we educate students on the difference between grants, loans, and work programs. We also offer the Loan Repayment Assistance Program (LRAP) because we believe our education is so worth it that graduates will obtain a position paying $51,000 annually or we will help pay back their loans.

We know every family is unique and when it comes to assembling a financial aid offer, no two families have the same circumstances, but we do our best to work with each student and their family individually to make Saint Mary's as accessible to them as possible. We know Saint Mary's is a special place. A great fit for many students. We are proud of both our Lasallian Catholic heritage and how we can offer a quality education as affordable as possible. Our desire is for every student to find the university that is their "best fit." Our beautiful Winona, Minnesota campus as well as the City of Winona has much to offer. The cost of a private education, at Saint Mary's, is well worth the investment.

Academic Programs

Accounting
Biochemistry
Biology: Health Sciences
Biology: Pre-Physical Therapy
Biology: Pre-Physician Assistant Studies
Biology: General Biology track
Biology: Life Science track

182

Biology: Pre-Medical Professions track
Biology: Pre-Laboratory Scientist
Biology: Pre-Medical Imaging
Business Intelligence and Analytics
Chemistry
Computer Science: Cybersecurity track
Computer Science: Data Analytics track
Computer Science: Management Information Systems track
Computer Science: Software Design track
Criminal Justice: Corrections track
Criminal Justice: Law Enforcement track
Educational Studies: Adult Education Contexts
Educational Studies: Child and Family Contexts
Educational Studies: Youth Development and Leadership
Elementary Education (K-6)
Elementary Education: Communication Arts and Literature
Endorsement for Grades 5-8
Elementary Education: General Science
Endorsement for Grades 5-8
Elementary Education: Mathematics
Endorsement for Grades 5-8
Elementary Education: Social Studies
Endorsement for Grades 5-8
Elementary Education: World Languages and Culture:
Spanish Endorsement for Grades 5-8
Environmental Biology and Conservation
Finance
Health Humanities
IHM Seminary Philosophy
Management
Marketing
Mathematics
Mathematics: Education track
Nursing: pre-licensure
Philosophy
Psychology
Public Relations and Digital Media
Secondary Education Grades 5-12 and K-12
Sport Management

TWENTY-THREE: **MONMOUTH COLLEGE**

College Name: Monmouth College
City, State: Monmouth, IL
Website: https://www.monmouthcollege.edu/
Admissions email address: admissions@monmouthcollege.edu
Admissions phone: 309.457.2345
Full-time undergraduate enrollment: 764
Number of full-time undergraduate students living on campus: 702
Average class size: 13
Student-faculty ratio: 9:1

Submitted by Stephanie Levenson, Vice President for Enrollment Management, Monmouth College

We get it. You're trying to decide on a college, and the more you look into it, the more they all kind of blend together. And now you're on the Monmouth College page. What makes this school any different from all the others?

We'll answer that question with a question: When you go to college, would you like to major in SUBJECT 1 and SUBJECT 2, play for the SPORTS TEAM, be involved in THIS ACTIVITY and THAT ORGANIZATION, and maybe even join a FRATERNITY/SORORITY?

You can at Monmouth – to all of that, you can.

(Not sure if you're ready for ALL that yet? That's OK. Hang on a bit – we'll get to that, too.)

Along the way, your campus experiences will serve as the springboard for all types of possible accomplishments – having the confidence to take on a leadership role at your job or in your community, starting your own company, or maybe even working in a foreign country. Monmouth gives its students the tools to do amazing things.

But let's start at the beginning. You're not a student yet, but you've read this page and decided to come for a visit. You'll quickly notice our beautiful, residential campus – the attractive brick buildings, the well-maintained grounds. A common refrain we hear from our students is that they "feel at home" at Monmouth. Many say that's the case from the moment they set foot on campus on that first visit.

What you'll notice next is that the campus community is a welcoming one, with friendly faces at every turn. It's the people who make Monmouth the supportive college it is. Many of those friendly faces belong to our faculty, the very same professors whose classes you'll be taking, rarely in groups of more than 20.

Let's jump ahead a bit. You're now a Monmouth student! Not being an anonymous body in a classroom full of more than 100 others is already a win; it helps you stay better connected to your academics, knowing that it's easy – even encouraged – to stop by your professor's office with questions.

But there's more to it than that. Your Monmouth professors really get to know you – your goals, your concerns, your talents, your idiosyncrasies, maybe even your dog's name – and will be able to connect you with opportunities throughout your time on campus, and even beyond, long after you've taken a class with them. You'll receive the personalized attention that will help you realize your full potential.

And it's not just your professors who'll befriend you. We are family here. Head residents, other student leaders, and members of our enthusiastic staff also get to know you so they can find out – or help you discover – what your goals are and how to achieve them. Every student is different, so our faculty and staff meet students where they

186

are and help them free the possibilities inside them, building their self-confidence every step of the way. Maybe your potential has been underestimated up to now. That won't happen at Monmouth.

It's not uncommon for students to come to us not fully prepared for what college is like. Perhaps our greatest strength as a campus community is our ability to meet our students here (picture our hand at waist level) and get them here (hand over our head). It happens time and again, often surprising our students themselves with what they're able to achieve.

Monmouth's alumni network provides some of those same advantages as our faculty and staff, as they often return to campus to meet students or stay connected to their alma mater through the College's Wackerle Center for Career, Leadership & Fellowships. An outstanding resource for students looking for opportunities with internships, graduate schools, and employers, the Wackerle Center is part of our Center for Academic and Career Excellence – we call it The ACE, for short.

Along the way to finding your future vocation, there's plenty of time for fun and games. More than half of our incoming students join at least one of our 22 Fighting Scot athletic teams, and they're able to practice and compete in Monmouth's top-notch athletic facilities.

Winning games and championships is a nice bonus, but as our athletes advance in post-college life, what they tell us over and over again is how important it is to them that they formed lifelong bonds with their teammates. Those fellow Scots who worked out with you, practiced with you, took road trips with you, and competed with you, will be the same ones who attend your wedding and your children's weddings.

Speaking of sports, there is perhaps no better place to be on a beautiful autumn Saturday than a college campus, and Monmouth is an ideal example. The college community turns out to watch the championship-caliber football team, and various music, cheer, and dance groups perform. If it's Homecoming weekend, there was a big Spirit Shout with fireworks the night before the game and a full parade on Saturday morning. Bagpipe music fills the air – you know, 'cause we're the Fighting Scots!

Greek letters can be seen throughout the stands and the surrounding hillside at the football stadium, as Monmouth boasts a vibrant Greek life community, which stresses leadership and service. In fact, two national women's fraternities were founded at Monmouth – Pi Beta Phi and Kappa Kappa Gamma.

Still thinking that you might not have time for such activities as the Fighting Scots Marching Band, or being in the cast or crew of a theatre production, or participating in the annual moot court competition, or continuing to play your favorite sport? Think again! Monmouth offers all those opportunities but without the mindset of turning any of them into an exclusive commitment of your time. Many of our students are involved with several campus organizations, often acquiring valuable leadership skills while taking on important roles.

The same holds true for academics. Many of our students are double majors – sometimes in vastly different subjects, such as physics and music, or computer science and political science. Our curriculum is set up so that there's time to do that, as well as to gain valuable experience from a variety of opportunities outside the classroom.

So where will your Monmouth career take you? Will you be a member of Sigma Phi Epsilon, who plays soccer, sings in the Chorale, and studies chemistry and economics? Perhaps a member of the marching band, a head resident, a First Year Mentor, and a double major in classics and education?

Those combinations, and infinitely many more, are available to you here. Come to Monmouth College. Free YOUR possible.

Editor's note: The next portion is scholarship information taken from the Monmouth College website. I worked for Monmouth for 27 years, and families were amazed at the low cost, after gift assistance, even for higher income families. The below quotes are all about merit aid not based on income. Note: Financial aid and scholarship amounts and policies change from year to year, so keep in mind that this information is accurate as of May 2023. If you are considering applying to Monmouth, please check with them first to make sure you have up-to-date information.

All applicants to Monmouth are automatically considered for Dean's Scholarships, which are awarded based on a holistic review of a student's application. Dean's Scholarships are offered up to $29,000 per year for new first-year students, and up to $25,000 per year for new transfer students.

Full tuition scholarships for first-year students: Each year, select students are eligible based on academic criteria to apply and compete for a small number of full-tuition scholarships. First-year students with a cumulative high school GPA of 3.6 or above are eligible to compete for the [full tuition scholarships].

In addition to these full-tuition awards, eligible Scholarship Competition event participants may also receive one of a select number of President's Scholarships, a $30,000 annual, renewable award replacing their previously awarded Dean's Scholarship.

Other merit scholarships:

- Chemistry/Biochemistry Scholarships: The Richard "Doc" Kieft scholarship is awarded to a limited number of incoming domestic students majoring in chemistry or biochemistry.

- Bagpipe and Highland Drumming Scholarships: Students with experience participating or competing with a pipe band are invited to audition for our pipe band scholarships.

- Presbyterian Scholarship: The Presbyterian Scholarship is for first-time freshmen and transfer students interested in connecting their Presbyterian faith to education at Monmouth College.

Editor's note: Bottom line: Monmouth is one of the more affordable colleges in the Midwest. It's an excellent college with wonderful people. I highly recommend that you visit!—V. Peter Pitts

Academic Programs

Accounting
Anthropology Minor
Art
Arts Management
Asian Studies
Biochemistry
Biology
Biopsychology
Business and Economics
Chemistry
Classics
Communication Studies
Data Science Minor
Educational Studies
Engineering
English
Environmental Studies and Sustainability
Global Food Security Studies
Global Public Health Studies
Greek Minor
History
Integrated Studies
Interdisciplinary Studies
International Business
International Studies
Investigative Forensics Minor
Journalism Minor
Kinesiology
Latin American Studies Minor
Mathematics, Statistics, and Computer Science
Media Minor
Modern Languages, Literatures, and Cultures
Music
Neuroscience
Peace, Ethics, and Social Justice Minor
Philosophy and Religious Studies

Physics
Political Science
Psychology
Sociology Minor
Sociology and Anthropology
Sports Information and Media
Theatre
Women's Studies Minor

TWENTY-FOUR: **MORAVIAN UNIVERSITY**

College Name: Moravian University
City, State: Bethlehem, PA
Website: https://www.moravian.edu/
Admissions email address: admission@moravian.edu
Admissions phone: 610.861.1320
Full-time undergraduate enrollment: 1,900
Number of full-time undergraduate students living on campus: 1,000
Average class size: 15.6
Student-faculty ratio: 10:1

Submitted by Michael Corr, Assistant Vice President for Marketing and
Communications, Moravian University

Who We Are

Moravian University in Bethlehem, PA offers students a private
education they will not find anywhere else: personal attention and
preparation for life with a history of success longer than America's.

With small class sizes and expansive academics, Moravian
University is both selective and accessible, rooted in an education-
for-all inclusiveness that we pioneered. The first school to open its
doors to women, Moravian has constantly evolved over 280 years
and now carries university recognition, reflecting the richness of our
undergraduate, graduate, and research offerings.

Open to students of every faith and background, we are deeply proud
of our distinction as the only school with ties to the Moravian
Church, carrying its ideals of purpose, service, truth, and justice.
Founded in 1742 and set in charming Bethlehem and the picturesque

Lehigh Valley of eastern Pennsylvania, Moravian is the place for those expecting remarkably dedicated faculty, the latest technology, the warmest of spirits, and the power to truly transform your life.

How We're Different

Moravian University's distinctiveness begins with its extraordinary commitment to students. The faculty know you; the alumni help you, the career strategists guide you. The dedication is authentic and everywhere, starting before students even show up to campus and lasting long after they graduate. We have designed our university to ensure it, with one faculty member for every 10 students. Yet it is also in our identity. We take your education personally.

For a small school, the Moravian experience has a broad reach. Undergraduates can choose from more than 70 areas of study – and have the freedom to design their own majors. The graduate program provides more than 50 doctorate and master's degrees and certification options.

So many other touches set us apart, too. As an Apple Distinguished School, Moravian University gives every incoming undergraduate student a MacBook Pro, an iPad, and an Apple Pencil. It's part of our determination to ensure every student has the tools to succeed, regardless of their background. Moravian was the first to launch an honor society just for first-generation students, Alpha Alpha Alpha, creating a model for other colleges and universities across America. We run the oldest continuously operating bookstore in the world. And we feel so strongly about the return on investment that we guarantee it: The Moravian Career Promise offers to help pay student loans or offer more courses for free for eligible graduates not employed or in graduate school within one year.

How it Feels Here

Set on the north side of the Lehigh River, the University is actually two campuses, famously linked by the Moravian Mile of Main Street that runs right through the historic downtown. The iconic Moravian star is engraved in our history and is present everywhere you turn.

Moravian University's feel is entwined with that of Bethlehem's, carrying both the resilience of its steel-town lore and the lightness of the window candles that glow each night in Moravian tradition.

Bethlehem pulses with concerts, restaurants, arts, and all the local appeal of a college town. Yet it also sits in just the right spot for an easy drive to New York City, Washington, D.C., and Philadelphia. Known as the Christmas City, Bethlehem is so regarded for its history that it's been added to the UNESCO World Heritage site shortlist, hoping to join such historic sites as Independence Hall, the Statue of Liberty, and the pyramids of Egypt.

We are also committed to being a place of equity and diversity. Every ongoing step to ensure this comes from the entire reason Moravian University was founded: education for all. The Moravian Bishop John Amos Comenius inspired that belief, and his values loom as large today as his statue on campus.

How You Benefit

Our history demonstrates our staying power since 1742; only five schools in all of America have been educating as long as us, and that means we have centuries of traditions and success stories. Yet for today's students, what's even more relevant is what we offer now: the skills that employers want and that graduates need to succeed as dynamic thinkers and engaged citizens.

Moravian University is highly regarded for the career preparation, employability, and earnings of our graduates. Undergraduates get hands-on research experience with senior faculty. About 95 percent of our students graduate within four years, and 99 percent move into the workforce or advanced education within 10 months of graduation. The return on investment here is real.

And our commitment to it is stronger than ever through Elevate – Moravian's distinctive undergraduate experience for every incoming student. It provides what students have asked for and employers demand: work experience, global study, and teamwork and leadership skills, all backed by an extraordinary level of career support for individual students. We promise it will pay off and we back it up.

And at the graduate level, Moravian University gives students an exceptional chance to work with the businesses and mission-driven organizations of tomorrow through partnerships we create just for them. That's just one of many ways our graduate program is infused with energy, urgency, and innovation to fit the needs of students no matter where they are in life.

The benefits extend in even deeper ways. We see our students transform year to year – always curious about what's next, ever confident they will achieve it. Just as our "Via Lucis" motto means The Way of Light, we believe education should illuminate a path for a more just society and prepare the young people who will lead it. And ultimately, that is how Moravian University graduates benefit the most: As people of values who leave campus ready to take on the world.

Affordability [*editor's note: the following section was taken from the Moravian University website*]

Merit Scholarships for First-Year Students: Moravian University awards merit-based academic scholarships to incoming first-year undergraduate students based on their academic performance in high school and demonstrated involvement in school and community activities. Students are automatically considered for an academic scholarship upon the review of their application for admission. Academic scholarships can range between $20,000-$29,000 and are awarded regardless of financial need. These scholarships are renewable at the same amount each year for up to five years of payment (or completion of the undergraduate degree, whichever comes first); provided students maintain continuous, full-time enrollment and satisfactory academic progress. Note: Presidential scholars must also maintain a 3.0 cumulative GPA in addition to the aforementioned requirements.

Some other merit scholarship opportunities at Moravian University include:

- The Legacy Grant – Awarded to incoming full-time undergraduate students whose sibling, parent, grandparent, and/or great-grandparent graduated from Moravian University. Eligible recipients receive up to $2,000 annually.

- The Sibling Grant – Awarded to an incoming full-time undergraduate student enrolling at Moravian University who has a sibling currently enrolled at the college. Eligible recipients receive up to $2,000 annually.

- The Moravian Church Scholarship – Awarded to incoming full-time undergraduate students who are official documented members of a Moravian Church congregation. Eligible recipients receive up to $2,000 annually.

- Endowed and Annual Giving Scholarships – Alumni and friends of Moravian University donate millions of dollars every year to the many scholarship funds established to support our students. Incoming first-year students are encouraged to file the Free Application for Federal Student Aid (FAFSA) as soon as possible to maximize funding consideration.

Editor's note: Amounts and types of scholarships can vary from year to year, so if you are applying to Moravian University, make sure to check with them for an updated list.

Academic Programs

Art
Art, B.A.
  The following tracks are available:
  Art Education
  Art History and Criticism
  Graphic and Information Design
  Studio Art - Photography-Media Concentration
  Studio Art

Art, B.F.A.
  The following tracks are available:
  Graphic and Information Design
  Studio Art - Photography-Media Concentration
  Studio Art
Biochemistry
Biochemistry, B.S.
Biological Sciences
Biology, B.S.
Chemistry
Chemistry, B.S.
Clinical Counseling
Master of Arts in Clinical Counseling, MACC
Communications & Media Studies
Communications & Media Studies, B.A.
Business & Economics
Accounting, B.A.
Business Management, B.A.
Economics, B.A.
  The following tracks are available:
  Managerial Economics
  Public Policy Economics
  Quantitative Economics
Finance, B.A.
International Management (French/German/Spanish), B.A.
Management, B.A.
  The following track:
  Sport Management
Marketing Analytics, B.A.
Marketing Management, B.A.
Organizational Leadership, B.A. (open to degree-completion students only)
Master of Business Administration, MBA
Master of Health Administration, MHA
Master of Science in Data Analytics, MSDA
Master of Science in Human Resource Management, MSHRM
Education
Art Education (pre-K to grade 12 certification)
Early Childhood Education (pre-K to grade 4 certification)
Early Childhood Education Special Education
Foreign Language Education (pre-K to grade 12 certification) in the
following disciplines:
  French

German
Spanish
Middle Level Education (grades 4-8 certification)
Music Education (pre-K to grade 12 certification)
Secondary Education (7-12 certification) in the following disciplines:
  Biology
  English
  General Science
  Mathematics
  Social Studies
English as a Second Language Program Specialist
Reading Specialist (pre-K to grade 12 certification)
Principal Certification
Supervisory Certification
Autism Endorsement
Online Instruction Endorsement
Social Emotional and Behavioral Wellness (SEBW) Endorsement
Master of Art in Teaching, MAT
Master of Education in Curriculum & Instruction, M.Ed.
English & Writing Arts
English, B.A.
  with option of Certification in Writing Arts
Environmental Science & Studies
Environmental Policy and Economics, B.A.
Environmental Science, B.S.
Global Religions
Religion, B.A.
History
Historical Studies, B.A.
History, B.A.
Integrative Studies, B.A. (open to degree-completion students only)
  Concentrations in:
  Art
  Business
  English
  History
  Philosophy
  Self-Design
Mathematics and Computer Science
Computer Science, B.S.
  The following tracks are available:
  Computer Science

Data Science
Mathematics, B.S.
  The following tracks are available:
  Actuarial Science
  Applied Mathematics
  Pure Mathematics
Modern Languages & Literatures
French, B.A.
French and Francophone Studies, B.A.
German, B.A.
German Studies, B.A.
Spanish, B.A.
International Management (French/German/Spanish), B.A.
Music
Music, B.A.
  The following tracks are available:
  Music (general)
  Music technology and audio recording
  Pre-music therapy
Music, B.Mus.
  The following tracks are available:
  Composition
  Music Education
  Performance
  Sacred Music
Neuroscience
Neuroscience, B.S.
  The following tracks are available:
  Behavioral Neuroscience
  Cellular Neurobiology
  Cognitive Neuroscience
Nursing
Nursing, B.S.N.
Master of Science in Nursing M.S.N.
Performance Creation, MFA
Philosophy
Philosophy, B.A.
Physics
Physics, B.A. or B.S.
Engineering (Cooperative), B.A.
Geology (Cooperative), B.S.
Political Science

Political Science, B.A.
   The following tracks are available:
   Citizenship in Theory and Practice
   Global Politics and International Political Awareness
Psychology
Psychology, B.A.
Public Health
Public Health, B.A. or B.S.
Rehabilitation Sciences
Health Sciences, B.S.
   The following tracks are available:
   Pre-Athletic Training
   Pre-Occupational Therapy
   Pre-Physical Therapy
   Communication Sciences & Disorders
Athletic Training, M.S., D.A.T.
Occupational Therapy, M.S.O.T.
Physical Therapy, DPT
Speech-Language Pathology, MS-SLP
Sociology and Anthropology
Sociology, B.A.
   The following tracks are available:
   General Sociology
   Criminal Justice and Law
Minors and Certificates
Minors are available in all departments and programs, except for
Biochemistry, Engineering, Historical Studies, and Nursing.

Minors are also available in:Africana Studies
Anthropology
Art History
Dance
Environmental Studies
Ethics
Graphic Design
International Studies
Medieval Studies
Peace and Justice Studies
Photography
Psychology
Statistics
Theatre

Women's, Gender and Sexuality Studies

Certificates are also available in:
Ethics
Indigenous Studies
Spanish for Healthcare Professionals

Post-Secondary Certificates:
Design
Philosophy
Graduate Business Certificates:

Business & Economics

Post-Master's Certificates:
Nursing
Nurse Educator Certificate
Nurse Administrator Certificate
Clinical Nurse Leader Certificate
Family Nurse Practitioner Certificate
Adult-Gerontology Primary Care Nurse Practitioner Certificate
Adult-Gerontology Acute Care Nurse Practitioner Certificate
Self-Design Majors or Minors
Students may also self-design majors or minors.

TWENTY-FIVE: **SPRINGFIELD COLLEGE**

College Name: Springfield College
City, State: Springfield, MA
Website: https://www.springfield.edu
Admissions email address: admissions@springfield.edu
Admissions phone: 413.748.3136
Full-time undergraduate enrollment: 2,050
Number of full-time undergraduate students living on campus: 1,661
Average class size: 20
Student-faculty ratio: 11:1

Submitted by Nikki Levine, Director of Undergraduate Admissions, Springfield College

Founded in 1885, Springfield College's commitment to Humanics has been our guiding principle and what sets us apart. You may be asking yourself, "What is Humanics"? The Humanics philosophy calls for educating students in spirit, mind, and body for leadership in service to others. In short, we are helping students educate their whole person so that they are prepared to serve their communities as leaders. We've graduated some pretty amazing people. Among our more notable alumni, we can count a professional wrestler and philanthropist who has granted the most wishes through the Make-a-Wish foundation of any celebrity, a ground-breaking Harvard medical researcher, and the highest-ranking three-star general in the U.S. Marine Corps.

Springfield College is a small, private co-educational institution. Nearly 3,500 undergraduate and graduate students currently attend Springfield College, both at the main campus in Springfield,

Massachusetts and through our regional and online options. Springfield College is accredited by the New England Commission for Higher Education.

Springfield College offers a wide range of undergraduate and graduate programs in the fields of health science, human and social services, sport management and movement studies, education, business, and the arts and sciences. We also offer doctoral programs in physical education, physical therapy, counseling psychology, educational leadership, exercise physiology, occupational therapy, and sport and exercise psychology. With an undergraduate student-to-faculty ratio of 11:1 and an average undergraduate class size of 20, students benefit from the individualized attention and support from their faculty. Undergraduate students also work with a faculty advisor (a faculty member from their major) for their four undergraduate years. Faculty advisors assist students with course selection each semester, make sure students are on track to graduate, and assist with placement and searching for internships, fieldwork, and practicum opportunities. Most of our majors require students to have some form of hands-on experience prior to graduation. With a 98% post-graduate placement rate, our students graduate prepared for success.

A focus on the whole person means a focus on both academics and co-curricular activities. Springfield College students take full advantage of opportunities to be involved on campus. We offer more than 60 clubs and organizations in a variety of areas including major-specific, special interest, community service, leadership, campus media and publication, and visual and performing arts. Students interested in athletics have a variety of opportunities as well, including four seasons of intramural sports, 12 club sports, and 24 Division III varsity teams. Springfield College's commitment to service is evident throughout our co-curricular activities. With more than 120,000 hours of community service annually, there are plenty of opportunities for students to give back during their time at Springfield College.

Located in Springfield, Massachusetts, our lakeside campus is beautiful any time of the year! Our main campus is comprised of 100 acres, making it a quick 10-minute walk to get from one side to the other. Just a mile and a half down the road you'll find our East Campus, made up of 57 acres of forest and ecosystem. East Campus is the perfect location for a restful retreat or for team-building activities like our high and low ropes courses. While some wellness-based classes, such as archery and our adventure education courses, are facilitated at East Campus, this is also a great recreational space for our students, clubs, athletic teams, and other organizations.

Our Western Massachusetts campus allows students easy access to lots of great local attractions. Springfield is home to the Naismith Memorial Basketball Hall of Fame, the Dr. Seuss Museum, the Springfield Museums, and great shopping and dining options. Just down the road, students can check out the Big E New England state fair each fall, head over to Six Flags New England, or check out other local cities such as Northampton, Amherst, the Berkshires, or Hartford, Conn. Hiking trails can be found throughout the area, and the beach is only about an hour away. Boston and New York City are also easily accessible.

Springfield College is known as the birthplace of basketball, and for good reason! Springfield College graduate student James Naismith invented the game on our campus in 1891. Another notable alumnus, William Morgan, invented volleyball in 1894. The first game was played on our campus, where it was also given the name "volleyball."

Small private colleges oftentimes are stereotyped as not affordable to students. However, we are trying to break that stereotype at Springfield College. Springfield College is ranked among America's best colleges by *U.S. News & World Report*, and in addition, is ranked very high as a best value college. This ranking means that the value of a Springfield College education is a great investment for students. There are many ways that we work to make Springfield College an affordable option for students. Our average financial aid award for our fall 2022 first-year class was $33,500. Additionally, 100% of all incoming first-year students receive a financial aid award. All students are considered for a merit-based scholarship at the point of admission. Additionally, all domestic students who submit a Free Application for Federal Student Aid and international students who submit a CSS profile are considered for a need-based financial aid award.

"Learning I would have the opportunity of starting field experience during the second week of my first semester of college was incredible. After just 14 days, I was able to see firsthand what I am committing to with my major. I also have had four other placements in different areas within Springfield leading up to my full-time field placement senior year. All of this allows me to visualize myself in the profession I chose, which truly validated my decision in this investment in Springfield College. I entered my senior year more confident and prepared than ever to start my lifelong career." —Madison Tubman '23 Elementary Education and Psychology

"I am proud of my classroom accomplishments and leadership experiences I gained at Springfield College. The lessons and skills I learned helped me become confident in my interpersonal skills and communication skills when working with patients. Springfield College taught me to work in a team setting and be able to build rapport with my patients. I have found great success in providing care for my patients with therapeutic exercise, manual therapy, and modalities. I value evidence-based practice and am eager to participate in continuing education via mentors and post-graduate courses in order to become the best physical therapist I can become. The Springfield College physical therapy program is the best, the faculty members provide the perfect amount of support to get you ready for a career as a PT." —Zach Varnauskas '21 Health Science/Pre-Physical Therapy, Physical Therapist, Access Physical Therapy & Wellness, Inc.

Academic Programs

Undergraduate Programs
Accounting Major

Adventure Education Minor

Animation Minor

Art and Design Major

Art and Design Education Major | Teacher Licensure Option

Art Therapy Major | Minor

Athletic Coaching Minor

Athletic Training Major

Biology Major | Minor

Biology Education Major | Teacher Licensure Option

Business Management Major | Minor

Chemistry Minor

Communication Sciences and Disorders Major | Minor

Communications/Sports Journalism Major

Community Arts Minor

Community Nutrition Minor

Computer and Information Sciences Major

Computer Programming Minor

Computer Science Minor

Computer Science/Criminal Justice Major

Computer Science/English Major

Creative Writing Minor

Criminal Justice Major | Minor | Online

Criminal Justice/Human Services Major | Online

Dance Major | Minor

Early Childhood Education Major | Teacher Licensure Option

Education Major | Minor | Teacher Licensure Option

Education: Grades PK-2 Major | Online

Elementary and Special Education Major | Teacher Licensure Option

Elementary Education Major | Teacher Licensure Option

English Major | Minor

English Education Major | Teacher Licensure Option

Environmental Science Major

Environmental Studies Minor

Exercise Science Major

Finance Major

General Studies Major | Online

Gerontology Undergraduate Certificate

Health Care Management Major | Minor

Health Promotion Minor

Health Promotion Major

Health Science Major | Minor

Health/Family and Consumer Sciences Major | Teacher Licensure Option

History Major | Minor
History Education Major | Teacher Licensure Option
Human Services Major | Online
Human Services - Addiction Studies Major
Human Services - Early Childhood Education Major | Online
Marketing Major | Minor
Mathematics Major | Minor
Mathematics and Computer Technology Major
Mathematics Education Major | Teacher Licensure Option
Movement and Sports Studies Major
Music Minor
Nutritional Sciences Minor
Occupational Therapy Major
Philosophy Minor
Physical Education Major | Teacher Licensure Option
Physical Education and Health/Family and Consumer Sciences Major |
Teacher Licensure Option
Physical Therapy Major | Doctoral Program
Physician Assistant Studies Major | Master's Program
Political Science Minor
Professional Writing Minor
Psychology Major | Minor
Public Health Major | Minor
Public History and Museum Studies Minor
Recreation Industries and Therapeutic Recreation: Recreation Professional
Studies Major
Recreation Industries and Therapeutics Recreation: Recreation, Youth and
Sports Leadership Major | Online
Religious Studies Minor
Social Justice Minor
Social Work Major | Minor
Sociology Minor
Spanish Minor
Special Education Major | Teacher Licensure Option
Speech-Language Pathology Undergraduate Certificate
Sport Management Major
Sports Analytics Minor
Sports Biology Major
Theater Arts Minor
Undeclared Major
Web Design Minor
YMCA Professional Studies Minor

Graduate Programs

Adapted Physical Education Master's Program
Art Therapy/Counseling Master's Program
Athletic Counseling Master's Program
Athletic Counseling (CAGS) Certificate of Advanced Graduate Study
Athletic Leadership Master's Program
Athletic Training Professional Preparation Master's Program
Clinical Mental Health Counseling Master's Program
Counseling Post-Master's Certificate
Counseling Psychology (PsyD) Doctoral Program
Early Childhood Education Master's Program | Teacher Licensure Option
Educational Leadership (PhD) Doctoral Program
Educational Studies: Non-licensure Master's Program
Elementary Education Master's Program | Teacher Licensure Option
Exercise Physiology Master's Program
Exercise Physiology (PhD) Doctoral Program
Gerontology Post-Baccalaureate Certificate
Health Disparities and Health Equity Post-Baccalaureate Certificate
Health Education for Schools and Communities Post-Baccalaureate
Certificate
Health Promotion and Health Equity Master's Program | Online
Industrial/Organizational Psychology Master's Program
MBA - Business Administration Master's Program
MBA - Non-Profit Management Master's Program
Occupational Therapy (MSOT) Master's Program
Occupational Therapy (OTD) Doctoral Program
Organizational Leadership Master's Program | Online
Physical Education (CAGS) Certificate of Advanced Graduate Study
Physical Education (PhD) Doctoral Program
Physical Education: Initial Licensure Master's Program | Teacher Licensure
Option
Physical Education: Professional Licensure Master's Program | Teacher
Licensure Option
Physical Therapy (DPT) Doctoral Program
Physician Assistant Studies Master's Program
Rehabilitation Counseling Master's Program
School Counseling Certificate of Advanced Graduate Study | Master's
Program
Secondary Education Master's Program | Teacher Licensure Option
Social Work Master's Program

Social Work/Juris Doctor Dual Degree Master's Program | Doctoral Program
Social Work: Advanced Standing Program Master's Program
Special Education Certificate of Advanced Graduate Study | Master's Program | Teacher Licensure Option
Sport and Exercise Psychology Master's Program
Sport and Exercise Psychology Master's Program | Online
Sport and Exercise Psychology (PhD) Doctoral Program
Sport Management and Recreation Master's Program
Strength and Conditioning Master's Program
Student Affairs Administration Master's Program

Online Programs

Criminal Justice Major | Minor | Online
Criminal Justice/Human Services Major | Online
Education: Grades PK-2 Major | Online
Educational Leadership (PhD) Doctoral Program
General Studies Major | Online
Gerontology Undergraduate Certificate
Gerontology Post-Baccalaureate Certificate
Health Promotion and Health Equity Master's Program | Online
Human Services Major | Online
Human Services - Addiction Studies Major
Human Services - Early Childhood Education Major | Online
MBA - Non-Profit Management Master's Program
Organizational Leadership Master's Program | Online
Recreation Industries and Therapeutics Recreation: Recreation, Youth and Sports Leadership Major | Online
Recreation, Youth and Sports Leadership Minor
Speech-Language Pathology Undergraduate Certificate
Sport and Exercise Psychology Master's Program | Online

TWENTY-SIX: **MOUNT MERCY UNIVERSITY**

College Name: Mount Mercy University
City, State: Cedar Rapids, IA
Website: https://www.mtmercy.edu/
Admissions email address: admissions@mtmercy.edu
Admissions phone: 800.248.4504
Full-time undergraduate enrollment: 1,145
Number of full-time undergraduate students living on campus: 502
Average class size: 13
Student-faculty ratio: 17:1

Submitted by J. Todd Coleman, Vice President for Enrollment & Marketing, Mount Mercy University

Mount Mercy University is a private Catholic liberal arts university in Cedar Rapids, IA United States. The enrollment at Mount Mercy is comprised of 1100 undergraduate students in addition to 500 graduate and adult students. The university attracts students from 24 states and 28 countries to provide a vibrant and diverse student body in the second largest city in Iowa on the "hill" overlooking the city. Just four hours by interstate from Chicago, St. Louis, Minneapolis, and Kansas City, Mount Mercy University is perfectly positioned to provide close- to-home experience.

Mount Mercy was founded in 1928 by the Sisters of Mercy, a Catholic religious order. It began as a two-year college for women and evolved into a four-year college in 1960 before becoming a university in 2012. The university has continued to expand its academic offerings and facilities over the years. The campus is situated on 40 acres on top of the "hill," the highest natural elevation in Cedar Rapids at 932 feet. The campus contains a mixture of historic and modern buildings, including the iconic Warde Hall, which dates back to 1906. The campus provides a serene and conducive environment for learning and personal growth.

Mount Mercy University is accredited by the Higher Learning Commission (HLC), a regional accrediting agency recognized by the Department of Education. This accreditation ensures the university meets standards of high quality and academic rigor. The University offers a wide range of undergraduate and graduate programs across various disciplines. The University comprises four academic divisions; Business, Education, Health Professions and Humanities, Arts and Sciences. Some popular majors are Nursing, Business Administration, Psychology, Criminal Justice, Social Work, Education, Data Science, and Graphic Design.

Mount Mercy is home to a diverse student body, with students from various backgrounds and cultures. The university emphasizes a supportive and inclusive community, where students can engage in a variety of extracurricular activities, clubs, and organizations. These opportunities foster personal development, leadership skills, and a sense of belonging.

Being a McAuley Scholar (one of our many scholarships) allowed Lauren Imhoff '22 to attend the school of her dreams—Mount Mercy University. During her time on campus, she created Gen 1—a club to support first-generation college students.

When Lauren first stepped on campus, it felt like a piece of home. Once she toured Mount Mercy, she knew she didn't need to see another school—she had made her decision.

"I just got so excited—I didn't really think about the financial aspect of things," said Lauren.

Lauren was a first-generation student and paying for college on her own. Being awarded the Catherine McAuley Scholarship allowed her to be more involved on campus and focus on her studies.

Lauren Imhoff '22 talks about the ability of being immersed in campus life through the McAuley Scholarship.

"We wanted Gen 1 to be a home away from home for individuals on campus who felt like they needed their questions answered."
– Lauren Imhoff '22

Lauren had the opportunity to join a supportive network of McAuley Scholars, and she took advantage of her time on campus by finding ways to support students who were in similar situations. She was a Mustang Mentor, a student leader for AmeriCorps, a Project Connect Mentor, and—with inspiration and help from Project Connect Director Jennifer McNabb—started a new club to uplift fellow first-generation students: Gen 1.

"We wanted Gen 1 to be a home away from home for individuals on campus who felt like they needed their questions answered," said Lauren. "It's led by a group of students who knew exactly what they were going through and could help them with any aspect of their life."

At the end of Gen 1's first official year as a club, it was granted the Student Organization of the Year Award at the Mustang Leadership Awards. For Lauren, this moment is a highlight in her time at Mount Mercy.

"It showed that what we were doing had an impact," said Lauren.

Lauren gives Project Connect a lot of credit for the leadership skills she used to start Gen 1. As a Project Connect Mentor, she was able to build leadership and communication skills and network.

"The person I am now and the person I was as a freshman are two completely different people, and I give 100% of the credit to Project Connect," said Lauren.

Joining Project Connect and being a McAuley Scholar allowed Lauren to make meaningful connections and join a supportive community at the start of her Mount Mercy career.

"I know some of my best friends today from the McAuley Scholarship," shared Lauren.

Her connections don't stop with fellow students. Jennifer McNabb has been an inspiration for Lauren during her entire time on the Hill. Jennifer gave the initial inspiration for Gen 1, and continued to work with Lauren to fulfill their goal of creating a supportive space for first-generation students.

"She saw potential in me that I didn't necessarily see in myself," Lauren shared. "That's given me the confidence to do a lot of things that I've been able to do here. Mount Mercy is my favorite place in the world, and I'm so happy that I chose to come here," said Lauren. "I think that the opportunities I've gotten here are really unique, and I don't know if I would have gotten it at a bigger university." In her classes, Lauren learned skills that have a real-life application. These came in handy during her internship as a Healthcare Administrator Assistant at Mercy Medical Center.

"The McAuley Scholarship meant I was able to come to my dream school," said Lauren.

Mount Mercy University graduate Tiara Muñoz '23 received the Sister Catherine McAuley Award during Mount Mercy's 2023 Commencement ceremony on Sunday, May 14.

Tiara graduated with a bachelor's degree in psychology and criminal justice.

The Sister Catherine McAuley Award is presented to the graduate who best exemplifies our university mission in how they reflect, engage, serve, and live a purposeful life during their time at Mount Mercy. The award is named for Sister Mary Catherine McAuley, who founded the Sisters of Mercy in Ireland in 1831.

Tiara, also known as T, came to the Hill excited to be involved on the women's soccer team, eventually as a captain. She excelled in the classroom and graduated summa cum laude. Much of her campus impact occurred beyond the field and classroom, specifically as President of the Student Government Association.

Our Director of Diversity, Equity & Inclusivity described Tiara's presence as, "Like the sun: bright, warm, and often shining in your face at eight in the morning before you had breakfast."

Her classmates noted, "Her abilities to communicate and empathize with teammates are like no other. She is so unbelievably compassionate to those around her. T has inspired so many students to be their best individual self each day. The best mentor is the one that has faith in you even when you lack that faith within yourself. To me and many others, that is Tiara Muñoz."

The native of Sterling, Illinois leads thought-provoking class discussions on scholarly research assigned for the class.

Tiara has impacted many student, employee, and community lives in the last four years—from the tours she gave in Admissions to the dedication of the JEDI Room.

Tiara has been accepted into Mount Mercy's Master of Arts in Marriage & Family Therapy program. She will also serve as a Graduate Assistant in the Admissions Office upon graduating.

Mount Mercy University is an athletic scholarship-granting NAIA institution that is a member of the Heart of America Athletic Conference (HAAC). The university sponsors 19 Men's and Women's sports including basketball, baseball, softball, soccer, track and field, volleyball, cross country, bowling, competitive cheer & dance, golf and our newest sport of Women's lacrosse.

Mount Mercy University follows the tradition of the Sisters of Mercy, emphasizing service to others and social justice. The university encourages students to engage in community service and volunteerism, both locally and globally. Through initiatives like Campus Ministry and various service-learning programs, students have opportunities to make a positive impact on society.

In addition to its undergraduate programs, Mount Mercy University offers a full complement of graduate degrees including PhD's in Marriage and Family Counseling and Nurse Practitioner. The other graduate degree offerings are Master of Business Administration, (MBA), Master of Strategic Leadership, (MSL), Master of Nursing (MSN), Master of Marriage and Family Therapy (MFT), Master of Science of Education (MSEd), and Master of Arts in Education (MAEd).

Mount Mercy University maintains a strong relationship with the local community and encourages students to actively engage in the surrounding area. The university collaborates with organizations, businesses, and nonprofits to create internships, service opportunities, and experiential learning experiences for students.

Mount Mercy University strives to provide a holistic education that integrates academic excellence, personal development, and a commitment to service and social justice. It prepares students to become ethical leaders in their profession and in their communities.

Mount Mercy University is proud to support our students' academic and co-curricular experience by awarding scholarships ranging from $18,000 per year up to full-tuition (currently $38,070 for 2023-24). Mount Mercy University, in addition to academic scholarships, awards music and athletic scholarships, and provides financial aid to 100 percent of the students attending.

Mount Mercy University puts tremendous emphasis on assisting students in their quest for a college degree and works to provide meaningful financial literacy to families as they strive to achieve the student's goal of a college degree. The average net tuition price (2023-24) for Mount Mercy University is $12,000 with the average net total price (including housing and food) being $24,000. Mount Mercy University serves first-generation students well. In fact, 95% of our undergraduate students receive university, state, and federal aid to assist in their education pursuits.

More words from our students:

"Mount Mercy University taught me so much about myself, my values, and how to lead a courageous life while living it with purpose and meaning" —Tiara Munoz, '23, Rock Falls, IL (2021-22 Student Body President; Women's Soccer)

"The person I am now and the person I was as a freshman are two completely different people, and I give 100% of the credit to Mount Mercy University. Being a McAuley Scholar allowed me to make meaningful connections and join a supportive community at the start of my Mount Mercy career." —Lauren Imhoff, '22, Keota, Iowa

Academic Programs

Accounting
Art
Art & Design
Biology
Business Administration
Career Development
Chemistry
Child and Adolescent Studies
Communication
Computer Science
Creative Writing
Criminal Justice
Data Science
Diversity Studies
Early Childhood Education
Economics
Education
English
English as a Second Language
Environmental Justice
Exercise Science
Finance

Gender Studies
General Studies
Health Care Administration
Health Care Navigation
History
Honors Seminars
Human Resource Management
Information Systems Security
Journalism
Leadership
Legal Studies
Management
Marketing
Marriage and Family Therapy
Mathematics
Mercy Education
Music
Nursing
Philosophy
Physical Science
Political Science
Psychology
Public Health
Public Relations
Religious Studies
Service Learning
Social Work
Sociology
Software Development
Spanish
Writing

TWENTY-SEVEN: **MIDWAY UNIVERSITY**

College Name: Midway University
City, State: Midway, KY
Website: https://www.midway.edu/
Admissions email address: admissions@midway.edu
Admissions phone: 800.952.4122
Full-time undergraduate enrollment: 777
Number of full-time undergraduate students living on campus: 401
Average class size: 17
Student-faculty ratio: 15:1

This first segment was submitted by Ellen Gregory, Vice President, Marketing & Communications, Midway University

Midway University is a private, coeducational institution located in the greater Lexington, Kentucky area. Founded in 1847, Midway University's student body consists of 777 traditional undergraduate students attending classes on its residential campus in Midway, Kentucky. Total enrollment (including traditional and online undergraduate, graduate, and dual credit students) is more than 1900 students from across Kentucky, the United States, and several foreign countries.

Undergraduate students can select from 20+ career-focused majors within the University's three schools—the School of Arts & Sciences, the School of Business, Equine and Sport Studies, and the School of Health Sciences. The University has 28 athletic teams including two equestrian teams. Academic and athletic scholarships are available. Graduate programs are offered in the areas of business (MBA), education (MED), nursing (MSN), and a unique MSN-MBA dual degree.

Located on a 200-acre working horse farm and in a bucolic rural location, the campus is both beautiful and safe. The charming town of Midway includes fine dining, boutiques, antique stores, and art galleries, and a train that runs through town (and campus) daily. The larger urban areas of Lexington, Louisville, and Cincinnati, Ohio are within easy driving distance and offer opportunities for internships and jobs.

For students looking for a unique private education, Midway University has a long history of providing support to its students, and always making college affordable. In fact, Midway University is the *"Most Affordable Private University in Central Kentucky."*

Visit us on campus or online to find out more about admissions, academic programs, and scholarships: www.midway.edu/experience. Students interested in athletics can also express their interest by completing a recruitment form at www.gomidwayeagles.com

Spotlight program: Equine Studies (Management, Rehabilitation or Science)
Quote from the Midway Website: "Midway University is located at the epicenter of the equine industry and is a renowned equine studies college. From boarding and breeding operations, sales and racing, equine association headquarters, therapy centers, animal health and pharmaceutical companies, and renowned veterinary practices, our campus is perfectly situated to give future equestrians the chance to put their education into practice.

"As a part of our holistic approach to equestrian studies and equine training, our campus is a working horse farm providing true access to hands-on learning with our large equine herd of varying breeds and disciplines. Students can walk from their residence hall to the barns in minutes.

"The Equine Studies program at Midway provides students with the essential skills they need to enter the broad equine industry or prepare for graduate school. Equine science degree students have opportunities throughout the program to work with a variety of breeds. Students are also able to perform tasks of varying levels in assisting with managing our farm and herd. Students learn basic horse-handling techniques as well as barn and farm management principles and practices. Through academic preparation in theories and methods of equine characteristics and needs, students acquire the basis on which to make decisions affecting horse care.

"Midway University currently fields two riding teams in the Intercollegiate Horse Show Association (IHSA)-Hunt Seat and Western. We compete in Region 6, Zone 3. Students interested in one of the teams should complete an admissions application and state their interest or complete an interest form on our Athletics Recruitment Center at https://GoMidwayEagles.com.

"Midway's equine education centers allow students to pursue equestrian studies regardless of the weather. Three centers are used for equestrian classes and by Midway's equestrian teams. Equine students also enjoy an outdoor riding arena, a jumping field, and 163 acres of pastureland. View our equine facilities online.

"The 36,000-square foot Equine Education Center houses a 105 x 235-foot indoor riding arena, eight stalls, laboratory, classroom, a large tack room, audio-visual room, wash stall, and equine staff offices.

"Bud's Barn and Spy Coast Farm Education Center was completed in August 2022. The new facility is adjacent to the Midway University Equestrian Center, which overlooks the main campus, and creates an equine hub on the north side of campus. This facility includes a 5,376 square foot barn with 18 stalls, tack room, feed room, and a 6040 square foot education center classroom.

"The Ashland stables and Theurkauf outdoor riding arena complement the two large equine centers, thus creating a comprehensive facility that meets the demands of all riding disciplines and equine training needs. The Ashland stables include eight stalls, tack room, washroom, office, and classroom. The

Theurkauf outdoor riding arena measures 227 x 117 feet and has a stonedust footing."

This second segment is a collection of quotes from the Midway University Website:

"Why Midway?

"At Midway, we'll support you all the way. Here you'll find a career-based curriculum that prepares you for a fulfilling job. You'll learn from caring faculty who know your name. We are invested in you as a person, not a number.

"Regardless of your background — traditional undergraduate student or working adult learner — we have your back."

From one of our students:

"Midway helped me get here by setting me up for success. Midway offers a more intentional classroom experience with a smaller teacher-to-student ratio, therefore you can ask your professors questions and they know you by name. Midway also really showed me how to work with people from all backgrounds and walks of life. I was fortunate to be a part of the Midway Activities Council, the Women's Soccer Team and to be the Ruth Slack Roach Scholar of the 2021 class. In all of these roles, I had to make plans, work events, lead community service, and present projects with these groups. I am thankful for my years at Midway because they taught me how to be a servant leader." —Cameron K. Faris, MBA

From Financial Aid section of the Midway website:

"Understanding the true costs of your education can sometimes be difficult. That is why our Financial Aid staff is here to assist our students with their financial aid planning, processing of federal, state aid, grants, loans, and scholarships.

"When comparing schools and costs, students should schedule a time to speak with a counselor in our Financial Aid Office to best understand their true costs. The published tuition rates are only there as a starting point but students need to understand what aid they qualify for and what will truly be their out-of-pocket costs versus the published rates.

"Each year, 99% of our traditional undergraduate students receive some type of aid to assist with their college expenses. Financial aid options vary by student type and many other factors so our advice is to start with completing the FAFSA and then schedule a time to speak with one of our Financial Aid Counselors."

Editor notes taken from the Midway website:

Midway University Traditional Undergraduate Student Scholarships: Pinkerton Scholarship (a high academic achievement award): High school GPA of 3.7 or higher and ACT – 28: Must be a U.S. citizen and compete during Scholarship Day on campus (interview/essay): Up to two full tuition awards per year will be decided by faculty and is renewable for up to four years with a renewal GPA of 3.5. Note: Scholarship Day is typically the first week in February.

New Freshman Merit Scholarships/Grants (awarded upon acceptance) range from $5,000 to $11,000 per year. Transfer Merit Scholarships (awarded upon acceptance) range from $6,000 to $11,000 per year

There are also athletic, chorale, minority, out-of-state, legacy, sibling, and many other types of awards. Check with the Midway admission office for details.

These scholarships and scholarship amounts were taken from the Midway website in June of 2023. Colleges often change the names, types, and amounts of awards from year to year, so make sure, if you plan to apply to Midway, to check with them for the most current information.

Academic Programs

Majors:
Accounting
Biology
Business Administration
Coaching and Sport Leadership
Computer Science
Criminal Justice
Education
Education Studies
English
Equine Studies
Health Care Administration
Health Science
Interdisciplinary Studies
Marketing Communications
Mathematics
Nursing
Psychology
Public Health
Sport Management
Sport Marketing

Minors:
Biology
Business Administration
Chemistry
Criminal Justice
English
Equine Studies
Finance
Human Resource Management
Interdisciplinary Studies
Mathematics
Music
Psychology
Sport Management

TWENTY-EIGHT: **CATAWBA COLLEGE**

College Name: Catawba College
City, State: Salisbury, NC
Website: https://www.catawba.edu/
Admissions email address: admission@catawba.edu
Admissions phone: 800.CATAWBA
Full-time undergraduate enrollment: 1,094
Number of full-time undergraduate students living on campus: 683
Average class size: 12
Student-faculty ratio: 12:1

Submitted by Jodi Bailey, Director of Marketing and Communications, Catawba College

Why Catawba College?

Yes, going to college is worth the investment. But going to the *right* college is just as important.

Nestled in the Piedmont region of North Carolina, Catawba is ideally situated between the Carolina Coast to the East and the Appalachian Mountains to the West. Located in charming, historic Salisbury, Catawba College offers a stunning campus with state-of-the-art facilities conducive to learning, growth, and exploration. The College's location provides students with a safe environment while also offering easy access to cultural, recreational, and career opportunities in the surrounding area.

From the moment students step foot on Catawba's campus, they will feel like they belong. Students aren't just a number, but a member of our inclusive, welcoming, diverse family united in the exploration of what's possible. They'll join a community of over 16,000 alumni who have gone on to change the world.

Founded in 1851, Catawba College has a rich legacy of academic excellence. Rooted in the liberal arts tradition, Catawba has a commitment to fostering intellectual curiosity, critical thinking, and practical skills – empowering students to develop a strong foundation for life-long learning.

We inspire students to think harder and dream bigger. Catawba allows our students to explore what fascinates them most and explore new interests through over 70 academic programs through our four schools: the School of Arts & Sciences, Goodman School of Education, School of Health Sciences and Human Performance, Ketner School of Business, and the Shuford School of Performing Arts. We are proud of our distinctive programs that provide unique learning opportunities. All of our schools are equipped with state-of-the-art facilities and expert faculty members dedicated to supporting and nurturing our students.

Catawba's engaging and dynamic learning environment blends theory and practice, encouraging students to become active participants in their education. Before the start of classes, students are paired with a success coach who works to ensure they excel in their chosen major and leave prepared for a successful career. Our small class sizes ensure personalized attention from dedicated faculty members who serve as mentors, guiding students along their academic journeys.

Catawba emphasizes experiential learning, providing opportunities for internships, research opportunities, and community service initiatives, where students gain real-world perspectives and develop practical skills. In our increasingly interconnected world, Catawba prepares students to be global citizens. We offer both domestic and international travel opportunities that enable students to immerse themselves in different cultures, broaden their perspectives, and develop a deeper understanding of the world.

Catawba College is also mindful of our impact on the environment, which is why we are constantly striving to make our campus and community greener and more renewable with a variety of initiatives. We are the first college in the Southeast, in North Carolina, and the thirteenth in the nation to be certified as carbon neutral. We continue to lead our higher education peers in embracing clean energy innovations and environmental stewardship efforts. In addition, our 189-acre Fred Stanback, Jr. Ecological Preserve lies adjacent to the campus and provides uncommon opportunities for research, fieldwork, and outdoor recreation.

College isn't just about homework, group projects, lectures, and tests. What happens outside of the classroom is also an essential part of going to college. Students also learn outside the academic buildings – on stage, on the field, in church, in the midst of campus, and in the community. Whether it's participating in athletics, joining student governments, working on a performing arts production, engaging in community service, or joining a choral group, students can share their talents and be inspired to try new things.

Students fill their days with everything from music to magicians, speakers to the arts, athletic events, and everything in between. More than 40 student clubs and organizations, countless music and theatre performances, Division II and intramural athletics, all keep them involved.

Living and studying with students from across the country and around the world provides plenty of opportunities to develop meaningful friendships, exchange ideas, and learn from across cultures. Catawba is a residential college with approximately 71% of our students living on-campus within our traditional residence halls, apartments, and living-learning communities. Each residence hall has its own unique community, but every hall becomes "home."

We also provide plenty of variety of delicious, nutritious options to meet different tastes and dietary needs. The Cannon Dining Commons was renovated in the summer of 2022 and serves everything from home-style dining, salads, and deli sandwiches to pizza and desserts for a diversity of diets. We also have a pure eats station specifically designed with foods that are not made with the top nine food allergens. You can also grab a Starbucks coffee or quick snack from Blue51 upstairs in our Student Center.

Catawba College is more than just an academic institution. It is a close-knit community where every individual is valued and supported. Our commitment to inclusivity and diversity creates an environment where students from all backgrounds feel welcomed and celebrated. Through clubs, organizations, and cultural events, Catawba fosters a sense of belonging, encouraging students to engage with each other and explore their passions.

College is an opportunity for students to discover who they are and what they want to do with their lives. For over 170 years, Catawba College has cultivated our students' creativity, talent, and curiosity. Whether the goal is to be an accountant, teacher, scientist, musician, minister, or CEO, Catawba will help them get there. Our students have grit and drive, and are curious and involved. If that sounds like you or your student – visit us to learn more about how we prepare students for graduate or professional school, the workplace, and the world.

Value of a Catawba College Degree
Going to college is an investment. A Catawba education is a smart investment for students and their futures. We are committed to making our high-quality private education affordable.

Catawba College is ranked among North Carolina's Highest Return on Investment Colleges. Catawba students graduate with an average of 28% less in student loan debt than students at other private schools. They also have 9% less debt than students at other ranked public schools.

Every undergraduate student at Catawba receives financial aid which includes federal, state, private, and college awards. All students are automatically considered for academic scholarships upon acceptance, and freshmen receive scholarships ranging up to full tuition. We also offer merit, need-based, and athletic scholarships. We award over

$120 million in gift aid to our students each year – these are awards that don't need to be paid back.

Our expert financial aid staff helps students and their families apply for financial aid, grants, loans, scholarships, and work-study, then walk them through their personalized financial aid packages.

A college education is one of the most important investments someone may make to ensure their future. A top-tier private school education doesn't have to come with the burden of high debt. Don't assume you can't afford Catawba College. The first step is submitting the FAFSA and applying!

Academic Programs

Accounting
Administration of Justice
Athletic Coaching
Biochemistry
Biology
Birth to Kindergarten (B-K)
BSN Pre-Licensure Nursing
Business Administration
Business Management
Chemistry
Communication
Computer Science
Counseling
Creative Writing
Dance
Digital Media & Production
Ecology
Economics
Economics & Finance
Educational Studies
Elementary Education (K-6)
English
Entrepreneurship

Environment & Sustainability
Environmental and Outdoor Education
Environmental Policy & Advocacy
Exercise Science
Forestry and Environmental Studies
General Management
General Studies
GIS & Technology (GIST)
History
Information Systems
Information Systems and Technology (IST)
Information Technology
Integrated Marketing Communication
International Business
Literature
Marketing
Mathematical Finance
Mathematics
MBA, Business Administration
MBA, General Management
MBA, Healthcare Administration
MHS, Clinical Mental Health Counseling
Middle School Education (6-9)
MS, Exercise & Nutrition Sciences
MSPM, Sport Management
Music
Music Business
Music Education
Music Performance
Natural Resource Management
Nutrition
Politics
Popular Music
Pre-Dentistry
Pre-Law
Pre-Medical
Pre-PA
Pre-Pharmacy
Pre-Veterinary Medicine
Professional Accounting
Psychology
Public Administration

Public and Professional Writing
Religion
RN to BSN Nursing
Sacred Music
Secondary Education (9-12) Minor
Sociology
Spanish
Special Education
Special Subjects (K-12)
Sport Management
Studio Art
Sustainable Planning and Leadership
Theatre Arts
Theatre Arts Administration
Theatre Arts: Design and Production
Theatre Arts: Performance
Theatre: Musical
Therapeutic Recreation
Worship Music and Production
Zoology

TWENTY-NINE: **WARTBURG COLLEGE**

College Name: Wartburg College
City, State: Waverly, IA
Website: https://www.Wartburg.edu/
Admissions email address: admissions@Wartburg.edu
Admissions phone: 319.352.8264
Full-time undergraduate enrollment: 1,444
Number of full-time undergraduate students living on campus: 1150 (approx.)
Average class size: 20
Student-faculty ratio: 14:1

Submitted by Tara Winter, Executive Director of Admissions, Wartburg College

Wartburg College is a private liberal arts college located in Waverly, Iowa, one of the top 20 fastest-growing cities in the state and part of the Waterloo-Cedar Falls metropolitan area of approximately 150,000 residents. Wartburg stands out as an exceptional institution with several distinguishing characteristics.

The college is renowned for its commitment to academic excellence. Wartburg offers more than 60 areas of study in various disciplines, including the arts, humanities, social sciences, natural sciences, and professional fields. With a low student-to-faculty ratio, Wartburg ensures that students receive personalized attention and guidance from highly qualified professors who are experts in their fields. This individualized approach to education fosters a vibrant learning environment and encourages students to explore their interests deeply.

Wartburg also distinguishes itself through its emphasis on experiential learning and the practical application of knowledge. The college provides numerous opportunities for students to engage in internships, research projects, and community-based learning experiences. These hands-on experiences allow students to apply what they have learned in the classroom to real-world situations, enhancing their understanding and preparing them for successful careers or further education.

Another remarkable aspect of Wartburg is its strong sense of community and inclusivity. The college prides itself on creating a welcoming and supportive environment for all students, regardless of their background or identity. Wartburg fosters a close-knit community where students, faculty, and staff form meaningful relationships, collaborate on projects, and support each other's personal and academic growth. The college's commitment to diversity and inclusion is reflected in its various student organizations, cultural events, and support services, which ensure that every student feels valued and included.

Wartburg also stands out for its international focus and commitment to global engagement. The college offers numerous study abroad programs, allowing students to gain valuable cross-cultural experiences and develop a global perspective. Additionally, Wartburg welcomes a diverse community of international students representing more than 50 countries, creating a multicultural environment that enriches the educational experience for everyone. The college also emphasizes global issues and intercultural competence through its curriculum, promoting an understanding of global challenges and fostering responsible global citizenship.

Athletics and co-curricular activities are another area in which Wartburg excels. Nearly one-third of the student body participates in 25 intercollegiate teams and more than a quarter participate in one of the college's 18 renowned music ensembles. The college is a member of the NCAA Division III and competes in the American Rivers Conference. Wartburg's athletic teams, known as the Knights, have achieved significant success, with more than 100 conference championships in the last 20 years and a combined 28 straight years of national titles. Wartburg also offers a wide range of co-curricular activities, including clubs, organizations, and performing arts groups, providing students with opportunities for personal growth, leadership development, and creative expression.

Wartburg prides itself on its strong alumni network and student success. The college has a dedicated Student Success Center that fosters connections between alumni and current students, offering mentorship, internships, and career networking opportunities. This commitment to alumni engagement and career development ensures that Wartburg students are well-prepared for success after graduation.

Wartburg College is committed to making higher education accessible and affordable for students and their families. The college recognizes the financial challenges that many students face and has implemented various initiatives to ensure affordability.

One of the primary ways Wartburg addresses affordability is through its robust financial aid program. The college offers a range of need-based grants, scholarships, and work-study opportunities to eligible students. These financial aid options are designed to help offset the cost of tuition, fees, and other educational expenses. Wartburg College is dedicated to meeting the demonstrated financial need of its students, and the financial aid office works closely with families to create comprehensive financial aid packages that make attending Wartburg a realistic possibility.

In addition to need-based aid, the college also offers merit-based scholarships. These scholarships are awarded to students based on their academic achievements, leadership qualities, and other talents. Merit scholarships recognize and reward students for their accomplishments, and they can significantly reduce the overall cost of attending Wartburg College.

Wartburg takes a proactive approach to cost management. The college is committed to keeping tuition increases as low as possible while maintaining the high quality of education it provides. Wartburg regularly reviews its operating expenses and seeks efficiencies to control costs. This commitment to cost management helps to minimize the financial burden on students and their families.

Another aspect that contributes to Wartburg's affordability is its emphasis on timely graduation. The college provides academic advising with faculty and support services to ensure that students can progress through their degree programs efficiently and graduate on time. By completing their degrees in the standard timeframe, students can avoid incurring additional costs associated with extra semesters or years of study.

Additionally, Wartburg offers work-study opportunities for students who wish to earn money to contribute towards their educational expenses. These on-campus employment options provide students with valuable work experience while helping to offset the cost of attendance. Work-study programs can provide financial stability and reduce the need for additional loans or personal expenses.

Wartburg is committed to transparency in its financial processes. The college provides clear and comprehensive information regarding tuition, fees, and financial aid on its website and in its communications with prospective and enrolled students. This transparency allows students and families to make informed decisions about their educational investment and understand the resources available to them.

Academic Programs

Major
- Accounting, B.A.
- Actuarial Science, B.A.
- American History Teaching (5-12), B.A.
- Art, B.A.
- Biochemistry, B.A.
- Biology Teaching (5-12), B.A.
- Biology, B.A.
- Business Administration, B.A.

- Chemistry Teaching (5-12), B.A.
- Chemistry, B.A.
- Computer Information Systems, B.A.
- Computer Science, B.A.
- Economics, B.A.
- Elementary Education, B.A.
- Engineering Science, B.A.
- Engineering, B.S.
- English, B.A.
- English, Language Arts Teaching (5-12), B.A.
- Environmental Science and Studies, B.A.
- Exercise Science, B.A.
- German Studies, B.A.
- German, B.A.
- Graphic Design, B.A.
- Health and Fitness Studies, B.A.
- History, B.A.
- Individualized, B.A.
- Interdepartmental, B.A.
- International Relations, B.A.
- Journalism and Communication, B.A.
- Leadership, M.A.
- Mathematics Teaching (5-12), B.A.
- Mathematics, B.A.
- Music Education (K-12), B.M.E.
- Music Education/Music Therapy (K-12), B.M.E.
- Music Therapy, B.M.
- Music, B.A.
- Neuroscience, B.A.
- Performance, B.M.
- Physical Education (K-12), B.A.
- Physics Teaching (5-12), B.A.
- Physics, B.A.
- Political Science, B.A.
- Psychology, B.A.
- Public Health, B.A.
- Religion, B.A.
- Secondary Education (5-12), B.A.
- Social Work, B.A.
- Sociology, B.A.
- Spanish Teaching (5-12), B.A.
- Spanish, B.A.

- World History Teaching (5-12), B.A.

Minor

- Accounting Minor
- Art Minor
- Biology Minor
- Business Minor
- Chemistry Minor
- Computer Information Systems Minor
- Computer Science Minor
- Creative Writing Minor
- Data Analytics Minor
- Digital Cinema and Production Minor
- Economics Minor
- Engineering Management Minor
- Engineering Science Minor
- Environmental Studies Minor
- German Minor
- German Studies Minor
- Graphic Design Minor
- History Minor
- Intercultural Studies Minor
- International Relations Minor
- Leadership Minor
- Literature and Film Minor
- Mathematics Minor
- Multimedia Journalism Minor
- Music Minor
- Organizational and Public Relations Minor
- Peace and Justice Studies Minor
- Philosophy Minor
- Physics Minor
- Political Science Minor
- Psychology Minor
- Public Health Minor
- Religion Minor
- Social Welfare Minor
- Sociology Minor
- Spanish Minor
- Speech Communication Minor
- Sports Media Minor
- Theatre Minor
- Women's Studies Minor

- Worship Studies Minor

THIRTY: **FLORIDA SOUTHERN COLLEGE**

College Name: Florida Southern College
City, State: Lakeland, FL
Website: flsouthern.edu/
Admissions email address: fscadm@flsouthern.edu
Admissions phone: 863.680.4131
Full-time undergraduate enrollment: 2,600
Number of full-time undergraduate students living on campus: 2,100
Average class size: 18
Student-faculty ratio: 13:1

Submitted by John Grundig, Vice President of Enrollment Management, Florida
Southern College

Cultivating Tomorrow's Difference Makers Today

More than just an institution of higher education, Florida Southern
College catalyzes transformative experiences. Emphasizing learning
by doing, it is nationally recognized for fostering a nurturing
environment that shapes learners into leaders. At the core of the
Florida Southern philosophy is a commitment to providing
meaningful experiences that open doors to intellectual growth,
personal development, and a strong sense of purpose. By cultivating
a familial spirit on a sun-soaked campus, providing immersive real-
world learning steered by expert faculty, and offering individualized
guidance that jumpstarts careers, Florida Southern College
empowers students to become change-makers who positively impact
our world.

Founded in 1883, the oldest private college in the Sunshine State,
Florida Southern College provides a distinctive synthesis of a
traditional liberal arts curriculum and professional learning.

Delivered through an engaged learning model recognized by the Society for Experiential Education as the best in the country, the College offers more than 70 rigorous undergraduate degree programs and career tracks in business, communication, fine arts and humanities, nursing, social sciences, STEM fields, and pre-professional programs in medicine, dentistry, law, and others. A range of 4+1 options provides an accelerated pathway into the College's distinctive business administration, education, and nursing graduate programs, saving students time and money and equipping them to take on leadership roles in the workplace.

Though Florida Southern's 2,600 undergraduate students represent nearly 50 countries and almost all 50 states, they share a few common traits. Self-described as "compassionate, motivated, and highly involved," FSC students are passionate about learning. High achievers, most have taken AP, IB, or honor-level courses, often ranking at the top of their high school class. They enjoy being part of a close-knit community; they're not afraid to put their skills to work, and most of all, they appreciate that their education isn't confined to inside the walls of a classroom but encourages them to actively participate in making the world a better place.

Florida Southern College prioritizes learning experiences that take knowledge acquisition beyond memorization and enable critical thinking, creativity, and problem-solving. Through intimate, discussion-based classes, one-on-one advising sessions, and even impromptu conversations over lunches in the "caf," faculty engage with their students. That student-faculty connection grows stronger while working side-by-side on everything from collaborative research and life-changing service projects to adventures across the globe. Most recently, students traveled with faculty to provide much-needed healthcare to patients in Costa Rica. They researched local crab populations and presented their findings at a national conference. They also worked together to find solutions for preventing post-surgical infections, leading to life-saving patents.

This type of collaboration isn't isolated to the sciences, however. For example, Political science students regularly present original research at conferences such as the Citadel Symposium on Southern

Politics, and the Florida Political Science Association. The Center for Free Enterprise and Entrepreneurship has helped students turn their ideas into 35 start-ups earning more than $45,000 in seed money to develop their prototypes and business plans, including an affordable product that can be used by island nations to help regrow coral reef. Student and faculty drive to contribute new knowledge and address the world's most complex challenges has led to the College earning the title of Fulbright "Top Producer" three times in the past four years.

At Florida Southern, making connections is the overarching goal: connecting students with professional practice, organizations outside the institution, and each other. Co-curricular experiences like internships and practicums allow students to practice what they've only theorized, gaining resume-building experience before graduation. In addition to scoring coveted internships at organizations nationwide, our Central Florida location puts students at the heart of innovation. Lakeland provides a wealth of opportunities for young, motivated professionals, from networking organizations that facilitate connections with the business community to internships with Fortune 500 companies, including Amazon, Disney, GEICO, FedEx, Publix Super Markets, and Truist. Florida Southern is also one of the few institutions in the state with a formal internship agreement with the prestigious Washington Center, enabling students to dig deeper into politics, journalism, and government relations.

FSC's Office of Career Services, ranked No. 24 in the country by *The Princeton Review*, gives students an added advantage. In addition to the wealth of job-preparation resources the Center provides, it also hosts professionals from leading corporations to connect with, interview, and even hire students. Ready to stand out in a competitive job market, 95 percent of Florida Southern graduates report meeting their post-baccalaureate degree goals within a year.

Consistently named one of the most beautiful in the nation, Florida Southern's 100-acre campus sits on the shores of the beautiful Lake Hollingsworth. Designated a National Historic Landmark in 2012, the campus boasts the world's largest collection of Frank Lloyd Wright architecture. In addition to the 13 Wright-designed structures, the campus features lush gardens, state-of-the-art academic facilities, and housing options ranging from ivy-clad traditional residence halls to modern garden apartments.

The distinctive physical setting of the Florida Southern campus serves as a constant source of inspiration, stimulating creativity and encouraging a strong sense of community. Through 100 student-run clubs and organizations, 12 national fraternities and sororities, music ensembles and theatre productions, and a Smithsonian-affiliated museum, students make the time spent outside the classroom as meaningful as the time spent in class. Whether partnering with local businesses to bring fresh food to low-income families or volunteering with nonprofit organizations such as Habitat for Humanity, students gain practical experience that further develops their leadership abilities and instills a sense of civic responsibility.

Florida Southern is also home to 22 men's and women's varsity sports teams with 30 NCAA Division II national championships. Students can participate in four club sports: esports, equestrian, ice hockey, and cheerleading, as well as 20+ intramural sports.

While splendid lakes and mild weather may lure families to visit, students ultimately choose Florida Southern College for the personalized support provided. Before students arrive on campus, advisors work with them to assess their strengths and explore potential majors and co-curricular opportunities, establishing a four-year plan to move them toward their career goals. And because transitioning into adulthood isn't always seamless — whether a student has difficulty with time management, study skills, or a personal problem, students have a vast network of administrators, advisors, and counselors dedicated to seeing them excel.

Knowing the value of the education they received, more than 30,000 alums give generously, helping to advance the mission and enhance the Florida Southern experience for the student community by sponsoring internships, assisting with case studies, and involving students in research. As one undergrad notes: "It is truly like a family here, and everyone wants to see each other succeed."

Worth the Investment

For 140 years, Florida Southern College has provided students with a career-launching education at an exceptional value. *U.S. News & World Report* consistently includes Florida Southern in its "Best Value Universities in the South" category, considering the College's academic quality, cost of attendance, and career outcomes of graduates. The guidebook recognizes FSC as delivering the most outstanding value among private universities in Florida, affirming Florida Southern is a wise investment for families seeking the best return.

Guidebooks also consistently tout the life-changing experiences Florida Southern delivers. *U.S. News & World Report* ranks Florida Southern No. 8 among the "Best Regional Universities in the South." It also includes the institution among the country's "Most Innovative" and as a "Top Performer in Social Mobility." *The Princeton Review* also includes Florida Southern in its "Best Colleges" guide, citing the school's career and job placement services as the No. 24 "Best Career Services" and campus theater productions as the No. 25 "Best College Theatre" in the nation. *U.S. News & World Report, Colleges of Distinction,* and *The Princeton Review* all laud the Barney Barnett School of Business and Free Enterprise and the Ann Blanton Edwards School of Nursing and Health Sciences as foremost programs in the nation for business and nursing education. Florida Southern is also honored as a three-time Top Producing Fulbright Student institution.

Understanding the importance of affordability, FSC has developed various financial aid programs to support students pursuing higher education. Each year, the College offers more than $58 million in institutional aid based on academic merit, talent in athletics or fine arts, demonstrated leadership or service, need, and other factors. Combined with federal, state, and other private funding sources, FSC students receive $66 million in overall assistance, with 99 percent receiving aid. Many students spend less for a degree from FSC than they would at a public university.

Finishing college in four years is critical to reducing costs. Yet, most undergraduate degrees take at least five years, which adds 20 percent to the total cost. FSC's Four-Year Graduation Guarantee minimizes expenses while providing a personalized, four-year plan that includes an internship and travel-study adventure — experiences that provide students a competitive advantage in the job market and when applying to graduate schools.

Because Florida Southern students are deeply engaged in every level of their education, from first-year support programs to internships and other hands-on experiences, they are uniquely positioned to forge productive careers at some of the world's leading organizations.

"My courses continuously challenged me to learn in ways that prepared me for my career," explained Brandy Pikus '12, J.D. and litigation counsel at Raymond James Financial, Inc. "My faculty stressed the development of portable skills such as communication, critical analysis, and the ability to infer meaning. These skills helped me thrive in internships, impress at interviews, and approach any situation with confidence."

Within a year of graduation, 95 percent of Florida Southern students report having achieved their post-bachelor's degree goals by securing gainful employment, entering into military or volunteer service, or beginning an advanced degree program. Because our students gain so much so quickly and carry those advantages through life, the value they receive is outstanding.

Some words from our students:

"I chose FSC for the opportunities! Having mentors within my career field was a pushing factor. Also, the ability to follow in dad, grandpa, and aunt's footsteps is incredible! I get to live and learn in the same place as my family did!" —Avery Standifer '24

"I remember touring the college when I was 13 with my sister, who had begun her college search, and I fell in love with the campus. I could picture myself walking around, enjoying classes, making good friends, and being really happy here - I tugged my mom's arm and told her, "This is where I'm going to college," and five years later, I put down my deposit." —Anna Grace Chandler '24

"In the middle of a global pandemic two years ago, I decided to come to Florida Southern College on a random Tuesday night at the dinner table! Florida Southern College currently holds the number one education program for pre-service teachers in the state. With the constant engaged learning experiences in the classroom, I knew I would be ready to teach! The small class sizes, campus community, guarantee to travel, and research opportunities have made me stand out here at FSC- definitely more than a number!" —James Houle '24

"Florida Southern has been able to offer me so much! The Nursing program is direct-entry, and we start our clinicals in the fall of our sophomore year, so I did not have to worry about competing against my peers, a lot less stressful! I have attended clinicals all around central Florida, from Lakeland Regional Health Medical Center to Winter Haven Hospital to All Children's in St. Petersburg. I was super involved in high school, and that was something I wanted to carry on when I got to college; Florida Southern made that possible. I have made great relationships with the professors and faculty at FSC and have made some of my best friends." —Claire Winters '23

"Two years ago, I decided to enroll at FSC due to its quaint community and immersive atmosphere. Everywhere I go on campus, I always see a friend, pass someone new, or enjoy the campus's scenic beauty. With 100+ clubs and organizations that almost always have something going on every day, I knew I'd have a hard time being bored. From petting the campus cats, to the study sessions at Tutu's Cyber Cafe, to video game tournaments in Wesley's lounge, every day is an adventure here." —Colton Dawson '24

"In my college search, I was looking for a school with a tight-knit community where I could form strong connections with my peers and professors. FSC had an engaging and hands-on Marine Biology program, which fit what I wanted in a degree. I have the opportunity to work closely with professors on research projects and do research of my own my senior year. FSC offered the extracurricular opportunities I was looking for, too, namely being able to compete with the school's equestrian team. My Scholar's Weekend experience sealed the deal with my choice to attend FSC, where I had an incredible weekend filled with fun memories, and I met my future roommates!" — Rose Laconto '24

"As a Florida native, I always said if I stayed in Florida for college, I would only want to go to FSC. Florida Southern offered the small campus size I was looking for and hands-on learning experiences, small class sizes, and one-on-one relationships with advisors and professors." — Ruby Silver '24

"The main problem with graduating college students is that they have their degree but lack job-related experience. So when I was looking at colleges, I was hooked on Florida Southern when I saw that one of their guarantees is that every student gets an internship! After spending a year on campus and learning about more of their programs dedicated toward students at the Rogers building, I am glad that I made this choice knowing that I'll have a loaded resume with tons of work experience when I graduate." — Ezra Cooper '24

"I looked at several schools when considering college, but I hadn't stumbled across Florida Southern until my aunt spoke to me about it. I attended Scholars Weekend and immediately felt at home. Everything about the campus, faculty, and students gave me the 'wow' factor. Though I am only in my first year, I know that if I attended elsewhere, I wouldn't have the same experience. The teacher relationship in classroom settings is phenomenal. I am more willing to ask for help because of the class sizes and am able to build relationships with my classmates that large lecture halls

prevent. The ability to start research your first year is also a major plus! I am currently in the process with the psychology department to plan out my research." — Emi Shannon '24

Academic Programs

Accounting
Applied Mathematics and Statistics: Actuarial Foundations
Applied Mathematics and Statistics: Business
Applied Mathematics and Statistics: STEM
Art Education
Art History and Museum Studies
Biochemistry and Molecular Biology
Biology
Biotechnology
Business Administration
Business Administration: International Business
Business Administration: Management
Business Analytics
Chemistry
Chemistry: Environmental Chemistry
Chemistry: Forensic Chemistry
Communication: Advertising and Public Relations
Communication: Interpersonal and Organizational Communication
Communication: Media Strategies & Production
Communication: Multimedia Journalism
Computer Science
Computer Science: Artificial Intelligence and Machine Learning
Computer Science: Cybersecurity
Computer Science: Web and Cloud Computing
Criminology
Dance
Dance Performance and Choreography
Data Analytics
Economics
Elementary Education
English: Literature
English: Writing
Environmental Studies

Exercise Science
Film
Finance
Graphic Design
History
Humanities
Integrative Biology
Interactive and Game Design
Marine Biology
Marketing
Mathematics
Medical Laboratory Sciences
Music
Music Education
Music Performance
Music: Music Management
Nursing (BSN)
Philosophy
Political Communication
Political Science
Psychology
Religion
Religion: Youth Ministry
Secondary Education: Biology 6-12
Secondary Education: English Literature 6-12
Secondary Education: English Writing 6-12
Secondary Education: Mathematics 6-12
Secondary Education: Social Science 6-12
Social Sciences
Spanish
Sport Business Management
Sports Communication and Marketing
Studio Art
Theatre Arts (B.A.)
Theatre Arts: Musical Theatre (B.F.A.)
Theatre Arts: Technical Theatre/Design (B.F.A.)
Theatre Arts: Theatre Performance (B.F.A.)
Undeclared

THIRTY-ONE: **ELMHURST UNIVERSITY**

College Name: Elmhurst University
City, State: Elmhurst, IL
Website: https://www.elmhurst.edu/
Admissions email address: admit@elmhurst.edu
Admissions phone: 630.617.3400
Full-time undergraduate enrollment: 3,780
Number of full-time undergraduate students living on campus: 886
Average class size: 18
Student-faculty ratio: 13:1

Submitted by Christine Grenier, Vice President of Admission, Elmhurst University

Torn between braving the big city or having the classic college experience? At Elmhurst University, you don't have to choose. Our gorgeous 48-acre arboretum campus is nestled in the heart of Elmhurst, Illinois – a close-knit community with delicious restaurants, beautiful nature preserves, and entertainment galore, all while being a quick 30-minute train ride from downtown Chicago. Whether grabbing a bite at student hotspot Nu Crepes, attending a local music festival, or catching a Chicago-bound train to explore some of the world's best museums, Elmhurst students are never bored. Plus, many local businesses, like York Movie Theatre and Brewpoint Coffee, offer discounts with your student ID!

Elmhurst not only has the most popular majors students are looking for but continues to be innovative, adding new majors each year. Explore some of our newest majors such as Digital Media, Music Industry, and Cybersecurity, or check out some of our favorites like Business, Nursing, Biology, and Computer Science. Don't worry if you can't decide, you can always pick more than one major to study here and it usually won't take you any longer.

Beyond academics, Elmhurst has the resources to make sure you're taken care of throughout your time on campus. Elmhurst University's Learning Center is your go-to for all things for academic success and development. Our talented and patient team is always prepared to act as a study buddy for an upcoming exam, provide feedback on essays and presentations, or help you review any subject you're struggling with. Most importantly, the Learning Center offers workshops and tutoring sessions that will empower you to become the best student you can be. Develop the skills, strategies, and behaviors needed to be a successful lifelong learner. The Office of Access and Disability Services provides various accommodations and accessibility programs to students with a wide range of differing needs and abilities. Some of their offerings include extended test time, educational coaching, and housing accommodations.

Our Wellness Center puts your needs first. Whether you require mental health counseling, vaccinations, or basic health care, such as primary care visits or medication, our skilled clinicians are here to help. While some services may require a small fee, most are free to students!

Additional services include nutrition counseling, group sessions, stress management workshops, and our visiting service dogs to combat seasonal depression. During finals week, be sure to sign up for one of their free back massage sessions! If that doesn't get you feeling good, take advantage of all that the Tyrrell Fitness Center has to offer, whether or not you're a student athlete. Equipped with a weightroom, workout spaces, a dance studio, and more, it's easy to stay active at Elmhurst. Consider joining a yoga or martial arts class or checking out an open gym!

Elmhurst University wants you to thrive off campus as well. The Weigand Center for Professional Excellence (WCPE) provides a wide variety of professional and career development programs for current students and alumni alike. From identifying a major and career path to shadowing, internships, and job placements, the WCPE supports Bluejays every step of their professional journey. Once you're ready to spread your wings and venture into the job market, the WCPE can also assist with resume building, job searches, mock interviews, and even dressing for the job you want with our closet of interview-ready apparel!

However, don't make your college experience all work and no play! You can relax on the lush green grass on the college "mall" with friends, take in one of our men's competitive basketball games, or join one of the sororities or fraternities. And if that's not your thing, there are almost 100 clubs and activities to keep you busy and active throughout the year! If you want to spread your wings a little further, O'Hare International Airport is just eight miles from campus. Hop a short flight to visit your friends anywhere in the country or take in the sights abroad through one of our short-term or longer study abroad programs. There are no boundaries to your Elmhurst Experience.

As a Bluejay, you'll be part of a community here that goes beyond the four walls of your house. Your new friends and mentors will be professors who are understanding of your "life" situations and want to see you succeed despite the stresses you might have. You don't have to worry when you know that you have someone you can talk to about your struggles and successes and who is there to help you learn.

Still wondering if you'll fit in, you will! Our campus is diverse in so many ways. One-third of our students each year are first-year students, another third are transfer students, and the last piece of the pie are graduate students. Whether you commute or live on campus, you'll find students, staff, and faculty from all backgrounds including racial, socio-economic, first-generation, and more. We value what everyone brings to the Elmhurst family.

Elmhurst University understands that the cost of college can be both intimidating and overwhelming. There's tuition and housing, fees, and miscellaneous expenses that you have to also prepare for such as books, notebooks, and a laptop, not to mention the cost of transportation these days. How can you make it all work? It's important to look beyond the "sticker price" because the question you should ask yourself is "How much **will I pay** for my Elmhurst experience?" You won't pay full price! In fact, you'll pay way less with our generous scholarships and financial aid. We work to make Elmhurst affordable for all students who want to join our community. There are many financial paths and creative financing that we can help you with, all you need to do is apply and let us do the rest! We'll guide you every step of the way through all of the scholarships that you qualify for and then some! Our admission counselors are constantly looking out for you and helping you take advantage of all of the financial aid that's available to you.

Even after that, our staff can walk you through ways that you can make Elmhurst even more affordable! For example, take advantage of our January Term class, a short-term class that's included in the cost of tuition! What else is there to do in the winter? Or transfer in a few courses from your local community college before you begin Elmhurst. We'll even let you know which courses are the best for what you want to study. Or maybe think about commuting to Elmhurst instead of living on campus. You can save money by living at home and still have a spectacular Elmhurst experience. We'll work on a payment plan with you to spread out your payments so you don't feel such a pinch. After all, you may want to fit in a little Starbucks coffee on your way to class. It's important to look at the big picture of affordability, but we're here to help.

Academic Programs

Accounting
Actuarial Science
Art
Art Business
Biochemistry
Biology
Business Administration
Chemistry
Communication
Communication Sciences and Disorders
Communication Sciences and Disorders (Grad Prep Program)

Computer Game and Entertainment Technology
Computer Science
Criminal Justice
Cybersecurity
Digital Marketing Communications
Digital Media
Digital Media - Audio and Video
Digital Media - Writing for Film and Television
Digital Media - Animation Game Design
Distance Accelerated BSN
Economics
Educating Young Children (Early Childhood Education)
Elementary Teacher Education
Elmhurst Learning and Success Academy (ELSA)
Elmhurst Management Program (Business Administration)
English: Literature
English: Writing
Environmental Studies
Exercise Science
Finance
French
Geographic Information Systems
Geography
German
Graphic Design
Health Science Technology
History
Information Systems
Information Technology
International Business
Latino Studies
Logistics and Supply Chain Management
Management
Marketing
Mathematics
Mathematics/Secondary Education
Middle Level English Language Arts (5-8)
Middle Level Mathematics (5-8)
Multi-Language
Multimedia Journalism
Music Business
Music Education

Music Industry
Music Performance
Music Production
Music Theory/Composition
Music: General
Music: Jazz Studies
Musical Theatre
Nursing
Philosophy
Physical Education
Physics
Political Science
Psychology
Psychology (Evening Program)
Public Health
Religious Studies
Secondary English Language Arts Education (9-12)
Secondary Mathematics Education (9-12)
Secondary Science Education with Biology (5-12)
Secondary Science Education with Chemistry (5-12)
Secondary Science Education with Physics (5-12)
Social Science Education with History (5-12)
Social Science Education with Political Science (5-12)
Sociology
Spanish
Special Education
Sport Management
Theatre
Theatre Arts Education (PK-12)
Undeclared/Undecided
Urban Studies
World Language Education with French
World Language Education with Spanish

SECTION TWO

333 Small Colleges to check out. What caught my eye!

There are over 700 small private colleges in the U.S. The 333 colleges on this list caught my eye due to the exceptional job they do in helping families keep their costs low. They also tend to be very accessible to a wide array of students and make the college application process very streamlined and straightforward.

About these 333 colleges:
Average enrollment 1,665
Avg Sticker Price for tuition, housing, food, and fees: $51,000
However…Average Out of Pocket Cost (without loans) is $22,000 and typically ranges from $15,000 to $39,000 for most families. Some a little higher, some a lot lower.
Average amount of Merit Aid awarded: $20,000

✓ *95% Have rolling admission*
✓ *65% Have no application fee*
✓ *96% Are some form of test-optional*
✓ *99% Admit some C+ students*
✓ *99% Give institutional merit aid to all domestic incoming freshmen*
✓ *Most, if not all, accept applications and admit students even after May 1*
✓ *83% Admit 70% or more of their applicants*
✓ *Most do not require extra essays in addition to the CA essays*
✓ *99% Do not require the CSS Profile*
✓ *Most, if not all, have over 90% placement rates (work or graduate school) within 6 months of graduation*

- ✓ *Median ACT Test Range 20-26*
- ✓ *Average Niche Grade is "B"*
- ✓ *45% offer some full tuition scholarships*
- ✓ *61% offer some performing arts scholarships without having to major in the arts*

For each college, as I "surfed their website," I took notes about "what caught my eye." I hope the reader will find this both interesting and helpful.

Important note regarding "what caught my eye:" Programs and policies do change at colleges from time to time, so please check with the colleges directly to receive any updates. These are not necessarily the biggest, best, or most popular programs at the college, but they are the ones that just "caught my eye" as unique, special, interesting, or just plain awesome. My eyes are not perfect, of course, so if the reader knows of a program I missed, I apologize.

I also researched the colleges for two kinds of scholarships: Full tuition academic merit scholarships, and talent/performance scholarships NOT based on the major the student chooses. Scholarship programs at colleges change often, so I cannot guarantee 100% accuracy. Make sure to check directly with the college to receive updates.

At the end of this section, there is a geographic index. There are also separate lists of colleges offering the full tuition and/or performing arts scholarships, also sorted geographically.

[Note: these 333 colleges are listed alphabetically. For a geographic breakdown, go to the end of this list]

Agnes Scott College (GA)

https://www.agnesscott.edu/
1,063 students (Women)
Full Tuition Scholarships? Y

Performing Arts Scholarships w/o majoring in the arts? N
What programs caught my eye? **Astrophysics; Human Rights; Foundations of Artificial Intelligence; Women's, Gender and Sexuality Studies**

Albertus Magnus College (CT)

https://www.albertus.edu/
1,031 students
Full Tuition Scholarships? N
Performing Arts Scholarships w/o majoring in the arts? Y
What programs caught my eye? **Art Therapy; Urban Studies; Project Management; Health Care Management; Game & Computer Arts**

Albion College (MI) *Chapter ONE in this book*

https://www.albion.edu/
1,444 students
Full Tuition Scholarships? N
Performing Arts Scholarships w/o majoring in the arts? Y
What programs caught my eye? **Paleontology; EMS Club / Student EMT's on campus (Wilson Medical Institute); Value Theory; Sexuality Studies; Geology; Environmental Geology**

Alfred University (NY)

https://www.alfred.edu/
1,485 students
Full Tuition Scholarships? N
Performing Arts Scholarships w/o majoring in the arts? N
What programs caught my eye? **Biomaterials Engineering; Ceramic Engineering; Glass Engineering; Renewable Energy Engineering; Art; Ceramic Art; Equine Business Management; Performance Design and Technology**

Allegheny College (PA)

https://allegheny.edu/
1,600 Students
Full Tuition Scholarships? N

Performing Arts Scholarships w/o majoring in the arts? Y
What programs caught my eye? **The Playshop Theatre;
Journalism in the Public Interest; Global Health Studies;
Environmental Writing**

Alma College (MI)

https://www.alma.edu/
1340 students
Full Tuition Scholarships? Y
Performing Arts Scholarships w/o majoring in the arts? Y
What programs caught my eye? **The Alma Venture; New Media
Studies; Dance; Biotechnology; Special Education LD; Highland
Arts (Highland Dancing and Bagpipes)**

Alverno College (WI) *Chapter EIGHTEEN in this book*

https://www.alverno.edu/
864 students (Women)
Full Tuition Scholarships? Y
Performing Arts Scholarships w/o majoring in the arts? N
What programs caught my eye? **No grades (narrative feedback);
Community Engagement and Activism; Music Therapy;
Creative Arts in Practice; Women in STEM; Alverno College
Greenhouse; Social Work (also Abolitionist MSW)**

Andrews University (MI)

https://www.andrews.edu/
1,358 students
Full Tuition Scholarships? N
Performing Arts Scholarships w/o majoring in the arts? N
What programs caught my eye? **Architecture; Aviation; Speech-
Language Pathology & Audiology; Biology; Nursing; Animal
Science; Medical Laboratory Science; Social Work; Wellness;
Nutrition Science and Dietetics; Biophysics; Informatics;
Christian Discipleship; Missions; Sustainable Horticulture**

Antioch College (OH)

https://antiochcollege.edu/

116 students

Full Tuition Scholarships? N

Performing Arts Scholarships w/o majoring in the arts? N

What programs caught my eye? **Self-Designed Majors; Anthropology; Environmental Science; Gender & Sexuality Studies; Sustainability**

Aquinas College (MI)

https://www.aquinas.edu/

1,238 students

Full Tuition Scholarships? Y

Performing Arts Scholarships w/o majoring in the arts? Y

What programs caught my eye? **Sustainable Business; Jazz; Child Life; Irish Studies; Music Entrepreneurship; Physically & Otherwise Health-Impaired Education**

Augsburg University (MN)

https://www.augsburg.edu/

2,363 students

Full Tuition Scholarships? N

Performing Arts Scholarships w/o majoring in the arts? N

What programs caught my eye? **American Indian, First Nations, and Indigenous Studies; Biopsychology; Sexuality Studies; Music Business; Directing/Dramaturgy/Playwriting; Space Physics; Biophysics; Music Creativity**

Augustana College (IL)

https://www.augustana.edu/

2,338 students

Full Tuition Scholarships? N

Performing Arts Scholarships w/o majoring in the arts? Y

What programs caught my eye? **Communication Sciences and Disorders; Library and Information Science Advising; Scandinavian Studies; Landscape Architecture; Environmental Management & Forestry; Japanese; Food Studies; Geology**

Augustana University (SD)

https://www.augie.edu/
1,715 students
Full Tuition Scholarships? N
Performing Arts Scholarships w/o majoring in the arts? Y
What programs caught my eye? **Fintech; Brewing and Fermentation; Fitness Management; Multimedia Entrepreneurship; Northern Plains Studies; Science Writing; Sign Language**

Austin College (TX)

https://www.austincollege.edu/
1,212 students
Full Tuition Scholarships? N
Performing Arts Scholarships w/o majoring in the arts? Y
What programs caught my eye? **Social Justice and Community Engagement; Global Science, Technology & Society; Western Intellectual Tradition; PPE: Philosophy, Politics, and Economics**

Ave Maria University (FL)

https://www.avemaria.edu/
1,245 students
Full Tuition Scholarships? N
Performing Arts Scholarships w/o majoring in the arts? N
What programs caught my eye? **Marine Biology; Classics & Early Christian Literature; Catholic Studies; Catechetics; Marriage and Family Studies; Shakespeare in Performance; Medieval Studies**

Avila University (MO)

https://www.avila.edu/
1,058 students
Full Tuition Scholarships? N
Performing Arts Scholarships w/o majoring in the arts? Y
What programs caught my eye? **Biochemistry & Molecular Biology; Criminology and Justice Studies; Healthcare Management; Nursing; Wellness Studies**

Baker University (KS)

https://www.bakeru.edu/
1,147 students
Full Tuition Scholarships? Y
Performing Arts Scholarships w/o majoring in the arts? Y
What programs caught my eye? **Health Humanities; Human Biology; Mass Media; Exercise Science**

Baldwin Wallace University (OH)

https://www.bw.edu/
2,829 students
Full Tuition Scholarships? N
Performing Arts Scholarships w/o majoring in the arts? N
What programs caught my eye? **Theatre: Design and Technical; Arts Management & Entrepreneurship; Digital Media and Interactive Design; Enterprise Risk Analytics; Hospitality & Tourism Management; Music Theatre Direction**

Bay Path University (MA)

https://www.baypath.edu/
1,524 students (Women)
Full Tuition Scholarships? Y
Performing Arts Scholarships w/o majoring in the arts? N
What programs caught my eye? **Forensic Science; Interior Design: Residential & Commercial; Hospitality Management; Severe**

Special Needs Education; Cybersecurity: Digital Forensics & Incident Response; Professional Writing; Paralegal Studies; Forensic Psychology; Neurobiology

Belhaven University (MS)

https://www.belhaven.edu/
1,713 students
Full Tuition Scholarships? N
Performing Arts Scholarships w/o majoring in the arts? N
What programs caught my eye? **Biblical Studies; Dance; Fashion Merchandising; Intercultural Studies; Leadership and Coaching; Sales Management**

Bellarmine University (KY)

https://www.bellarmine.edu/
2,407 students
Full Tuition Scholarships? Y
Performing Arts Scholarships w/o majoring in the arts? Y
What programs caught my eye? **Senior Living Management; Respiratory Therapy, Aging Studies; Design, Arts, & Technology; Health, Culture, and Compassion; Esports; Refugee & Forced Migration Studies; TV News & Sports Broadcasting**

Beloit College (WI)

https://www.beloit.edu/
1,011 students
Full Tuition Scholarships? N
Performing Arts Scholarships w/o majoring in the arts? Y
What programs caught my eye? **CELEB Center for Entrepreneurship; Critical Identity Studies; Environmental Geology; Japanese Language and Culture; Museum Studies; Ancient Mediterranean Studies; Comparative Literature; Medieval Studies**

Berea College (KY)

https://www.berea.edu/
1,468 students
Full Tuition Scholarships? N
Performing Arts Scholarships w/o majoring in the arts? N
What programs caught my eye? **No Tuition Charged; Agriculture and Natural Resources; Appalachian Studies; Forest Resource Management**

Berry College (GA)

https://www.berry.edu/
2,172 students
Full Tuition Scholarships? N
Performing Arts Scholarships w/o majoring in the arts? Y
What programs caught my eye? **Professional Tennis Management Program; Animal Science; Creative Technologies; Digital Storytelling; Geology; Applied Behavior Analysis**

Bethany Lutheran College (MN)

https://blc.edu/
781 students
Full Tuition Scholarships? N
Performing Arts Scholarships w/o majoring in the arts? N
What programs caught my eye? **Global and Cross Cultural Studies; Legal Studies; Paralegal Certification; Special Education**

Birmingham-Southern (AL)

https://www.bsc.edu/
1,058 students
Full Tuition Scholarships? Y
Performing Arts Scholarships w/o majoring in the arts? Y
What programs caught my eye? **E-Term (Exploration Term in January); Urban Environmental Studies; Spanish for the**

Workplace; Arabic Studies; Chinese; Musical Theatre; Architectural Studies; Mathematical Finance; Human Rights and Conflict Studies

Blackburn College (IL) *Chapter NINETEEN in this book*
https://blackburn.edu/
350 students
Full Tuition Scholarships? N
Performing Arts Scholarships w/o majoring in the arts? N
What programs caught my eye? **Only Student Managed Work Program in the United States; Justice Administration; Creative Writing; Human Resource Management**

Bob Jones University (SC)
https://www.bju.edu/
2,705 students
Full Tuition Scholarships? N
Performing Arts Scholarships w/o majoring in the arts? N
What programs caught my eye? **Film and Digital Storytelling; Interior Architecture and Design; Biblical Counseling; Music and Church Ministries; Culinary Arts; Fashion Design**

Brenau University (GA)
https://www.brenau.edu/
1,427 students (Women in the Women's College)
Full Tuition Scholarships? Y
Performing Arts Scholarships w/o majoring in the arts? N
What programs caught my eye? **Costuming for Film and Theatre; interior design; Fashion Design/Merchandising; Conflict Resolution and Legal Studies; Logistics and Supply Chain Management; Theatre Design and Technology**

Brescia University (KY)

752 students
Full Tuition Scholarships? N
Performing Arts Scholarships w/o majoring in the arts? Y
What programs caught my eye? **Social Work; Professional Writing; Catholic Studies; Sports Management; Communication Sciences and Disorders; Graphic Design**

Brigham Young Hawaii (HI)

3,180 students
Full Tuition Scholarships? N
Performing Arts Scholarships w/o majoring in the arts? N
What programs caught my eye? **Anthropology and Cultural Sustainability; Hawaiian Studies; Hospitality & Tourism Management; Intercultural Peacebuilding; Pacific Island Studies**

Buena Vista University (IA)

1,506 students
Full Tuition Scholarships? N
Performing Arts Scholarships w/o majoring in the arts? Y
What programs caught my eye? **Scientific Illustration; Agricultural Business/Science; Animation; Art Therapy; Corporate Mathematics; Music Production and Technology; Rehabilitation Health Sciences; Social Innovation**

Calvin University (MI)

3,068 students
Full Tuition Scholarships? N
Performing Arts Scholarships w/o majoring in the arts? N
What programs caught my eye? **Financial Planning; Marketing Professional Selling; Music Composition; Speech Pathology and**

Audiology; Therapeutic Recreation; Recreational Leadership;
Archaeology; Linguistics; Ministry Leadership; Naturalist
Environmental Science; International Designation; Optics;
Dutch; Korean

Campbell University (NC)

https://www.campbell.edu/
3,325 students
Full Tuition Scholarships? N
Performing Arts Scholarships w/o majoring in the arts? N
What programs caught my eye? **PGA Golf Management; Exercise
and Sport Science; Converged Journalism; Homeland Security;
Emergency Management; Financial Planning**

Canisius College (NY)

https://www.canisius.edu/
1,866 students
Full Tuition Scholarships? N
Performing Arts Scholarships w/o majoring in the arts? Y
What programs caught my eye? **Animal Behavior; Animal
Behavior, Ecology, and Conservation; Anthrozoology;
Computer Theory; Conservation; Industrial/Organizational
Psychology; Neuropsychology; Neuroscience; Zoo Biology**

Capital University (OH)

https://www.capital.edu/
2,090 students
Full Tuition Scholarships? Y
Performing Arts Scholarships w/o majoring in the arts? N
What programs caught my eye? **Bonner Leader Program; Music
Technology; Contemporary Worship Arts; Film and Media
Production Minor; Screenwriting; Performance Technology;
Therapeutic Art**

Carroll College (MT)
https://www.carroll.edu/
1,098 students
Full Tuition Scholarships? N
Performing Arts Scholarships w/o majoring in the arts? Y
What programs caught my eye? **Anthrozoology; Animal Studies; Catholic Studies; Public Health; Reading Education; Ethics & Value Studies**

Carroll University (WI)
https://www.carrollu.edu/
2,884 students
Full Tuition Scholarships? Y
Performing Arts Scholarships w/o majoring in the arts? Y
What programs caught my eye? **Freshwater Sciences; Animal Behavior; Marine Sciences; Actuarial Science; Music Therapy; Neurodiagnostic Technology; Photography; Video Game Studies**

Carthage College (WI) *Chapter EIGHT in this book*
https://www.carthage.edu/
2,634 students
Full Tuition Scholarships? Y
Performing Arts Scholarships w/o majoring in the arts? Y
What programs caught my eye? **Climatology & Meteorology; Space Studies (college campus for NASA in Wisconsin); Business Design and Innovation; Environmental Conservation; Geographic Information Science; Geoscience; Nursing; Paleontology**

Catawba College (NC) *Chapter TWENTY-EIGHT in this book*
https://catawba.edu/
1,094 students
Full Tuition Scholarships? Y

Performing Arts Scholarships w/o majoring in the arts? Y
What programs caught my eye? **Popular Music; Environmental and Outdoor Education; Forestry and Environmental Studies; GIS & Technology; Natural Resource Management; Nutrition; Sustainable Planning and Leadership**

Cedar Crest College (PA)
https://www.cedarcrest.edu/
1,053 students (Women in traditional UG)
Full Tuition Scholarships? Y
Performing Arts Scholarships w/o majoring in the arts? Y
What programs caught my eye? **Criminal Justice/Crime Science; Audiology; Art Therapy; Genetics & Counseling Psychology; Genetic Engineering and Biotechnology; Global Diseases; Child Welfare**

Centenary College of Louisiana (LA)
https://www.centenary.edu/
552 students
Full Tuition Scholarships? Y
Performing Arts Scholarships w/o majoring in the arts? Y
What programs caught my eye? **Centenary in Paris Program for incoming freshmen; Environment & Society; Geology; Museum Management; Business/Foreign Language Coordinate Program**

Central College (IA) *Chapter NINE in this book*
https://central.edu/
1,150 students
Full Tuition Scholarships? Y
Performing Arts Scholarships w/o majoring in the arts? Y
What programs caught my eye? **Glass Blowing; Steel Pan Drum Band; Musical Theatre; Personal Training; Strength and Conditioning; Environmental and Sustainability Studies; Cultural Anthropology; Actuarial Science**

Centre College (KY)

https://www.centre.edu/
1,320 students
Full Tuition Scholarships? Y
Performing Arts Scholarships w/o majoring in the arts? Y
What programs caught my eye? **Chemical Physics; African & African American Studies; Behavioral Neuroscience; Linguistics; Health and Medical Studies; Social Justice; Film Studies**

Chaminade University Honolulu (HI)

https://chaminade.edu/
1,028 students
Full Tuition Scholarships? N
Performing Arts Scholarships w/o majoring in the arts? N
What programs caught my eye? **Surf Studies; Hawaiian and Pacific Studies; Asian and Pacific Studies; Environmental + Interior Design**

Charleston Southern University (SC)

https://www.charlestonsouthern.edu/
2,725 students
Full Tuition Scholarships? N
Performing Arts Scholarships w/o majoring in the arts? Y
What programs caught my eye? **Supply Chain Management; Aeronautics; Hospitality & Tourism; Laboratory Technology; Missions**

Chatham University (PA)

https://www.chatham.edu/
1,460 students
Full Tuition Scholarships? Y
Performing Arts Scholarships w/o majoring in the arts? N

What programs caught my eye? **Food Studies; Cultural Studies; Immersive Media; Interior Architecture**

Christian Brothers University (TN)
https://www.cbu.edu/
1,321 students
Full Tuition Scholarships? Y
Performing Arts Scholarships w/o majoring in the arts? N
What programs caught my eye? **5 year BS/MS in Engineering; Cultural Studies; English for Corporate Communications; Cognitive Neuroscience; Banking; Construction Management; Packaging; Cybersecurity and Digital Forensics**

Claflin University (SC)
https://www.claflin.edu/
1,779 students
Full Tuition Scholarships? N
Performing Arts Scholarships w/o majoring in the arts? N
What programs caught my eye? **HBCU; African and African American Studies; Bioinformatics; Biotechnology; Performing Ensembles; Sport Management; Applied Computing; Early Childhood Education**

Clarke University (IA)
https://www.clarke.edu/
707 students
Full Tuition Scholarships? N
Performing Arts Scholarships w/o majoring in the arts? Y
What programs caught my eye? **Justice and Activism; Nutrition & Food Science; Health, Wellness & Behavioral Sciences; Digital Media Studies**

Clarkson College (NE)
https://www.clarksoncollege.edu/

616 students
Full Tuition Scholarships? N
Performing Arts Scholarships w/o majoring in the arts? N
What programs caught my eye? **Radiography; Medical Imaging; Community Health; Physical Therapy Assistant; Nursing; Health Information Technology; Healthcare Business Management**

Cleary University (MI)
https://www.cleary.edu/
586 students
Full Tuition Scholarships? N
Performing Arts Scholarships w/o majoring in the arts? N
What programs caught my eye? **Business Ethics; Project Management; Sports Promotion and Management; Nonprofit Management**

Coe College (IA)
https://www.coe.edu/
1,371 students
Full Tuition Scholarships? Y
Performing Arts Scholarships w/o majoring in the arts? Y
What programs caught my eye? **Organizational Science; Molecular Biology; Neuroscience; English as a Second Language - ESL; Writing; Creative Writing**

College of Saint Mary (NE)
https://www.csm.edu/
634 students (Women)
Full Tuition Scholarships? N
Performing Arts Scholarships w/o majoring in the arts? N
What programs caught my eye? **BOLD program for undecided freshmen; Medical Laboratory Science; Women's Studies; Gallery Management; Nursing Paralegal Studies; Early Childhood Education**

College of St. Benedict (MN)

https://www.csbsju.edu/
1,542 students (Women)
Full Tuition Scholarships? N
Performing Arts Scholarships w/o majoring in the arts? Y
What programs caught my eye? **Adventure Programs/Outdoor University; Ancient Mediterranean Studies; Book Arts; Forestry; Global Health; Numerical Computation; Nutrition**

College of the Atlantic (ME)

https://www.coa.edu/
374 students
Full Tuition Scholarships? N
Performing Arts Scholarships w/o majoring in the arts? N
What programs caught my eye? **Ethnography & Documentary; Field Ecology & Natural History; Farming & Food Systems; Climate Change & Energy; Culture & Place; Marine Science**

College of the Ozarks (MO)

https://www.cofo.edu/
1,468 students
Full Tuition Scholarships? N
Performing Arts Scholarships w/o majoring in the arts? N
What programs caught my eye? **"Hard Work U" (all students work); Agriculture; Conservation and wildlife management; Culinary Arts; Hospitality Management; Applied Nutrition; Biblical and Theological Studies**

College of Wooster (OH)

https://wooster.edu/
1,973 students
Full Tuition Scholarships? N

Performing Arts Scholarships w/o majoring in the arts? Y
What programs caught my eye? **Chemistry; Activism & Social Change; Archaeology; Biochemistry & Molecular Biology; Chemical Physics; Digital & Visual Storytelling; Environmental Geoscience; Museum & Archival Studies; Music Therapy**

Columbia International University (SC)

https://www.ciu.edu/
905 students
Full Tuition Scholarships? N
Performing Arts Scholarships w/o majoring in the arts? N
What programs caught my eye? **Bible; Youth Ministry, Family, & Culture; Social Media Strategist; Middle Eastern Studies; International Community Development; Disaster Relief and Emergency Management**

Concordia College-Moorhead (MN)

https://www.concordiacollege.edu/
1,883 students
Full Tuition Scholarships? Y
Performing Arts Scholarships w/o majoring in the arts? Y
What programs caught my eye? **TESOL / Chinese; Accelerated BSN; Astrophysics; Clinical Practice, Rehabilitation and Therapy; Dietetics; Long-term Care Administration; Neurochemistry; Social Activism**

Concordia University-Nebraska (NE)

https://www.cune.edu/
2,550 students
Full Tuition Scholarships? N
Performing Arts Scholarships w/o majoring in the arts? Y
What programs caught my eye? **Agricultural Science; American Sign Language; Digital Marketing; Mandarin; Music Therapy; Public Health and Fitness; Recreation and Sport Studies; Special Education**

Concordia University-Ann Arbor (MI)

https://www.cuaa.edu/
1,002 students
Full Tuition Scholarships? N
Performing Arts Scholarships w/o majoring in the arts? Y
What programs caught my eye? **Sport and Entertainment Business; Christian Thought; Diagnostic Medical Sonography; Family Life Ministry; Hospitality and Event Management; Pharmaceutical Sciences**

Concordia University-Chicago (IL)

https://www.cuchicago.edu/
1,381 students
Full Tuition Scholarships? Y
Performing Arts Scholarships w/o majoring in the arts? Y
What programs caught my eye? **Center for Gerontology; Sports Nutrition; Strength & Conditioning; Church Music; Early Childhood Education; Human Communication & Culture**

Concordia University-St. Paul (MN)

https://www.csp.edu/
3,355 students
Full Tuition Scholarships? N
Performing Arts Scholarships w/o majoring in the arts? Y
What programs caught my eye? **Orthotics and Prosthetics; Actuarial Science; Church Work; Hmong studies; Family Science; Trauma and Resilience**

Concordia University-Wisconsin (WI)

https://www.cuw.edu/
2,908 students
Full Tuition Scholarships? N

Performing Arts Scholarships w/o majoring in the arts? Y
What programs caught my eye? **Hospitality and Event Management; Animal-Assisted Therapy Certificate; Bioethics; Earth and Space Sciences Certificate; Environmental Health and Water Quality Technology; Horticulture; Interior Architecture & Design; Illustration**

Cornell College (IA)

https://www.cornellcollege.edu/
1,045 students
Full Tuition Scholarships? N
Performing Arts Scholarships w/o majoring in the arts? Y
What programs caught my eye? **One-Course-At-A-Time Curriculum; 3+3 Law Program with U of Iowa; 5-year B.A./M.P.H. with the University of Iowa College of Public Health/Epidemiology; Russian & Russian Studies**

Cottey College (MO)

https://cottey.edu/
303 students (Women)
Full Tuition Scholarships? Y
Performing Arts Scholarships w/o majoring in the arts? Y
What programs caught my eye? **Serenbetz Institute for Women's Leadership, Social Responsibility, and Global Awareness; Women, Gender, & Sexuality Studies; Organizational Leadership; Criminology; Women's Flag Football (scholarships too!)**

Covenant College (GA)

https://covenant.edu/
872 students
Full Tuition Scholarships? N
Performing Arts Scholarships w/o majoring in the arts? N
What programs caught my eye? **Art (2-D, 3-D, Art History, Graphic Design, Photography); Biblical & Theological Studies;**

Economics & Community Development; Church Music; Organ
Performance

Culver-Stockton College (MO)
https://culver.edu/
879 students
Full Tuition Scholarships? Y
Performing Arts Scholarships w/o majoring in the arts? Y
What programs caught my eye? **Agribusiness Management;
Supply Chain Management; Speech and Theatre Education;
Radiologic Science; Professional Sales; Musical Theatre; Esports
and Gaming Administration; Child Advocacy Studies**

Cumberland University (TN)
https://www.cumberland.edu/
2,257 students
Full Tuition Scholarships? Y
Performing Arts Scholarships w/o majoring in the arts? N
What programs caught my eye? **E-Commerce; Computational
Finance; Non-Profit Management; Technology Management;
Geography; Supply Chain Management; Child Growth and
Learning**

Daemen University (NY)
https://www.daemen.edu/
1,787 students
Full Tuition Scholarships? Y
Performing Arts Scholarships w/o majoring in the arts? Y
What programs caught my eye? **Social Entrepreneurship;
Professional Writing and Rhetoric; Global and Local
Sustainability; 3+4 Doctor of Veterinary Medicine Program;
Atlantic Studies; Leadership and Entrepreneurship in the Arts;**

Dakota Wesleyan University (SD)

https://www.dwu.edu/
759 students
Full Tuition Scholarships? N
Performing Arts Scholarships w/o majoring in the arts? Y
What programs caught my eye? **Wildlife Management / Law Enforcement; Christian Leadership; Nonprofit Administration; Web Design; Sports Management**

Davis and Elkins College (WV)

https://www.dewv.edu/
738 students
Full Tuition Scholarships? N
Performing Arts Scholarships w/o majoring in the arts? Y
What programs caught my eye? **Hospitality and Tourism; Sustainable Resource Management; Product Design; Outdoor Recreation Management; Criminology with Cybersecurity Concentration**

DePauw University (IN)

https://www.depauw.edu/
1,724 students
Full Tuition Scholarships? N
Performing Arts Scholarships w/o majoring in the arts? Y
What programs caught my eye? **Peace and Conflict Studies; Museum Studies; Astronomy; Design Studies; Environmental Geosciences; Italian Cultural Studies; Archaeology Pathway; Latin American and Caribbean Studies**

DeSales University (PA)

https://www.desales.edu/
2,309 students
Full Tuition Scholarships? Y
Performing Arts Scholarships w/o majoring in the arts? Y

What programs caught my eye? **Pharmaceutical Marketing; TV/Film; Behavioral Neuroscience; Biomechanics; Homeland Security; Law and Society**

Doane University (NE)
https://www.doane.edu/
1,107 students
Full Tuition Scholarships? Y
Performing Arts Scholarships w/o majoring in the arts? Y
What programs caught my eye? **Agribusiness; Natural Resources and Environmental Sciences; Policy and Values; Substance Use Counseling; Strategic Communication**

Dominican University (IL)
https://www.dom.edu/
2,063 students
Full Tuition Scholarships? N
Performing Arts Scholarships w/o majoring in the arts? N
What programs caught my eye? **Culinology; Art History; Black World Studies; Digital Journalism; Fashion Design/Merchandising; Informatics; Interfaith Studies; Italian Studies; Nutrition and Dietetics; Translation & Interpretation Studies; Photo-Cinema**

Dordt University (IA)
https://www.dordt.edu/
1,534 students
Full Tuition Scholarships? N
Performing Arts Scholarships w/o majoring in the arts? N
What programs caught my eye? **Agriculture Technology; Agriculture; Animal Science; Architecture; Biotechnology; Church Music; Construction Facilities Management; Dutch; Event Planning; Industrial Networks/Programming; Legal Studies; Linguistics; Mission and Ministry; Music Management;**

Natural Resource Management; Plant Science; Production and design; Retail and Sales

Drake University (IA)
https://www.drake.edu/
2,902 students
Full Tuition Scholarships? N
Performing Arts Scholarships w/o majoring in the arts? Y
What programs caught my eye? **Actuarial Science/Risk Management; 3+3 law/Journalism degree; Arabic Language and Culture Minor; Advertising; Artificial Intelligence; Astronomy; Chinese Language and Culture; Magazine Media; Quantitative Economics; Zoo & Conservation Science; Comparative Animal Behavior**

Drury University (MO)
https://www.drury.edu/
1,345 students
Full Tuition Scholarships? Y
Performing Arts Scholarships w/o majoring in the arts? Y
What programs caught my eye? **Design-Build Program; Design in Society; Cyber-risk Management; Architecture and Design; Animal Studies; Music Therapy; Architecture; Graphic Storytelling; Personal Branding**

Dunwoody College of Technology (MN)
https://dunwoody.edu/
1,382 students
Full Tuition Scholarships? N
Performing Arts Scholarships w/o majoring in the arts? N
What programs caught my eye? **Engineering Drafting and Design; Machine Tool Technology; Welding and Metal Fabrication; Automotive Collision Repair and Refinishing; Automotive Service Technology; Cloud Engineering Technology;**

Construction Management; Robotics; Architecture; Architectural Drafting and Design; Interior Design

D'Youville University (NY)

https://www.dyu.edu/
1,388 students
Full Tuition Scholarships? N
Performing Arts Scholarships w/o majoring in the arts? N
What programs caught my eye? **5 year Nutrition and Dietetics BS/MS; Pharmaceutical Science; Public Health; Health Services Management**

Earlham College (IN)

https://earlham.edu/
658 students
Full Tuition Scholarships? N
Performing Arts Scholarships w/o majoring in the arts? Y
What programs caught my eye? **Epic Journey/Epic Advantage; Anthrozoology (Human-Animal Studies); Archaeology; Art, Nature and Conservation; Comparative Languages and Linguistics; Contemplative Studies; Equestrian Management; Jewish Studies; Museum Studies; Peace Corps Prep; Shakespeare Studies; Quality Science; Sustainable Agriculture**

Eastern Mennonite University (VA)

https://emu.edu/
958 students
Full Tuition Scholarships? Y
Performing Arts Scholarships w/o majoring in the arts? N
What programs caught my eye? **Aviation; Bible, Religion, and Theology; Community Organizing; Criminology and Restorative Justice; Global Development; Peacebuilding and Development**

Edgewood College (WI) *Chapter SEVENTEEN in this book*

https://www.edgewood.edu/
1,194 students
Full Tuition Scholarships? N
Performing Arts Scholarships w/o majoring in the arts? Y
What programs caught my eye? **Geoscience; Art Therapy; Bilingual Education; Child life; Cytotechnology; Music Media and Production; Music Promotion and Industry; Masters in Thanatology (death and dying)**

Elizabethtown College (PA)

https://www.etown.edu/
1,691 students
Full Tuition Scholarships? Y
Performing Arts Scholarships w/o majoring in the arts? Y
What programs caught my eye? **Architectural Studies; Asian Studies; Cognitive Science; Computational Physics; Early Childhood Education; Family Business and Entrepreneurship; Japanese; Law Early Admissions Program (LEAP); Public Heritage Studies; Technical Design**

Elmhurst University (IL)

https://www.elmhurst.edu/
2,914 students
Full Tuition Scholarships? N
Performing Arts Scholarships w/o majoring in the arts? N
What programs caught my eye? **Jazz Studies; Urban Studies; Music Production; Multimedia Journalism; Computer Game and Entertainment Technology; Musical Theatre; Logistics and Supply Chain Management**

Elms College (MA)

https://www.elms.edu/
1,060 students

Full Tuition Scholarships? N
Performing Arts Scholarships w/o majoring in the arts? N
What programs caught my eye? **ASPIRE program for undecided freshmen; Biotechnology; Bioethics and Medical Humanities; Irish Studies**

Emory and Henry College (VA)

https://www.ehc.edu/
1,084 students
Full Tuition Scholarships? N
Performing Arts Scholarships w/o majoring in the arts? Y
What programs caught my eye? **Outdoor Program/Adventure Team; Animal Science; Appalachian Studies; Civic Innovation; Creative Communication; Equine Assisted Therapy; Equine Studies; Semester-A-Trail (hike of the Appalachian Trail); Intermont Equestrian Team**

Eureka College (IL)

https://www.eureka.edu/
476 students
Full Tuition Scholarships? Y
Performing Arts Scholarships w/o majoring in the arts? N
What programs caught my eye? **Agricultural Science; Child Life Specialist; Genre and Fandom Studies; Sports Management**

Fisk University (TN)

https://www.fisk.edu/
914 students
Full Tuition Scholarships? Y
Performing Arts Scholarships w/o majoring in the arts? N
What programs caught my eye? **HBCU;Bioinformatics; Homeland Security; Special Education; Social Work; Kinesiology; Healthcare Management**

Flagler College (FL)

https://www.flagler.edu/
2,630 students
Full Tuition Scholarships? N
Performing Arts Scholarships w/o majoring in the arts? N
What programs caught my eye? **Coastal Environmental Science; Hospitality And Tourism Management; Social Enterprise; Education of the Deaf and Hard of Hearing; American Sign Language; Cinematic Arts; Film Studies**

Florida College (FL)

https://floridacollege.edu/
528 students
Full Tuition Scholarships? N
Performing Arts Scholarships w/o majoring in the arts? N
What programs caught my eye? **Biblical Studies; Mass Media; Sport Management; Nursing**

Florida Southern College (FL)

https://www.flsouthern.edu/
2,600 students
Full Tuition Scholarships? Y
Performing Arts Scholarships w/o majoring in the arts? Y
What programs caught my eye? **Tiny Earth Network Member (Biology research); Technical Theatre and Design; Marine Biology; Advertising Design; Environmental Chemistry; Biotechnology; Artificial Intelligence and Machine Learning; Dance Performance and Choreography**

Fontbonne University (MO)

https://www.fontbonne.edu/
665 students
Full Tuition Scholarships? Y
Performing Arts Scholarships w/o majoring in the arts? N

What programs caught my eye? **American Culture Studies; Bioinformatics; Fashion Merchandising; Food Management; Management Information Systems; Nutrition; Social Entrepreneurship; Accelerated Bridge Program in Social Work; Deaf Education; University Major (design your own); Dietetics; Early Childhood Education; One Health; Chiropractic Partnership with Logan University**

Franciscan University of Steubenville (OH)

https://franciscan.edu/
2,610 students
Full Tuition Scholarships? N
Performing Arts Scholarships w/o majoring in the arts? N
What programs caught my eye? **Narrative Arts (screenwriting, playwriting, film making, stage production, set design, directing, acting, storyboarding, concept art, graphic novels and graphic illustration); Humanities and Catholic Culture; Anthropology**

Franklin College (IN)

https://franklincollege.edu/
899 students
Full Tuition Scholarships? Y
Performing Arts Scholarships w/o majoring in the arts? Y
What programs caught my eye? **Art; Art History; Photography: Digital Fine Art; Ceramics; Graphic Design; Painting; Ecology/Conservation; Biomedical Physics; Actuarial Science**

Franklin University (OH)

https://www.franklin.edu/
1,206 students
Full Tuition Scholarships? N
Performing Arts Scholarships w/o majoring in the arts? N
What programs caught my eye? **Business Forensics; Interactive Media Design; Public Safety Management and Leadership**

Fresno Pacific University (CA)

https://www.fresno.edu/
2,158 students
Full Tuition Scholarships? Y
Performing Arts Scholarships w/o majoring in the arts? Y
What programs caught my eye? **Arts Administration; Media Production; Peacemaking and Conflict Studies; Software Engineering; Wilderness Studies; Christian Ministry and Leadership**

Friends University (KS)

https://www.friends.edu/
1,190 students
Full Tuition Scholarships? N
Performing Arts Scholarships w/o majoring in the arts? Y
What programs caught my eye? **Zoo Science/Studies; Conservation Science; Radiologic Technology; Cyber Security; Christian Formation and Ministry**

Gallaudet University (DC)

https://gallaudet.edu/
1,012 students
Full Tuition Scholarships? N
Performing Arts Scholarships w/o majoring in the arts? N
What programs caught my eye? **College for the Deaf and Hearing Impaired; American Sign Language; Graphic Design; Deaf Studies; Black Deaf Studies; Deaf Cultural Studies; Educational Neuroscience; Hearing, Speech, and Language Sciences; Insurance; Interpretation and Translation; Linguistics; Sexuality and Gender Studies**

Gannon University (PA)

https://www.gannon.edu/

3,165 students
Full Tuition Scholarships? Y
Performing Arts Scholarships w/o majoring in the arts? Y
What programs caught my eye? **Freshwater and Marine Biology;
Mortuary Science; Industrial and Robotics Engineering;
Applied Intelligence; Sport Behavior; Cyber Engineering;
Innovation and Creativity**

Georgetown College (KY)

https://www.georgetowncollege.edu/
1,259 students
Full Tuition Scholarships? Y
Performing Arts Scholarships w/o majoring in the arts? Y
What programs caught my eye? **Maskrafters Theatre and Film
Studies Academy; Prototype Art Program; Forensic Chemistry;
Professional Spanish; Diplomacy and International Commerce;
Child Development; Certified Financial Planning Certificate**

Goshen College (IN)

https://www.goshen.edu/
749 students
Full Tuition Scholarships? N
Performing Arts Scholarships w/o majoring in the arts? Y
What programs caught my eye? **Agroecology; Anabaptist-
Mennonite Studies; Conflict Transformation Studies; Criminal
Justice and Restorative justice; Deaf Studies; Disability Studies;
Environmental & Marine Science; Music for Social Change;
Public Health; Sign Language Interpreting; Sustainable Food
Systems; Theatre Education**

Goucher College (MD)

https://www.goucher.edu/
1,067 students
Full Tuition Scholarships? N
Performing Arts Scholarships w/o majoring in the arts? N

What programs caught my eye? **100% study abroad; Equine Studies; Historic Preservation; Peace Studies; Summer Science Research Program; Visual and Material Culture**

Graceland University (IA)

https://www.graceland.edu/
959 students
Full Tuition Scholarships? Y
Performing Arts Scholarships w/o majoring in the arts? Y
What programs caught my eye? **Social Change; Agricultural Business; Agricultural Plant and Animal Sciences; Digital Content Creation; Esports; Peace and Social Transformation; Transformational Leadership**

Guilford College (NC)

https://www.guilford.edu/
1,192 students
Full Tuition Scholarships? N
Performing Arts Scholarships w/o majoring in the arts? N
What programs caught my eye? **Elon Law Program (3+3); Sport Marketing; Quaker Studies; Principled Problem Solving Experience; Money & Finance; Japanese; Experience Design; Analytics**

Gustavus Adolphus College (MN)

https://gustavus.edu/
2,247 students
Full Tuition Scholarships? N
Performing Arts Scholarships w/o majoring in the arts? Y
What programs caught my eye? **Scandinavian Studies; Theatre for Social Justice; Latin Teaching; Latin American, Latinx, and Caribbean Studies; Geography with GIS**

Gwynedd Mercy University (PA) *Chapter ELEVEN in this book*
https://www.gmercyu.edu/
1,412 students
Full Tuition Scholarships? Y
Performing Arts Scholarships w/o majoring in the arts? N
What programs caught my eye? **Sport Management; Respiratory Care; Voices of Gwynedd traveling choir; Radiation Therapy; Nursing; Artificial Intelligence and Machine Learning; Cyber Security and Computer Forensics; Web Design and Multimedia**

Hamline University (MN)
https://www.hamline.edu/
1,825 students
Full Tuition Scholarships? N
Performing Arts Scholarships w/o majoring in the arts? Y
What programs caught my eye? **Behavioral Economics; Communicating Across Differences; Computation (Applied Physics); Computational Data Science; Ecology and evolutionary biology; Energy and environmental science; Forensic Psychology; Investigative and forensic science**

Hanover College (IN)
https://www.hanover.edu/
1,004 students
Full Tuition Scholarships? N
Performing Arts Scholarships w/o majoring in the arts? Y
What programs caught my eye? **Medieval-Renaissance Studies; Data Science; Geology; Health and Movement Studies; Physics & Astronomy, Archaeology**

Hastings College (NE) *Chapter TEN in this book*
https://www.hastings.edu/
919 students

Full Tuition Scholarships? Y
Performing Arts Scholarships w/o majoring in the arts? Y
What programs caught my eye? **Wildlife Biology; Education; Pre-Law 100% acceptance; Art (even has glass blowing); Drafting and Design Technology; Welding Technology; Precision Agriculture; Construction Technology; Hospitality Management and Culinary Arts**

Heidelberg University (OH)

https://www.heidelberg.edu/
1,054 students
Full Tuition Scholarships? N
Performing Arts Scholarships w/o majoring in the arts? Y
What programs caught my eye? **Watershed Science Specialization; Video Game Production; Theatre Production; Supply Chain Management**

Hendrix College (AR)

https://www.hendrix.edu/
1,111 students
Full Tuition Scholarships? Y
Performing Arts Scholarships w/o majoring in the arts? Y
What programs caught my eye? **The Odyssey Program; Chemical Physics; Neuroscience; Miller Center for Vocation, Ethics and Calling; Molecular Biology**

Hiram College (OH)

https://www.hiram.edu/
1,315 students
Full Tuition Scholarships? N
Performing Arts Scholarships w/o majoring in the arts? N
What programs caught my eye? **The Hiram Plan (3-1-3-1); Biomedical Humanities; Esports and Gaming Administration; Supply Chain Management; Public Leadership;**

Entrepreneurship Minor - Chemistry; Entrepreneurship Minor - Biochemistry

Hollins University (VA)
https://www.hollins.edu/
713 students (Women UG)
Full Tuition Scholarships? Y
Performing Arts Scholarships w/o majoring in the arts? Y
What programs caught my eye? **Theatre/Hollins Theatre Institute; Children's Book Illustration; New Play Directing; Children's Book Writing MFA, Creative Writing, Dance**

Holy Family University (PA) *Chapter SIXTEEN in this book*
https://www.holyfamily.edu/
1,842 students
Full Tuition Scholarships? N
Performing Arts Scholarships w/o majoring in the arts? N
What programs caught my eye? **Neuroscience; Nursing ; Cybersecurity; Applied Behavior Analysis; Business Analytics; Childhood Studies; Fire Science & Public Safety Administration; Gerontology**

Hope College (MI)
https://hope.edu/
3,132 students
Full Tuition Scholarships? N
Performing Arts Scholarships w/o majoring in the arts? Y
What programs caught my eye? **Strong Research Focus; Biochemical Engineering; Biomedical-Bioelectrical Engineering; Biomedical-Biomechanical Engineering; Global Health; Japanese; Jazz Studies; Organizational Leadership Practice; Special Education (emotionally impaired/learning disabilities)**

Houghton University (NY)

https://www.houghton.edu/
871 students
Full Tuition Scholarships? Y
Performing Arts Scholarships w/o majoring in the arts? N
What programs caught my eye? **Behavioral Neuroscience; Equestrian; Music Industry; Applied Design and Visual Communication**

Husson University (ME) *Chapter TWO in this book*

https://www.husson.edu/
2,264 students
Full Tuition Scholarships? N
Performing Arts Scholarships w/o majoring in the arts? N
What programs caught my eye? **NESCOM Audio Engineering; Conservation Law; Extended Reality (XR); Financial Planning; Hospitality and Tourism Management; Software Development; Video and Film Production**

Illinois College (IL)

https://www.ic.edu/
1,097 students
Full Tuition Scholarships? Y
Performing Arts Scholarships w/o majoring in the arts? Y
What programs caught my eye? **Editing and Publishing; Public History; Agribusiness Management; Environmental Studies & Wildlife Management; Fine Arts Administration; Japanese Studies**

Illinois Institute of Technology (IL)

https://www.iit.edu/
2,998 students
Full Tuition Scholarships? Y
Performing Arts Scholarships w/o majoring in the arts? N

What programs caught my eye? **Architecture; Architectural Engineering; Aerospace Science; Artificial Intelligence; Astrophysics; Building Systems Engineering; Circuits and Systems; Computer Architecture; Electromechanical Design and Manufacturing; Environmental Engineering; Food Science and Nutrition; Information Architecture; Polymer Science**

Indiana Tech (IN)
https://www.indianatech.edu/
1,381 students
Full Tuition Scholarships? Y
Performing Arts Scholarships w/o majoring in the arts? N
What programs caught my eye? **Industrial & Manufacturing Engineering; Mechatronics and Robotics Engineering; Network Engineering; Recreation Therapy; Software Engineering**

Indiana Wesleyan University (IN)
https://www.indwes.edu/
2,463 students
Full Tuition Scholarships? N
Performing Arts Scholarships w/o majoring in the arts? N
What programs caught my eye? **Songwriting; Design for Social Impact; TESOL, Shakespeare in Performance; Music Therapy; Ceramics; Illustration; Composition; Design Thinking; Biblical Literature; Addictions Counseling**

Iona University (NY)
https://www.iona.edu/
2,994 students
Full Tuition Scholarships? N
Performing Arts Scholarships w/o majoring in the arts? N
What programs caught my eye? **Hynes Institute for Entrepreneurship and Innovation; Arts Leadership; Entrepreneurial Leadership; Media & Strategic Communication**

and Sports Media; Media, Politics & Society; Speech-Language
Pathology & Audiology

Jacksonville University (FL)

https://www.ju.edu/
2,650 students
Full Tuition Scholarships? N
Performing Arts Scholarships w/o majoring in the arts? N
What programs caught my eye? **Animation; Ceramics; Glass; Jazz;
Music Technology; Sculpture; Aviation and Aeronautics;
Fintech; Marine Science**

John Brown University (AR)

https://www.jbu.edu/
1,617 students
Full Tuition Scholarships? N
Performing Arts Scholarships w/o majoring in the arts? N
What programs caught my eye? **Construction Management; Bible,
Religion & Christian Ministry; Visual FX; Robotics; Renewable
Energy Engineering; Digital Cinema; Museum Studies; Visual
Effects; Robotics and Mechatronics Engineering; Humanitarian
and Disaster Relief; Outdoor Leadership Ministries**

John Carroll University (OH)

https://www.jcu.edu/
2,660 students
Full Tuition Scholarships? N
Performing Arts Scholarships w/o majoring in the arts? N
What programs caught my eye? **The Center for Service-Learning
and Social Action; Arrupe Scholars Program; Institute of
Catholic Studies; Peace, Justice, and Human Rights; Social
Innovation Fellows Program; Finance/Wealth Management and
Financial Planning**

Johnson University (TN)

https://johnsonu.edu/
758 students
Full Tuition Scholarships? N
Performing Arts Scholarships w/o majoring in the arts? N
What programs caught my eye? **Applied Linguistics; Bible and Theology; Family Studies; Teaching English as a Second Language**

Juniata College (PA)

https://www.juniata.edu/
1,256 students
Full Tuition Scholarships? N
Performing Arts Scholarships w/o majoring in the arts? Y
What programs caught my eye? **Wildlife Conservation; Fisheries and Aquatic Sciences; Environmental Geology; Environmental Engineering; Art History & Museum Studies; Visual and Material Culture Studies; Rural Experience; Astronomy; Medical Humanities; Global Village (International Housing)**

Kalamazoo College (MI)

https://www.kzoo.edu/
1,241 students
Full Tuition Scholarships? N
Performing Arts Scholarships w/o majoring in the arts? Y
What programs caught my eye? **K-Plan Curriculum that enables ultimate flexibility; Biological Physics; Arabic; Jewish Studies; Chinese; Critical Theory; East Asian Studies; French and Francophone Studies; German Studies**

Kansas Wesleyan University (KS)

https://www.kwu.edu/
760 students

Full Tuition Scholarships? Y
Performing Arts Scholarships w/o majoring in the arts? Y
What programs caught my eye? **Emergency Management;
Biomedical Chemistry; Environmental, Sustainability and
Resilience Studies; Marketing Communications**

King University-Tennessee (TN)

https://www.king.edu/
1,358 students
Full Tuition Scholarships? N
Performing Arts Scholarships w/o majoring in the arts? Y
What programs caught my eye? **Social Work; Digital Media Art &
Design; Nursing; Security & Intelligence Studies; Forensic
Science; Sport Management**

King's College-Pennsylvania (PA)

https://www.kings.edu/
1,831 students
Full Tuition Scholarships? Y
Performing Arts Scholarships w/o majoring in the arts? N
What programs caught my eye? **Exercise Science & Chiropractic
Track (3+4); Clinical Lab Science and Medical Technology
(B.S.); Nutrition and Dietetics 5-Year* (B.S. / M.S.N.D.);
Physician Assistant 5-Year* (B.S. / M.S.P.A.S.)**

Knox College (IL)

https://www.knox.edu/
1,154 students
Full Tuition Scholarships? N
Performing Arts Scholarships w/o majoring in the arts? Y
What programs caught my eye? **Creative Writing; KnoX-Factor
(merit scholarships for various talents); Africana Studies;
Japanese; Archaeology; Journalism; Art Museum Studies;
Asian Studies; Astronomy; Chinese; Design; Peace Corps Prep;
Playwriting**

La Salle University (PA)

https://www.lasalle.edu/
2,746 students
Full Tuition Scholarships? N
Performing Arts Scholarships w/o majoring in the arts? N
What programs caught my eye? **Spanish/Translation & Interpretation: 5-year (B.A./M.A.); Social Work: 5-year (BSW/MSW); Public Health: 5-year (BSPH/MPH); Nutrition: 5-year (B.S./M.S.); Information Technology/Cybersecurity: 5-year (B.S./M.S.); Communication Sciences and Disorders: 5-Year (B.S./M.S.)**

La Sierra University (CA)

https://lasierra.edu/
1,350 students
Full Tuition Scholarships? N
Performing Arts Scholarships w/o majoring in the arts? N
What programs caught my eye? **A well-known ENACTUS (social entrepreneurship) college; Archaeology; Biblical Languages; Biomathematics; Biophysics; Cognitive & Behavioral Neuroscience; Bioinformatics; Global Contexts of Health; Social Ecology; UI/UX**

Lake Forest College (IL)

https://www.lakeforest.edu/
1,661 students
Full Tuition Scholarships? N
Performing Arts Scholarships w/o majoring in the arts? Y
What programs caught my eye? **Dual Degree Law Program with 5 law schools (3+3); Asian Studies; African American Studies; Urban Studies, Print and Digital Publishing, Neuroscience; Museum Studies, Islamic World Studies; Ethics Center; Chinese**

Lasell University (MA)

https://www.lasell.edu/
1,392 students
Full Tuition Scholarships? N
Performing Arts Scholarships w/o majoring in the arts? N
What programs caught my eye? **Resort and Casino Management; Esports and Gaming Management; Fashion Design and Production; Fashion Media and Marketing ; Fashion Merchandising and Management; Hospitality Management; Interactive Design; Professional Sales; Radio and Video Production; Lasell Works Program; 3-year-degrees**

Lawrence Tech University (MI)

https://www.ltu.edu/
2,356 students
Full Tuition Scholarships? Y
Performing Arts Scholarships w/o majoring in the arts? N
What programs caught my eye? **Robotics Engineering; Aeronautical Engineering; Audio Engineering Technology; Artificial Intelligence; Construction Engineering Technology and Management; Energy Engineering; Interior Design; Nanotechnology; Product Design; Transportation Design**

Lawrence University (WI)

https://www.lawrence.edu/
1,483 students
Full Tuition Scholarships? N
Performing Arts Scholarships w/o majoring in the arts? Y
What programs caught my eye? **Music Conservatory; Innovation & Entrepreneurship; Dance; Biomedical Ethics; Geosciences; Jazz; Linguistics; Museum studies; Musicology; Organ; Opera Theatre; Russian; Statistics and Data Science; Forestry and Environmental Studies**

Le Moyne College (NY)

https://www.lemoyne.edu/
2,713 students
Full Tuition Scholarships? N
Performing Arts Scholarships w/o majoring in the arts? N
What programs caught my eye? **Direct Entry PA, PT, and OT; Risk Management and Insurance; Double Major (B.A.) in Political Science and Theatre; Dual Major in English (Creative Writing) and Theatre**

Lebanon Valley College (PA)

https://www.lvc.edu/
1,691 students
Full Tuition Scholarships? Y
Performing Arts Scholarships w/o majoring in the arts? N
What programs caught my eye? **Dutchmen First [program for incoming first generation students]; University of London Certificate in Higher Education in the Common Law; Music Business; Interaction Design; Audio & Music Production**

Lees-McRae College (NC)

https://www.lmc.edu/
872 students
Full Tuition Scholarships? Y
Performing Arts Scholarships w/o majoring in the arts? N
What programs caught my eye? **Cycling Studies, Ski Industry Business and Instruction, Wilderness Medicine and Rescue, Wildlife Rehabilitation; Appalachian Studies; Outdoor Recreation Management; Technical Theatre; Wildlife Biology**

LeTourneau University (TX)

https://www.letu.edu/
2,992 students
Full Tuition Scholarships? N

Performing Arts Scholarships w/o majoring in the arts? N
What programs caught my eye? **Aviation and Aeronautical Science; Materials Joining Engineering; Electrical, Automation and Robotics Engineering Technology; Mechatronics Engineering; Astrophysics**

Lewis University (IL)

https://www.lewisu.edu/
3,907 students
Full Tuition Scholarships? Y
Performing Arts Scholarships w/o majoring in the arts? Y
What programs caught my eye? **Aviation (airport on campus); Unmanned Aircraft Systems; Forensic Criminal Investigation; Vascular Ultrasound Technology; Paralegal Studies; Nuclear Medicine Technology; Dental Hygiene; East European: Polish/Russian Language and Culture; Forensic Criminal Investigation**

Linfield University (OR)

https://www.linfield.edu/
1,283 students
Full Tuition Scholarships? N
Performing Arts Scholarships w/o majoring in the arts? Y
What programs caught my eye? **Wine Studies; Japanese Language and Culture; Wine Marketing; Sports Economics; Musical Theatre; Leadership and Ethics Across Disciplines; Linguistics, Law, Rights, and Justice**

Lipscomb University (TN)

https://www.lipscomb.edu/
2,952 students
Full Tuition Scholarships? Y
Performing Arts Scholarships w/o majoring in the arts? Y
What programs caught my eye? **Animation; Art Therapy; Biblical Archaeology; Biomedical Physics; Biomolecular Science;**

Bioscience and Philosophy; Business as Mission; Commercial Music: Songwriting or Production; Event Planning; Fashion and Interior Merchandising; Fashion Design; Film Production; Music City New Media Academy ; Music Industry Studies

Loras College (IA)
https://www.loras.edu/
1,310 students
Full Tuition Scholarships? N
Performing Arts Scholarships w/o majoring in the arts? Y
What programs caught my eye? **Lynch Learning Center (support for neurodiverse students); Paramount EMS Academy; Rhetoric and Public Writing; Irish Studies; Financial Planning & Wealth Management; Analytics; Catholic Studies; Software Engineering**

Loyola University New Orleans (LA) *Chapter FIVE in this book*
loyno.edu/
3,369 students
Full Tuition Scholarships? Y
Performing Arts Scholarships w/o majoring in the arts? Y
What programs caught my eye? **Hip Hop and R&B; Digital Filmmaking; Design; Jazz Studies; Music Industry Studies; Music Therapy with Jazz Concentration; Popular and Commercial Music**

Lubbock Christian University (TX)
https://lcu.edu/
1,393 students
Full Tuition Scholarships? N
Performing Arts Scholarships w/o majoring in the arts? N
What programs caught my eye? **Animal Science and Pre-Vet; Biblical Text; Agribusiness; Children's Ministry; Museum and Heritage Studies; Natural Resources Ecology and Conservation**

Luther College (IA) *Chapter THIRTEEN in this book*
https://www.luther.edu/
1,600 students
Full Tuition Scholarships? N
Performing Arts Scholarships w/o majoring in the arts? Y
What programs caught my eye? **Rochester MN semester/Nursing and Mayo Clinic Affiliation; Seed Savers Exchange; Identity Studies; Nordic Studies; Center for Sustainable Communities; Ninety percent of Luther students study away, domestically or internationally; Rooftop Observatory and Planetarium; Makerspace; Human Anatomy Laboratory; Individualized Interdisciplinary; Engineering Science (new)**

Lycoming College (PA) *Chapter FOURTEEN in this book*
https://www.lycoming.edu/
1,200 students
Full Tuition Scholarships? N
Performing Arts Scholarships w/o majoring in the arts? Y
What programs caught my eye? **The Warrior Coffee Project; Archaeology; Astrophysics; Film and Video Arts; Entrepreneurship Minor, Neuroscience, 2D Animation Minor; Energy Science/Studies; 3D Animation; Astrobiology; Astrochemistry; Astronomy; Computational Physics; Multiculturalism**

Lyon College (AR)
https://www.lyon.edu/
580 students
Full Tuition Scholarships? Y
Performing Arts Scholarships w/o majoring in the arts? Y
What programs caught my eye? **Scottish Arts; Outdoor Leadership; Celtic Studies; Data Science; Bagpipe and Drum Band; Data Science; Design Your Own Major**

Madonna University (MI)

https://www.madonna.edu/
2,491 students
Full Tuition Scholarships? N
Performing Arts Scholarships w/o majoring in the arts? Y
What programs caught my eye? **Social Work; Sign Language; Animal Studies; Film Music Scoring; Forensic Science, Nutritional Sciences; Broadcast and Cinema Arts; Deaf Community Studies**

Manchester University (IN)

https://www.manchester.edu/
1,084 students
Full Tuition Scholarships? Y
Performing Arts Scholarships w/o majoring in the arts? Y
What programs caught my eye? **5 Year BS/MS in Athletic Training; Esports Management; Gerontology; Medical Technology; Nutritional Sciences; Orthopedic Studies; BS to MS in Pharmacogenomics; Population Health; Professional Sales**

Manhattan College (NY)

https://manhattan.edu/
3,166 students
Full Tuition Scholarships? N
Performing Arts Scholarships w/o majoring in the arts? Y
What programs caught my eye? **Game Design and Production; Arabic; Catholic Studies; Digital Arts and Humanities; Cultural Anthropology; Geography; Labor Studies; Italian; Nuclear Medicine Technology; Sound Studies; Real Estate**

Marian University (IN)

https://www.marian.edu/
2,980 students
Full Tuition Scholarships? Y

Performing Arts Scholarships w/o majoring in the arts? Y
What programs caught my eye? INnovation Through Engineering Camp; Medical School on campus (D.O.); Spanish for the Professions; Biomedical Engineering; Chemical Engineering; Civil Engineering; Computer Engineering; Mechanical Engineering; Logistics and Supply Chain Management; Sport Performance; Planetary Science

Marian University (WI)

https://www.marianuniversity.edu/
1,108 students
Full Tuition Scholarships? Y
Performing Arts Scholarships w/o majoring in the arts? N
What programs caught my eye? Biology-Cytotechnology; Construction Management; Diagnostic Medical Sonography; Marketing and Public Relations; Nursing; Radiologic Technology; Sport and Recreation Management

Marietta College (OH)

https://www.marietta.edu/
1,173 students
Full Tuition Scholarships? Y
Performing Arts Scholarships w/o majoring in the arts? Y
What programs caught my eye? Land and Energy Management; Investigative Studies Program; Petroleum Engineering and Geology; Earth, Energy & Environment; Clinical Mental Health Counseling; Energy Systems Studies

Mars Hill University (NC)

https://www.mhu.edu/
1,025 students
Full Tuition Scholarships? Y
Performing Arts Scholarships w/o majoring in the arts? Y
What programs caught my eye? Appalachian Studies; Webmaster; Recreation and Leisure Management; Biological Natural History;

Zoology; Web Development; Fashion Marketing; Ecology and Conservation Biology; Art Therapy

Maryville College (TN) *Chapter FIFTEEN in this book*
https://www.maryvillecollege.edu/
1,065 students
Full Tuition Scholarships? Y
Performing Arts Scholarships w/o majoring in the arts? Y
What programs caught my eye? **American Sign Language and Deaf Studies / ASL Interpreting / Hospitality and Regional Identity / Fermentation Sciences (science behind beer brewing); Appalachian Studies; Pharmacy / Biopharmaceutical Sciences; Outdoor Studies and Tourism; Design**

Maryville University (MO)
https://www.maryville.edu/
2,640 students
Full Tuition Scholarships? Y
Performing Arts Scholarships w/o majoring in the arts? Y
What programs caught my eye? **Direct Entry Speech Language Pathology; Accounting Information Systems; Forensic Psychology/Criminal Justice; Game Design; Interior Design; Music Therapy; Photography and Video; Sustainability and Environmental Stewardship**

Marywood University (PA)
https://www.marywood.edu/
1,790 students
Full Tuition Scholarships? N
Performing Arts Scholarships w/o majoring in the arts? N
What programs caught my eye? **Architecture/Interior Architecture; Biotechnology; Environmental Design; 3-Dimensional Studio Arts; Sequential Art and Storytelling; Aviation Management; Construction Management; Autism**

Spectrum Disorders Teaching Endorsement; Sports and Human Performance Nutrition; Art Therapy

McDaniel College (MD)

https://www.mcdaniel.edu/
1,757 students
Full Tuition Scholarships? Y
Performing Arts Scholarships w/o majoring in the arts? N
What programs caught my eye? **Research-Publish-Present-Repeat; Writing and Publishing; Popular Literature; Journalism and New Media; Food Studies; European Studies/History; Arabic/Arabic and Middle Eastern Studies**

McKendree University (IL)

https://www.mckendree.edu/
1,443 students
Full Tuition Scholarships? N
Performing Arts Scholarships w/o majoring in the arts? Y
What programs caught my eye? **Aerospace Studies; Cyber Defense; Financial & Actuarial Sciences; 3+3 Law Program; Music Marketing; Sport Psychology**

McMurry University (TX)

https://mcm.edu/
1,142 students
Full Tuition Scholarships? Y
Performing Arts Scholarships w/o majoring in the arts? Y
What programs caught my eye? **Neurocognitive Psychology; Servant Leadership; Public Health and Wellness; Multimedia and Graphic Design; Medical and Research; Film Studies**

Menlo College (CA)

https://www.menlo.edu/

826 students
Full Tuition Scholarships? Y
Performing Arts Scholarships w/o majoring in the arts? N
What programs caught my eye? **Real Estate; Professional Sales and Business Development; Business Analytics; Human Resource Management**

Mercyhurst University (PA)

https://www.mercyhurst.edu/
2,659 students
Full Tuition Scholarships? N
Performing Arts Scholarships w/o majoring in the arts? Y
What programs caught my eye? **Business and Competitive Intelligence; Sport and Event Management; Interior Architecture and Design; Music Therapy; Hospitality Management; Fashion Merchandising; Intelligence Studies; Anthropology/Archaeology**

Meredith College (NC)

https://www.meredith.edu/
1,427 students (Women)
Full Tuition Scholarships? Y
Performing Arts Scholarships w/o majoring in the arts? N
What programs caught my eye? **Interior Design; Web Development; Professional Writing & Presentation Media; Hospitality & Tourism Management; Fashion Design/Merchandising; Geoscience; Food and Nutrition; Dance/Private Studio Teaching**

Messiah University (PA)

https://www.messiah.edu/
2,495 students
Full Tuition Scholarships? Y
Performing Arts Scholarships w/o majoring in the arts? N

What programs caught my eye? **African American Religion and Culture; Bible; Chinese Studies; Church Media; Commercial Music; Composition; Conservation and Agriculture; Foods and Nutrition; Hospitality and Tourism Management; Mobile Application and Game Design; Multicultural Families; Organismal Biology; Robotics Engineering; World Christianity**

Mid-America Christian University (OK)

https://www.macu.edu/
1,601 students
Full Tuition Scholarships? Y
Performing Arts Scholarships w/o majoring in the arts? N
What programs caught my eye? **Cybersecurity; Accounting & Ethics; Christian Ministries; Digital Marketing; Sports Management**

Midland University (NE)

https://www.midlandu.edu/
1,512 students
Full Tuition Scholarships? N
Performing Arts Scholarships w/o majoring in the arts? Y
What programs caught my eye? **Agribusiness; Business Intelligence & Technology; Strength & Conditioning; Youth & Family Ministry; Applied Behavior Analysis; Politics and Citizenship**

Midway University (KY) *Chapter TWENTY-SEVEN in this book*

https://www.midway.edu/
777 students
Full Tuition Scholarships? Y
Performing Arts Scholarships w/o majoring in the arts? Y
What programs caught my eye? **Bourbon Studies Minor; Equine Studies (Management, Rehabilitation or Science); Sport Marketing; Alcohol & Drug Counseling; Equine Business &**

Sales; Coaching and Sport Leadership; Equine Business and Sales; Tourism and Hospitality Management

Milligan University (TN)
https://www.milligan.edu/
789 students
Full Tuition Scholarships? Y
Performing Arts Scholarships w/o majoring in the arts? N
What programs caught my eye? **3 Year Degrees (Business, Computer Science, Exercise Science, Information Systems, Psychology); Accelerated Bachelor's to Master's (MBA, MEduc; MA Humanities); Early Acceptance Programs (Counseling and OT); Bible; Worship Leadership; Photography; Human Anatomy and Physiology; Digital Illustration; Health Sector Management**

Millikin University (IL)
https://www.millikin.edu/
1,812 students
Full Tuition Scholarships? Y
Performing Arts Scholarships w/o majoring in the arts? Y
What programs caught my eye? **Arts Technology: Audio and Video Production; Live Event Technology; Arts Technology Administration; Art Therapy; Audio Engineering & Production; Commercial Music; Design Thinking; Graphic Design; Health & Wellness Coaching; Musical Theatre; Stage Management; Theatre & Dance; Video Production & Cinema**

Millsaps College (MS)
https://www.millsaps.edu/
697 students
Full Tuition Scholarships? N
Performing Arts Scholarships w/o majoring in the arts? Y
What programs caught my eye? **Neurophilosophy; Archaeology; Museum Studies; Interreligious Encounters; Jewish Studies;**

Neuroscience and Cognitive Studies; Vocation, Ethics, and
Society

Milwaukee Institute of Art & Design (WI)

https://www.miad.edu/
925 students
Full Tuition Scholarships? Y
Performing Arts Scholarships w/o majoring in the arts? N
What programs caught my eye? **Communication Design (graphic
design, advertising, interactive media); Illustration; Animation;
Product Design (invention, product development and design,
furniture design); Interior Architecture and Design; New Studio
Practice**

Milwaukee School of Engineering (WI)

https://www.msoe.edu/
2,574 students
Full Tuition Scholarships? Y
Performing Arts Scholarships w/o majoring in the arts? N
What programs caught my eye? **User Experience (UX);
Architectural Engineering; Biomolecular Engineering;
Construction Management; Industrial Engineering; Nursing;
Business Analysis and Improvement; Technical Communication;
Gerontology; Technical Sales**

Minneapolis College of Art & Design (MN)

https://www.mcad.edu/
676 students
Full Tuition Scholarships? N
Performing Arts Scholarships w/o majoring in the arts? N
What programs caught my eye? **Animation; Comic Art; Drawing
and Painting; Entrepreneurial Studies; Filmmaking; Fine Arts
Studio; Furniture Design; Graphic Design; Illustration;
Photography; Print Paper Book; Product Design; Sculpture;
Web and Multimedia Environments**

Misericordia University (PA) *Chapter FOUR in this book*
https://www.misericordia.edu/
1,663 students
Full Tuition Scholarships? Y
Performing Arts Scholarships w/o majoring in the arts? N
What programs caught my eye? **Popular Culture; Women with Children Program (housing/childcare on campus); Alternative Learners Program (LD support); Guaranteed Placement Program (paid internship if not placed); Public History; Patient Navigation; Forensic Accounting; Medical Imaging**

Mississippi College (MS)
https://www.mc.edu/
2,757 students
Full Tuition Scholarships? Y
Performing Arts Scholarships w/o majoring in the arts? Y
What programs caught my eye? **Graphic Design; Chemical Physics; Worship Leadership; Digital Media Production, Foreign Language and International Trade; Language, Writing, and Linguistics**

Monmouth College (IL) *Chapter TWENTY-THREE in this book*
https://www.monmouthcollege.edu/
764 students
Full Tuition Scholarships? Y
Performing Arts Scholarships w/o majoring in the arts? N
What programs caught my eye? **SOFIA program; Chemistry/Summer Chemistry Research Fellowship; Ceramics; Merida Mexico Program; Physics (Nuclear Physics Lab), Midwest Journal for Undergraduate Research; Sports Information & Media; Biopsychology; Global Food Security; Global Public Health**

Moody Bible Institute (IL)

https://www.moody.edu/
2,185 students
Full Tuition Scholarships? N
Performing Arts Scholarships w/o majoring in the arts? N
What programs caught my eye? **Missionary Aviation Technology (Flight or Maintenance); Applied Linguistics; Biblical Preaching; Ministry to Victims of Sexual Exploitation; Ministry to Women; Theology and Cultural Engagement; Music Ministry**

Moravian University (PA) *Chapter TWENTY-FOUR in this book*

https://www.moravian.edu/
1,900 students
Full Tuition Scholarships? N
Performing Arts Scholarships w/o majoring in the arts? N
What programs caught my eye? **Public Health; Art History and Criticism; Graphic and Information Design; Quantitative Economics; Autism Teaching Endorsement; Pure Mathematics; International Management (French/German/Spanish); Music technology and audio recording; Cellular Neurobiology; Cognitive Neuroscience; Behavioral Neuroscience; Nursing**

Morningside University (IA)

https://www.morningside.edu/
1,281 students
Full Tuition Scholarships? N
Performing Arts Scholarships w/o majoring in the arts? Y
What programs caught my eye? **Supply Chain Management; Agricultural and Food Studies; Agricultural Humanities; Aviation Management; Developmental Psychology; Biopsychology; Professional Flight; Respiratory Care**

Mount Mary University (WI)

https://mtmary.edu/
736 students (Women)
Full Tuition Scholarships? Y
Performing Arts Scholarships w/o majoring in the arts? N
What programs caught my eye? **Fashion Design/Fashion Marketing; Art Therapy; Merchandise Management; Baking; Food Science; Interior Architecture & Design; Interior Merchandising; User Experience Design (UX); Nursing**

Mount Mercy University (IA) *Chapter TWENTY-SIX in this book*

https://www.mtmercy.edu/
1,145 students
Full Tuition Scholarships? Y
Performing Arts Scholarships w/o majoring in the arts? Y
What programs caught my eye? **Outdoor Conservation (law enforcement track too); Environmental Justice; People Management; Remote & Virtual Workforce Certificate; Science Marketing; Health Care Navigation; Software Development; Diversity Studies**

Mount Saint Joseph University (OH)

https://www.msj.edu/
1,475 students
Full Tuition Scholarships? Y
Performing Arts Scholarships w/o majoring in the arts? Y
What programs caught my eye? **Criminology / Victimology; Addictions; Communication and New Media Studies; Social Computing; Socio-Psychology; Special Education**

Mount St. Mary's University (MD)

https://msmary.edu/
2,055 students

Full Tuition Scholarships? Y
Performing Arts Scholarships w/o majoring in the arts? N
What programs caught my eye? **PPE: Politics, Philosophy, and Economics; Biotechnology Management Dual Degree; Cyber Criminology; Conflict, Peace and Social Justice; Italian**

Muhlenberg College (PA)

https://www.muhlenberg.edu/
2,387 students
Full Tuition Scholarships? N
Performing Arts Scholarships w/o majoring in the arts? Y
What programs caught my eye? **Documentary Storymaking; Statistics; Acopian Center for Ornithology; Biological Field Station and Wildlife Sanctuary; Arboretum; Dance; Analytics**

Muskingum University (OH)

https://www.muskingum.edu/
1,578 students
Full Tuition Scholarships? Y
Performing Arts Scholarships w/o majoring in the arts? Y
What programs caught my eye? **Nursing; Animal Studies; Conservation Science; Molecular Biology; Music Theatre; Nutrition; Human Biology; Film Studies; PLUS Program for neurodiverse student support**

Nazareth University (NY)

https://www2.naz.edu/
2,057 students
Full Tuition Scholarships? N
Performing Arts Scholarships w/o majoring in the arts? Y
What programs caught my eye? **Business, Artificial Intelligence, and Innovation; Chinese; Digital Marketing Strategy; Ethical Data Science; Museums, archives, and Public History; Open Path Program (for exploring majors); Technology, Artificial Intelligence, and Society**

Nebraska Methodist College (NE)

https://www.methodistcollege.edu/
766 students
Full Tuition Scholarships? N
Performing Arts Scholarships w/o majoring in the arts? N
What programs caught my eye? **Nursing; Certified Nursing Assistant; Certifies Medication Aide; Cardiovascular Sonography; Imaging Sciences; Multispecialty Sonography; Respiratory Therapy; Healthcare Management**

Nebraska Wesleyan University (NE)

https://www.nebrwesleyan.edu/
1,706 students
Full Tuition Scholarships? Y
Performing Arts Scholarships w/o majoring in the arts? Y
What programs caught my eye? **Theatre is huge program; U.S. Minority Studies; Directing; Digital Marketing; East Asian Studies; Financial Planning; Theatre Design and Technology; Theatre Arts Education; Musical Theatre**

New York Institute of Technology (NY)

https://www.nyit.edu/
3,414 students
Full Tuition Scholarships? N
Performing Arts Scholarships w/o majoring in the arts? N
What programs caught my eye? **Construction Engineering; Architectural Technology; Architecture; Urban Design; biotechnology; bioengineering; Energy Science; Interior Design; UX/UI Design and Development**

Newman University (KS)

https://newmanu.edu/

1,577 students
Full Tuition Scholarships? Y
Performing Arts Scholarships w/o majoring in the arts? Y
What programs caught my eye? **Sports Media and Promotion;
Agribusiness; Respiratory Care; Sports Media & Promotion;
Sonography, Diagnostic Medical; Radiologic Technology;
Nursing**

Niagara University (NY)

https://www.niagara.edu/
2,785 students
Full Tuition Scholarships? N
Performing Arts Scholarships w/o majoring in the arts? N
What programs caught my eye? **Tourism and Recreation;
Vincentian Poverty Studies; Event Management; Law and
Jurisprudence; Italian Studies; Hotel and Restaurant
Management; Luxury Hospitality Operations; Fraud
Examination & Economic Crime; American Sign Language &
Deaf Studies; Food and Beverage Management**

North Central College (IL)

https://www.northcentralcollege.edu/
2,404 students
Full Tuition Scholarships? N
Performing Arts Scholarships w/o majoring in the arts? Y
What programs caught my eye? **The Coffee Lab; Social Innovation;
Professional and Technical Writing; Industrial/Organizational
Psychology; History of Ideas; Conflict Resolution; Chicago Area
Studies; Animation; Nuclear Medicine Technology;
Neuroscience; Jazz Studies**

North Greenville University (SC)

https://ngu.edu/
1,982 students
Full Tuition Scholarships? Y

Performing Arts Scholarships w/o majoring in the arts? N
What programs caught my eye? **Animal Concentration within Biology; Environmental Concentration within Biology; Chiropractic 3+3.5; Intercultural Studies; Film; Media Ministry; Outdoor Leadership; Sport Ministry; Worship Leading**

North Park University (IL)

https://www.northpark.edu/
1,866 students
Full Tuition Scholarships? N
Performing Arts Scholarships w/o majoring in the arts? Y
What programs caught my eye? **Bilingual Education/ESL teaching; Advertising; Arabic; Music Composition; Jazz Studies; Latino and Latin American Studies; Middle Eastern Studies; Scandinavian Studies**

Northland College (WI) *Chapter SIX in this book*

https://www.northland.edu/
500 students
Full Tuition Scholarships? N
Performing Arts Scholarships w/o majoring in the arts? N
What programs caught my eye? **Climate Science/Climate Change; Native American Studies; Sustainable Community Development and Natural Resources; "Superior Connections" cohort of students taking courses related to Lake Superior; Fisheries and Wildlife Ecology; Ecological Restoration; Environmental Education; Forestry; Humanity and Nature Studies; Sustainable Agriculture and Food Systems; Water Science**

Northwest Nazarene University (ID)

https://nnu.edu/
1,241 students
Full Tuition Scholarships? N
Performing Arts Scholarships w/o majoring in the arts? Y

What programs caught my eye? **Wildlife Biology and Ecology; Agricultural Engineering Concentration (focus on agricultural automation); Intercultural Ministry (Missions); Commercial Music**

Northwest University (WA)

https://www.northwestu.edu/
778 students
Full Tuition Scholarships? Y
Performing Arts Scholarships w/o majoring in the arts? Y
What programs caught my eye? **Center for Calling and Theological Formation; User Experience Design; Music Industry Business; Music Production; Church and Ministry Leadership; Audio Production**

Northwestern College (IA)

https://www.nwciowa.edu/
1,080 students
Full Tuition Scholarships? N
Performing Arts Scholarships w/o majoring in the arts? Y
What programs caught my eye? **Art and Art Therapy; Biophysics; Agricultural Business; Social Enterprise; Software Engineering; Sport Management–Media and Marketing; Youth Ministry and Christian Formation**

Northwood University (MI)

https://www.northwood.edu/
1,072 students
Full Tuition Scholarships? N
Performing Arts Scholarships w/o majoring in the arts? N
What programs caught my eye? **Automotive Aftermarket/Marketing/Management; Entrepreneurship; Fashion Marketing and Management; Esports Management; Hospitality Management; Franchising Management; Insurance Risk Management; Operations and Supply Chain Management**

Norwich University (VT)

https://www.norwich.edu/
2,988 students
Full Tuition Scholarships? N
Performing Arts Scholarships w/o majoring in the arts? N
What programs caught my eye? **Architecture and Art; Computer Security and Information Assurance; Construction Management; Design Arts; Geology; Engineering; Nursing; Neuroscience; Studies in War and Peace; Leadership**

Oglethorpe University (GA)

https://oglethorpe.edu/
1,446 students
Full Tuition Scholarships? Y
Performing Arts Scholarships w/o majoring in the arts? Y
What programs caught my eye? **Medical and Scientific Illustration; Filmmaking, Video and Photography; Japanese; Astrophysics; Computational Physics; Shakespeare & Renaissance Studies; Urban Leadership**

Ohio Dominican University (OH)

https://www.ohiodominican.edu/
907 students
Full Tuition Scholarships? Y
Performing Arts Scholarships w/o majoring in the arts? Y
What programs caught my eye? **Medical School Early Assurance Program; Sport Media; Risk Management and Insurance; Quantitative Methods and Data Management**

Ohio Northern University (OH)

https://www.onu.edu/
2,426 students

Full Tuition Scholarships? Y
Performing Arts Scholarships w/o majoring in the arts? Y
What programs caught my eye? **International Theatre Production;
Aerospace Engineering; Advanced Mathematical Studies;
Applied Robotics; Multimedia Production; Astronomy;
Construction Management; Environmental Engineering; Music
Sound Recording Technology; Pharmaceutical and Healthcare
Business; Public History and Museum Studies; Robotics**

Ohio Wesleyan University (OH)

https://www.owu.edu/
1,339 students
Full Tuition Scholarships? Y
Performing Arts Scholarships w/o majoring in the arts? N
What programs caught my eye? **OWU connection
(travel/internship/service/research); Astrophysics; Ancient
Studies; Black World Studies; Botany; Data and Society; Food
Studies; Genetics; Interdisciplinary Religious Studies;
Microbiology; Nutrition; Renaissance Studies; Zoology**

Oklahoma Baptist University (OK)

https://www.okbu.edu/
1,430 students
Full Tuition Scholarships? Y
Performing Arts Scholarships w/o majoring in the arts? Y
What programs caught my eye? **Learning Communities (freshman
cohort all taking same classes); Family Science; Forensic
Psychology; Global Marketplace Engagement; Music
Composition; Worship Studies**

Oklahoma City University (OK)

https://www.okcu.edu/
1,526 students
Full Tuition Scholarships? N
Performing Arts Scholarships w/o majoring in the arts? N

What programs caught my eye? **Music Theatre; Acting: On Camera; Acting: Stage and Screen; Cell and Molecular Biology; Dance Performance; Dance Teacher; Entertainment Business; Film Production; Music Composition; Theatre Innovation and Entrepreneurship; Theatre Design and Production**

Otterbein University (OH)

https://www.otterbein.edu/
2,253 students
Full Tuition Scholarships? Y
Performing Arts Scholarships w/o majoring in the arts? Y
What programs caught my eye? **Equine Assisted Activities and Therapies; Zoo and Conservation Science; Marketing Analytics; Equine Business Management; Theatre Design & Technology; Equine Veterinary Technology; Environmental Chemistry**

Ouachita Baptist University (AR)

https://obu.edu/
1,664 students
Full Tuition Scholarships? N
Performing Arts Scholarships w/o majoring in the arts? Y
What programs caught my eye? **Musical Theatre; Biophysics; Christian Missions; Music Industry; Worship Studies; Nutrition and Dietetics; Public History**

Pacific Lutheran University (WA)

https://www.plu.edu/
2,373 students
Full Tuition Scholarships? Y
Performing Arts Scholarships w/o majoring in the arts? Y
What programs caught my eye? **Chinese Studies; Chinese Language; Engineering and Industry; Exercise & Sport Psychology; Gender, Sexuality, & Race Studies; Geosciences; Holocaust & Genocide Studies; Innovation Studies; Native**

American & Indigenous Studies; Personal Training; Peace Corps Prep; Publishing & Printing Arts

Palm Beach Atlantic University (FL)

https://www.pba.edu/

2,837 students

Full Tuition Scholarships? N

Performing Arts Scholarships w/o majoring in the arts? N

What programs caught my eye? **Apologetics; Behavioral Neuroscience; Botany, Environmental Science, and Field Biology; Marine Biology; Zoology; Molecular and Biotechnology; Christian History; Franchising; Dance; Medicinal and Biological Chemistry; Worship Leadership; Oceanography; Play Therapy; Popular Music; Screenwriting**

Paul Smith's College (NY)

https://www.paulsmiths.edu/

711 students

Full Tuition Scholarships? N

Performing Arts Scholarships w/o majoring in the arts? N

What programs caught my eye? **Baking Arts & Service Management; Culinary Management; Disaster Management & Response; Ecological Restoration; Fisheries & Wildlife Sciences; Ecological Forest Management; Forest Operations; Forest Biology; Hotel, Resort & Tourism Management; Park and Conservation Management; Recreation, Adventure Education & Leisure Management; Arboriculture and Landscape Management; Baking and Pastry Arts; Botany; Craft Beer Studies & Management; Maple Production & Products; Wildland Firefighting**

Piedmont University (GA)

https://www.piedmont.edu/

1,255 students

Full Tuition Scholarships? N

Performing Arts Scholarships w/o majoring in the arts? N
What programs caught my eye? **Design and Technical Theatre;
Art Therapy; 5 year Athletic Training; Business Analytics;
Digital Marketing; Special Education**

Presbyterian College (SC)

https://www.presby.edu/
991 students
Full Tuition Scholarships? Y
Performing Arts Scholarships w/o majoring in the arts? Y
What programs caught my eye? **Southern Studies; Computational
Biology; Marine Studies-Gulf Coast Research Laboratory;
Medical Physics; Forestry/Environmental Management**

Principia College (IL)

https://www.principiacollege.edu/
340 students
Full Tuition Scholarships? N
Performing Arts Scholarships w/o majoring in the arts? N
What programs caught my eye? **Christian Science affiliation;
Music Technology; Sustainability; Entrepreneurship**

Queens University of Charlotte (NC)

https://www.queens.edu/
1,440 students
Full Tuition Scholarships? N
Performing Arts Scholarships w/o majoring in the arts? N
What programs caught my eye? **Interior Architecture and Design;
Multimedia Storytelling; Book Development; Change
Management; Conservation Biology; Environmental Chemistry;
Geospatial Sciences; Media Studies and Popular Culture; Music
Therapy; Music in Special Education; Theatre Stage Combat**

Quincy University (IL)

https://www.quincy.edu/
1,052 students
Full Tuition Scholarships? Y
Performing Arts Scholarships w/o majoring in the arts? Y
What programs caught my eye? **Radiologic Science; Advertising Production; Communication and Music Production; Theology and Philosophy; Forensic Psychology; Agribusiness; Aviation; Digital Forensics; Forensics Chemistry; Respiratory Care**

Randolph-Macon College (VA)

https://www.rmc.edu/
1,501 students
Full Tuition Scholarships? N
Performing Arts Scholarships w/o majoring in the arts? Y
What programs caught my eye? **Archaeology; Astrophysics; Applied Mathematics; Asian Studies; Behavioral Neuroscience; Black Studies; Geology**

Regis University (CO)

https://www.regis.edu/
3,197 students
Full Tuition Scholarships? Y
Performing Arts Scholarships w/o majoring in the arts? N
What programs caught my eye? **Applied Psychology; Computational Physics; Craft Brewing; Data Science; Environmental Biology; Nursing**

Rhodes College (TN)

https://www.rhodes.edu/
2,050 students
Full Tuition Scholarships? N
Performing Arts Scholarships w/o majoring in the arts? Y

What programs caught my eye? **Mock Trial (Mock Trial Academy); Ancient Mediterranean Studies; Archaeology; Biochemistry and Molecular Biology; Biomathematics; Health Equity; Jewish, Islamic, and Middle East Studies; Latin American and Latinx Studies; Music and Psychology; Statistics**

Ripon College (WI)
https://ripon.edu/
810 students
Full Tuition Scholarships? N
Performing Arts Scholarships w/o majoring in the arts? Y
What programs caught my eye? **Catalyst Curriculum; they have a full tuition "science and math" scholarship; Adapted P.E.; Ancient, Renaissance and Medieval Studies; Francophone Studies; Museum Studies; Psychobiology**

Roanoke College (VA)
https://www.roanoke.edu/
1,,865 students
Full Tuition Scholarships? N
Performing Arts Scholarships w/o majoring in the arts? Y
What programs caught my eye? **Screen Studies; African and African Diaspora Studies; Archaeological Studies; Classics and the Ancient Mediterranean World; Crime, Deviance and Social Control; Disability Studies; East Asian Studies; Foreign Politics; Materials and Nanoscience; Medicinal Chemistry; Parish Youth Leadership; Public History; Publishing and Editing**

Robert Morris University of Pennsylvania (PA)
https://www.rmu.edu/
3,007 students
Full Tuition Scholarships? Y
Performing Arts Scholarships w/o majoring in the arts? N

What programs caught my eye? **User Experience and User Interface Design, UX/UI; Financial Planning; News and Sports Communication; Manufacturing Engineering**

Rockhurst University (MO)

https://www.rockhurst.edu/
2,704 students
Full Tuition Scholarships? Y
Performing Arts Scholarships w/o majoring in the arts? Y
What programs caught my eye? **Film Arts; Analytics and Technology; Marketing Analytics; Materials Science; Medial Assisting; Medical humanities; Medical Spanish; Physics of Medicine**

Rocky Mountain College (MT)

https://www.rocky.edu/
817 students
Full Tuition Scholarships? N
Performing Arts Scholarships w/o majoring in the arts?
What programs caught my eye? **Equestrian Studies; Aviation; Environmental Management & Policy; Geology; Therapeutic Riding; Equine Science**

Saint Francis University (PA)

https://www.francis.edu/
1,647 students
Full Tuition Scholarships? N
Performing Arts Scholarships w/o majoring in the arts? N
What programs caught my eye? **Animal Assisted Health; Aquarium and Zoo Science; Autism Spectrum Disorder Education Endorsement; Aviation; Biological Diving; Ecological Engineering; Fermentation Chemistry; Marine Biology/Diving; Nanotechnology; Renewable Energy; Social Responsibility**

Saint Martin's University (WA)

https://www.stmartin.edu/
1,356 students
Full Tuition Scholarships? N
Performing Arts Scholarships w/o majoring in the arts? N
What programs caught my eye? **Native Voices Minor; Special Education; Public Health; Nursing; Social Work**

Saint Mary's College (IN)

https://www.saintmarys.edu/
1,438 students (Women)
Full Tuition Scholarships? N
Performing Arts Scholarships w/o majoring in the arts? N
What programs caught my eye? **Women's History; Statistical and Actuarial Mathematics; Speech Language Pathology; Social Work; Nursing; Musical Theatre; Autism Studies**

Saint Mary's University of Minnesota (MN) *Chapter TWENTY-TWO in this book*

https://www.smumn.edu
950 students
Full Tuition Scholarships? N
Performing Arts Scholarships w/o majoring in the arts? Y
What programs caught my eye? **First Generation Initiative; 3+2 PA Program; Business Intelligence and Analytics; Software Design; Sport Management; Artificial Intelligence; Accounting Leadership; Cybersecurity**

Saint Norbert College *(WI) Chapter SEVEN in this book*

https://www.snc.edu/
1,800 students
Full Tuition Scholarships? N
Performing Arts Scholarships w/o majoring in the arts? Y

What programs caught my eye? **The Village Project (service-learning); Global Seminars (NOT in other countries; during J-term); J-Term; Classical, medieval and Renaissance studies; Organismal Biology; Computer science major (graphic design and implementation systems; Geology; Liturgist Music; Data Analytics**

Saint Vincent College (PA)

https://www.stvincent.edu/
1,430 students
Full Tuition Scholarships? Y
Performing Arts Scholarships w/o majoring in the arts? Y
What programs caught my eye? **Fred Rogers Institute; Fred Rogers Scholars; Biological Psychology; Biotechnology; Children's Literature; Children's Studies; Classical Thought; Digital Humanities; Literary Translation; Music History; Operational Excellence; Public History; Sanctity of Life; Sacred Music**

Salem College (NC)

https://www.salem.edu/
651 students (Women)
Full Tuition Scholarships? Y
Performing Arts Scholarships w/o majoring in the arts? N
What programs caught my eye? **WISMP: Women in Science and Mathematics Program; Center for Women in Business; Health Advocacy and Humanitarian Systems; Design**

Seton Hill University (PA)

https://www.setonhill.edu/
1,653 students
Full Tuition Scholarships? N
Performing Arts Scholarships w/o majoring in the arts? N
What programs caught my eye? **Histotechnology; Art Therapy; Audiology; Dance; Graphic & Interactive Design; Commercial**

Music; Music Therapy; Nutrition and Dietetics; 3+4 Optometry; 6 year Pharmacy LECOM

Shenandoah University (VA)

https://www.su.edu/
2,416 students
Full Tuition Scholarships? N
Performing Arts Scholarships w/o majoring in the arts? Y
What programs caught my eye? **Virtual Reality Design; Professional and Popular writing; Outdoor Leadership; Artificial Intelligence; Pharmacy (2 + 4 & 3 + 4); Songwriting; Civil War Era Studies; Contemporary Musicianship & Entrepreneur Development; Costume Design; Jazz & Commercial Music; Lighting Design; Music Production & Recording Technology; Scenic Design**

Siena College (NY)

https://www.siena.edu/
3,498 students
Full Tuition Scholarships? N
Performing Arts Scholarships w/o majoring in the arts? N
What programs caught my eye? **Albany Medical College Program (liberal arts/humanities focus); Astronomy; Astrophysics; Brand Management; Chemical Physics; Chemistry-Business; Computational Physics; Economic Theory and Practice; Food Marketing; Fraud and Digital Forensics; Investment Fundamentals; Italian; Public History**

Simpson College (IA)

https://simpson.edu/
1,172 students
Full Tuition Scholarships? Y
Performing Arts Scholarships w/o majoring in the arts? Y

What programs caught my eye? **Sport Administration/Communication; Neuroscience; Multimedia Journalism; Interactive Media**

SOKA University of America (CA)

https://www.soka.edu/
392 students
Full Tuition Scholarships? N
Performing Arts Scholarships w/o majoring in the arts? N
What programs caught my eye? **Learning Across Disciplines: Environmental Studies, Humanities, International Studies, Life Sciences, or Social and Behavioral Sciences; Learning Cluster during January Block (small groups of students and faculty together)**

Southern Adventist University (TN)

https://www.southern.edu/
2,400 students
Full Tuition Scholarships? Y
Performing Arts Scholarships w/o majoring in the arts? Y
What programs caught my eye? **Vegetarian Culinary Arts; Outdoor Leadership; Outdoor Emergency Services; Kinesiology; Health Science; Health and Wellness; Health, Physical Education, and Recreation**

Southern Wesleyan University (SC)

https://www.swu.edu/
1,085 students
Full Tuition Scholarships? N
Performing Arts Scholarships w/o majoring in the arts? Y
What programs caught my eye? **Writing and Digital Studies; Early Childhood Education and Family Studies; Recreation and Sport Management; Special Education**

Southwestern Adventist University (TX)

https://www.swau.edu/
836 students
Full Tuition Scholarships? Y
Performing Arts Scholarships w/o majoring in the arts? Y
What programs caught my eye? **Ecology and Conservation Biology; Professional Sales; Esports and Gaming Administration**

Southwestern University (TX)

https://www.southwestern.edu/
1,505 students
Full Tuition Scholarships? N
Performing Arts Scholarships w/o majoring in the arts? Y
What programs caught my eye? **Independent Major (design your own major); Animal Studies; Architecture and Design Studies; Computational Mathematics; Design Thinking; Early Modern Studies; Feminist Studies; Latin American & Border Studies**

Spalding University (KY)

https://spalding.edu/
855 students
Full Tuition Scholarships? N
Performing Arts Scholarships w/o majoring in the arts? N
What programs caught my eye? **Innovation (Art); Nursing; Organizational Psychology; Social Work; Interdisciplinary Studies**

Spring Arbor University (MI)

https://www.arbor.edu/
1,215 students
Full Tuition Scholarships? N
Performing Arts Scholarships w/o majoring in the arts? N
What programs caught my eye? **Broadcasting; Freelance and Personal Branding; Financial Planning; Professional Writing;**

Reading; Special Education Learning Disabilities; Technology
Tools; Video/Film Production

Spring Hill College (AL)
https://www.shc.edu/
990 students
Full Tuition Scholarships? N
Performing Arts Scholarships w/o majoring in the arts? N
What programs caught my eye? **Digital Content Production;
Multimedia Journalism; Supply Chain Management; Marine
Biology; Digital Marketing**

Springfield College (MA) *Chapter TWENTY-FIVE in this book*
https://springfield.edu/
2,050 students
Full Tuition Scholarships? N
Performing Arts Scholarships w/o majoring in the arts? N
What programs caught my eye? **Sports Biology; Sports Analytics;
Adventure Education; Animation; Art Therapy; Sports
Journalism; Community Nutrition; Movement and Sports
Studies; Nutritional Sciences; Public History and Museum
Studies; Recreation Industries and Therapeutic Recreation;
Direct Entry Programs in PT, PA, OT, and AT**

St. Ambrose University (IA)
https://www.sau.edu/
2,228 students
Full Tuition Scholarships? Y
Performing Arts Scholarships w/o majoring in the arts?Y
What programs caught my eye? **Book Arts; Forensic Psychology;
Behavioral Neuropsychology; Biomedical Laboratory Science;
Cybersecurity; Industrial Engineering**

St. Bonaventure University (NY)

https://www.sbu.edu/
1,800 students
Full Tuition Scholarships? N
Performing Arts Scholarships w/o majoring in the arts? Y
What programs caught my eye? **Literary Publishing and Editing; Family Business; Broadcast Journalism; Arabic and Islamic Studies; Art History; Bioinformatics; Movement Studies; Native American and Indigenous Studies; Philosophy Pre-Law; Quantitative Analysis for Business**

St. Catherine University (MN)

https://www.stkate.edu/
2,585 students (Women)
Full Tuition Scholarships? Y
Performing Arts Scholarships w/o majoring in the arts? N
What programs caught my eye? **Talent Management and Human Resources; American Sign Language; Echocardiography ; Electronic Media Studies; Fashion Design and Merchandising; Immigrants and Refugees; Interpreting; Radiation Therapy; Respiratory Care; Sonography; Longevity and Aging; Critical Hmong Studies; Foods**

St. John Fisher (NY)

https://www.sjf.edu/
2,563 students
Full Tuition Scholarships? N
Performing Arts Scholarships w/o majoring in the arts? N
What programs caught my eye? **Pharmacy Early Assurance Program (2+4 Pharm.D); Museum Studies Certificate; Film and Television Studies; Gerontology; Professional Sales; Public and Professional Writing; Spanish for the Health Professions**

St. John's College (MD)

https://www.sjc.edu/
473 students
Full Tuition Scholarships? Y
Performing Arts Scholarships w/o majoring in the arts? N
What programs caught my eye? **No majors here! St. John's students don't have majors but they learn about Classical Studies and Greek; French; History, Politics, Law and Economics; Literature; Mathematics and the Natural Sciences; Music and the Arts; and Philosophy, Theology, and Psychology. All classes at St. John's are conducted seminar-style with 20 students or fewer and faculty facilitating the discussion.**

St. John's College (NM)

https://www.sjc.edu/
367 students
Full Tuition Scholarships? Y
Performing Arts Scholarships w/o majoring in the arts? N
What programs caught my eye? **No majors here! St. John's students don't have majors but they learn about Classical Studies and Greek; French; History, Politics, Law and Economics; Literature; Mathematics and the Natural Sciences; Music and the Arts; and Philosophy, Theology, and Psychology. All classes at St. John's are conducted seminar-style with 20 students or fewer and faculty facilitating the discussion.**

St. John's University (MN)

https://www.sjc.edu/
1,538 students (Men)
Full Tuition Scholarships? N
Performing Arts Scholarships w/o majoring in the arts? Y
What programs caught my eye? **Adventure Programs/Outdoor University; Ancient Mediterranean Studies; Book Arts; Forestry; Global Health; Numerical Computation; Nutrition**

St. Mary's University (TX)

2,139 students
Full Tuition Scholarships? Y
Performing Arts Scholarships w/o majoring in the arts? Y
What programs caught my eye? **Mexican American Studies; Business Analytics; Portuguese; Theology; Criminology; Bioinformatics; Engineering Management; Industrial Engineering; Software Engineering**

St. Michael's College (VT)

1,421 students
Full Tuition Scholarships? Y
Performing Arts Scholarships w/o majoring in the arts? Y
What programs caught my eye? **Equity Studies; Global Health; Health Equity; Human Geography; Medieval Studies; Public Health; Public History; Neuroscience**

St. Xavier University (IL)

3,101 students
Full Tuition Scholarships? N
Performing Arts Scholarships w/o majoring in the arts? N
What programs caught my eye? **Hospitality Management; Bilingual Education; Digital Humanities; Film and Media Studies; Middle Eastern Studies; Public Administration; Actuarial Science Mathematics; Early Childhood Education; Gerontology Studies; Spanish in the Professions; Strategic Communication; Technology Specialist**

Stephens College (MO)

443 students (Women)
Full Tuition Scholarships? Y
Performing Arts Scholarships w/o majoring in the arts? N

What programs caught my eye? **Pet-Friendly; Equestrian Studies; Fashion and Apparel programs; Art History; Content Creation; Costume Design; Event Planning; Fashion Communication; Fashion Design and Product Development; Fashion Marketing and Management; Apparel Studies; Women in STEM Research; Women's Studies**

Stetson University (FL)

https://www.stetson.edu/
2,884 students
Full Tuition Scholarships? Y
Performing Arts Scholarships w/o majoring in the arts? Y
What programs caught my eye? **Aquatic and Marine Biology; Business FLEX; Family Enterprise Management; Global Development; Molecular and Cellular Biology; Music Business; Music Composition; Music with a variety of different majors; Professional Sales; Public Management; Music Technology**

Susquehanna University (PA) *Chapter TWELVE in this book*

https://www.susqu.edu/
2,200 students
Full Tuition Scholarships? N
Performing Arts Scholarships w/o majoring in the arts? Y
What programs caught my eye? **Entrepreneurship and Corporate Innovation; Earth & Environmental Sciences, Luxury Brand Marketing & Management, Publishing & Editing, Global Opportunities – Requires every student to have an away/cross-cultural experience); Applied Linguistics; Professional and Civic Writing; Publishing and Editing**

Sweet Briar College (VA) *Chapter TWENTY-ONE in this book*

https://www.sbc.edu/
457 students (Women)

Full Tuition Scholarships? Y
Performing Arts Scholarships w/o majoring in the arts? Y
What programs caught my eye? **Engineering; Environmental
Science/Studies, Riding/Equestrian Programs; Archaeology;
Ancient Studies; Dance; Dance Teaching; Arts Management;
Equine Studies; Leadership in Sustainable Agriculture and Food
Systems**

Taylor University (IN)
https://www.taylor.edu/
2,076 students
Full Tuition Scholarships? N
Performing Arts Scholarships w/o majoring in the arts? N
What programs caught my eye? **Autism Studies & Intervention;
Biblical Literature; Biology Investigations & Applications;
Geology Environmental Science; Peace and Conflict Studies;
Music Worship Arts; Orphans and Vulnerable Children;
Scripture Engagement; Youth Ministry**

Tennessee Wesleyan University (TN)
https://www.tnwesleyan.edu/
988 students
Full Tuition Scholarships? Y
Performing Arts Scholarships w/o majoring in the arts? Y
What programs caught my eye? **Dental Hygiene; Sports
Psychology; Legal Studies; Worship Leader**

Texas Lutheran University (TX)
https://www.tlu.edu/
1,401 students
Full Tuition Scholarships? N
Performing Arts Scholarships w/o majoring in the arts? Y
What programs caught my eye? **Business Methods for Historians,
Mexican American Studies, Social Innovation and
Entrepreneurship; Computational Physics; Dramatic Media;**

Rehabilitation Science; Media Arts for Change; Sociological
Research

Texas Wesleyan University (TX)
https://txwes.edu/
1,480 students
Full Tuition Scholarships? N
Performing Arts Scholarships w/o majoring in the arts? Y
What programs caught my eye? **Forensic and Fraud Accounting;
Forensic Biochemistry; Pharmaceutical Biochemistry; Paralegal
Studies; Supply Chain Management; Interfaith Leadership;
Non-Profit Finance/Management; Recreation SCUBA Diving
Management, Database Administration**

The College of Idaho (ID)
https://www.collegeofidaho.edu/
1,100 students
Full Tuition Scholarships? N
Performing Arts Scholarships w/o majoring in the arts? Y
What programs caught my eye? **PEAK Curriculum allows for
multiple majors/minors; Medical Laboratory Science; Judaic
Studies; Geosciences; Communication Sciences and Disorders;
Human Performance**

The College of St. Scholastica (MN)
https://www.css.edu/
2,144 students
Full Tuition Scholarships? N
Performing Arts Scholarships w/o majoring in the arts? Y
What programs caught my eye? **Native American Studies / Ojibwe
Language; Catholic Studies; Civic Studies; Deaf Language and
Culture; Health Humanities; Photography; Social Work**

The Cooper Union (NY)

https://cooper.edu/welcome
806 students
Full Tuition Scholarships?
Performing Arts Scholarships w/o majoring in the arts?
What programs caught my eye? **Architecture; Engineering (chemical, civil, electrical, mechanical, general); Fine Arts (drawing, film/video, graphic design, painting, photography, printmaking, and sculpture)**

The Culinary Institute of America (NY)

https://www.ciachef.edu/
2,854 students
Full Tuition Scholarships? N
Performing Arts Scholarships w/o majoring in the arts? N
What programs caught my eye? **Culinary Arts; Baking and Pastry Arts; Hospitality Management; Food Business; Wine and Beverage Management; Food Studies and Sustainability; Culinary Science**

The Master's University (CA)

https://www.masters.edu/
1,649 students
Full Tuition Scholarships? N
Performing Arts Scholarships w/o majoring in the arts? N
What programs caught my eye? **Agribusiness; Animal Science; Artificial Intelligence; Audio Production; Biblical Counseling; Constitutional Law; Creative Writing & Publishing; Global Studies & Missions Abroad; Paleontology; One Year Bible Program; Pure Mathematics**

Thomas Aquinas College (CA)

https://www.thomasaquinas.edu/
407 students

Full Tuition Scholarships? N
Performing Arts Scholarships w/o majoring in the arts? N
What programs caught my eye? **Great Books, not textbooks; The Discussion Method; No majors; They have a Massachusetts campus too.**

Thomas More University (KY)

https://www.thomasmore.edu/
1,836 students
Full Tuition Scholarships? Y
Performing Arts Scholarships w/o majoring in the arts? Y
What programs caught my eye? **Bioinformatics and Computational Biology; 4+1 MBA; Bioinformatics & Computational Biology; Marine Biology; Management Information Systems; Non-Profit & Public Administration; Special Education, Learning & Behavior Disorders; Sports & Entertainment Marketing; Tourism and Recreation Management**

Thomas University (GA)

https://www.thomasu.edu/
732 students
Full Tuition Scholarships? N
Performing Arts Scholarships w/o majoring in the arts? N
What programs caught my eye? **Creative Technologies; Data Intelligence; Homeland Security; Rehabilitation Studies; Supply Chain management; Addictions; GIS; Gerontology; Sports Studies**

Transylvania University (KY)

https://www.transy.edu/
971 students
Full Tuition Scholarships? Y
Performing Arts Scholarships w/o majoring in the arts? Y

What programs caught my eye? **Music Technology; Biology: Ecology, Evolution, and Behavior; Hospitality and Tourism; Education and Social Change; Diplomacy; Medical Humanities**

Trevecca Nazarene University (TN)

https://www.trevecca.edu/
1,924 students
Full Tuition Scholarships? Y
Performing Arts Scholarships w/o majoring in the arts? Y
What programs caught my eye? **Commercial Music; Composition; Film and Television; Game Design and Development; Information Technology; Jazz Studies; Music and Worship; Nutrition; Recording Technology; Songwriting; UX Design**

Trine University (IN)

https://www.trine.edu/
3811 students
Full Tuition Scholarships? Y
Performing Arts Scholarships w/o majoring in the arts? Y
What programs caught my eye? **Bioprocess Engineering; Energy Engineering; Aerospace Engineering; Environmental Engineering; Forensic Psychology; Game Design and Esports; Golf Management; Metallurgical Engineering; Nutrition Science; Plastics Engineering; Robotics; Structural Engineering; Design Engineering Technology; Extended Reality; Mechatronics and Robotics Engineering**

Trinity Christian College (IL)

https://www.trnty.edu/
1,015 students
Full Tuition Scholarships? Y
Performing Arts Scholarships w/o majoring in the arts? N

What programs caught my eye? **Theology and Christian Ministry; Speech-Language Pathology; Special Education; Computing and Data Analytics**

Trinity Washington University (DC)

https://www2.trinitydc.edu/
1,444 students (Women)
Full Tuition Scholarships? N
Performing Arts Scholarships w/o majoring in the arts? N
What programs caught my eye? **Public Health; Bioinformatics; Social Work; Women's Studies; Early Childhood Education**

Union College Nebraska (NE)

https://ucollege.edu/
579 students
Full Tuition Scholarships? N
Performing Arts Scholarships w/o majoring in the arts? N
What programs caught my eye? **International Rescue and Relief; Occupational Therapy Assistant; Photo and Video Imaging; Physician Assistant; Public Health; Social Work**

Union University (TN)

https://www.uu.edu/
2,096 students
Full Tuition Scholarships? N
Performing Arts Scholarships w/o majoring in the arts? N
What programs caught my eye? **Apologetics; Biblical Languages; Ethics and Public Policy; Mental Health Services; Photojournalism; Ceramics; Botany; Chemical Physics; Commercial Music (composition, performance, recording, producing, songwriting); Music Worship Leadership; Zoology**

University of Charleston (WV)

https://www.ucwv.edu/
2,115 students
Full Tuition Scholarships? Y
Performing Arts Scholarships w/o majoring in the arts? Y
What programs caught my eye? **Sport Analytics; Sport Business; Sport Media; Radiologic Science; Professional Selling; Pharmacy Direct; Game Development; Digital Marketing; Digital Media Design**

University of Dallas (TX)

https://udallas.edu/
1,447 students
Full Tuition Scholarships? N
Performing Arts Scholarships w/o majoring in the arts? N
What programs caught my eye? **Pastoral Ministry; Philology; Human Sciences and the Contemporary World; Ethics**

University of Detroit Mercy (MI)

https://www.udmercy.edu/
2,633 students
Full Tuition Scholarships? N
Performing Arts Scholarships w/o majoring in the arts? N
What programs caught my eye? **Addiction Studies; Architectural Engineering; Architecture; Bioinformatics; Biomedical Design; Cybersecurity/Intelligence Analysis; Dental Hygiene; Financial Economics; Museum Studies; Industrial/Organizational Psychology; Robotics and Mechatronic Systems Engineering**

University of Evansville (IN)

https://www.evansville.edu/
2,041 students
Full Tuition Scholarships? Y
Performing Arts Scholarships w/o majoring in the arts? Y
What programs caught my eye? **Creative Technologies; Archaeology; British Studies; Baccalaureate to Doctor of**

Medicine; Cognitive Science; Construction Management; Ethics and Social Change; Heritage Management; Logistics and Supply Chain Management; Nursing; Neuroscience; Statistics and Data Science

University of Health Sciences and Pharmacy (MO)
https://www.uhsp.edu/
286 students
Full Tuition Scholarships? N
Performing Arts Scholarships w/o majoring in the arts? N
What programs caught my eye? **Pharmaceutical Sciences; Exercise Physiology; Biomedical Sciences; Public Health; Neuroscience; Medicinal Chemistry; Medical Humanities; Health Care Administration and Management; Data Science; Computer Science; Biopsychology; Biochemistry**

University of Holy Cross (LA)
https://uhcno.edu/
881 students
Full Tuition Scholarships? N
Performing Arts Scholarships w/o majoring in the arts? N
What programs caught my eye? **Culinology; Food Business; Food Science (also has beverage specialization); Neurodiagnostic Technology; Radiologic Technology; School Counseling**

University of La Verne (CA) *Chapter THREE in this book*
https://laverne.edu/
2,509 students
Full Tuition Scholarships? N
Performing Arts Scholarships w/o majoring in the arts? N
What programs caught my eye? **UN Ambassador on faculty; Model UN; International Studies Institute ; 5 year Athletic Training Masters; Loans for students to start their own businesses (Integrated Business Program); E-Commerce; Internet Programming; Natural History; Public History; Center for Neurodiversity**

University of Lynchburg (VA)

https://www.lynchburg.edu/
1,640 students
Full Tuition Scholarships? N
Performing Arts Scholarships w/o majoring in the arts? Y
What programs caught my eye? **Graduate Pathways; Applied and Public Humanities; Criminal Forensics; Disability Services; Music for Children; Music Media; Popular Culture; Social Influence and Advocacy; Intelligence Studies**

University of Mary (ND)

https://www.umary.edu/
2,540 students
Full Tuition Scholarships? N
Performing Arts Scholarships w/o majoring in the arts? Y
What programs caught my eye? **Biomechanics; Catechesis & the New Evangelization; Catholic Studies; Construction Engineering; Construction Management; Liturgy; Sport and Leisure Management; Special Education; Sacred Music**

University of Mobile (AL)

https://umobile.edu/
1,654 students
Full Tuition Scholarships? N
Performing Arts Scholarships w/o majoring in the arts? N
What programs caught my eye? **Nursing; Kinesiology; Early Childhood Education; Christian Ministry; Digital Media & Advertising; Public History; Marine Science; Criminology; Production Technologies**

University of Mount Union (OH)

https://www.mountunion.edu/

1,891 students
Full Tuition Scholarships? Y
Performing Arts Scholarships w/o majoring in the arts? Y
What programs caught my eye? **Biomedical, Civil, Computer,
Electrical and Mechanical Engineering; Autism Studies;
Computer and Network Security; Multi-age Education; Human
Development and Family Science; Japanese; Leadership Studies;
Medical Spanish; Nursing; Peacebuilding and Social Justice;
Risk Management and Insurance; 3+3 B.A./J.D. Law Programs**

University of Providence (MT)

https://www.uprovidence.edu/
668 students
Full Tuition Scholarships? Y
Performing Arts Scholarships w/o majoring in the arts? N
What programs caught my eye? **Forensic Science, Paralegal
Studies, Sport Management; Nursing**

University of Saint Joseph (CT)

https://www.usj.edu/
906 students
Full Tuition Scholarships? N
Performing Arts Scholarships w/o majoring in the arts? N
What programs caught my eye? **Expressive Therapies; Nutrition;
Latino Community Practice; Justice & Peace; Disability Studies;
Conservatorship/Guardianship; Child Study; Catholicism and
Cultures; Sports Nutrition; Sport Management and Promotion;
3+3 Pharm.D. Program**

University of Saint Mary (KS)

https://www.stmary.edu/
858 students
Full Tuition Scholarships? Y
Performing Arts Scholarships w/o majoring in the arts? Y

What programs caught my eye? **Cybersecurity, Information Technology; Criminology; 3+4 Doctor of Osteopathic Medicine; 3+4 Doctor of Dental Science; Medical Laboratory Science; Nursing**

University of Sioux Falls (SD)

https://www.usiouxfalls.edu/
1,337 students
Full Tuition Scholarships? N
Performing Arts Scholarships w/o majoring in the arts? N
What programs caught my eye? **Computational Economics; Medical Laboratory Science; Nursing; Paramedic Technology; Radiologic Technology; Social Media Marketing; Sports Marketing and media**

University of St. Francis (IL)

https://www.stfrancis.edu/
1,572 students
Full Tuition Scholarships? Y
Performing Arts Scholarships w/o majoring in the arts? Y
What programs caught my eye? **Adventure Based Recreation Therapy; Business Analytics; Advertising/Marketing; Language & Cultural Diversity; Digital Audio Recording Arts (DARA); Music Industry Entrepreneur; Digital Humanities; Entrepreneurial & Small Business Finance; Industrial-Organizational Psychology; Information Technology & Network Support; Community Recreation & Park Resources; Recreation Therapy**

University of St. Francis (IN)

https://www.sf.edu/
1,572 students
Full Tuition Scholarships? Y
Performing Arts Scholarships w/o majoring in the arts? Y

What programs caught my eye? **Jesters Theatre Program (special needs/neurodiverse children's theatre); Special Education; Animation; Applied Science for Paramedics; Advanced Medical Imaging; Dance; Diagnostic Medical Sonography; Echocardiography; Medical Laboratory Technician; Music Technology; Nursing; Surgical Technology; Radiologic Technology; Graphic Design/Art**

University of St. Thomas-Texas (TX)
https://www.stthom.edu/Home/Index.aqf
2,463 students
Full Tuition Scholarships? Y
Performing Arts Scholarships w/o majoring in the arts? N
What programs caught my eye? **Diplomacy and Strategic Affairs; Catholic Studies; Applied Sport and Performance Psychology; Computational Biology; Social Innovation and Human Service**

University of the Ozarks (AR)
https://ozarks.edu/
784 students
Full Tuition Scholarships? N
Performing Arts Scholarships w/o majoring in the arts? N
What programs caught my eye? **LENS program (students pick one major and two minors); Sustainable Agriculture; Interfaith Studies; Strategic Communication**

University of Tulsa (OK)
https://utulsa.edu/
2,929 students
Full Tuition Scholarships? Y
Performing Arts Scholarships w/o majoring in the arts? Y
What programs caught my eye? **ACE: Arts, Culture, & Entertainment Management (funded London experience plus 5 internship opportunities), Film Scoring, Petroleum Engineering; High Performance Computing Science**

Ursinus College (PA)

https://www.ursinus.edu/
1,556 students
Full Tuition Scholarships? N
Performing Arts Scholarships w/o majoring in the arts? Y
What programs caught my eye? **The Philadelphia Experience Semester; African American and Africana Studies; Animal Behavior; Applied Ethics; Astrophysics; Biostatistics; Food Studies; Marine Science; Science and the Common Good; Scientific Computing; Screen Studies**

Ursuline College (OH)

https://www.ursuline.edu/
663 students
Full Tuition Scholarships? N
Performing Arts Scholarships w/o majoring in the arts? Y
What programs caught my eye? **LECOM Medical College Early Acceptance Program; Art Therapy; Fashion Design; Fashion Merchandising; Nursing; 3+3 Law Partnerships; 3+4 Pharmacy Partnerships; Women's Studies**

Utica University (NY)

https://www.utica.edu/
2,989 students
Full Tuition Scholarships? N
Performing Arts Scholarships w/o majoring in the arts? N
What programs caught my eye? **Aging Studies; Animal Behavior; Construction Management; Creativity Studies - Communication and Media; Criminal Intelligence Analysis; Dietetics and Nutrition; Fraud and Financial Crime Investigation; Geoscience; Human Rights Advocacy; Nursing; Performance and Public Address; Philosophy of Law; Therapeutic Recreation**

Valparaiso University (IN)

https://www.valpo.edu/
2,507 students
Full Tuition Scholarships? N
Performing Arts Scholarships w/o majoring in the arts? Y
What programs caught my eye? **Meteorology; Actuarial Science; Astronomy; Bioengineering; Computer Engineering; Environmental Engineering; Humanitarian Engineering; Mechatronics; Music History and Culture; Music Therapy; Urban Studies**

Vanguard University (CA)

https://www.vanguard.edu/
1,925 students
Full Tuition Scholarships? N
Performing Arts Scholarships w/o majoring in the arts? Y
What programs caught my eye? **Biotechnology; Ecology; Women and Justice; Sports Media; Theology**

Viterbo University (WI)

https://www.viterbo.edu/
1,660 students
Full Tuition Scholarships? Y
Performing Arts Scholarships w/o majoring in the arts? Y
What programs caught my eye? **Institute for Ethics in Leadership; Dietetics; American Sign Language Deaf Studies; Communication Disorders and Sciences; Ethics, Culture, and Society; Nutrition Sciences; Sport Science**

Wabash College (IN)

https://www.wabash.edu/
840 students (Men)
Full Tuition Scholarships? Y

Performing Arts Scholarships w/o majoring in the arts? N
What programs caught my eye? **Men's college; WabashX (innovate, advocate, create, transform); Accounting Pipeline to the Indiana University Kelley School of Business for Masters and CPA; Gender Studies**

Walla Walla University (WA)

https://www.wallawalla.edu/
1,419 students
Full Tuition Scholarships? N
Performing Arts Scholarships w/o majoring in the arts? N
What programs caught my eye? **Automotive Management/Service; Aviation Management/Technology; Biblical Languages; Bioengineering Science; Biophysics; Forensic Psychology; Music Production; Product Design; Portuguese; Arabic**

Walsh University (OH)

https://www.walsh.edu/
1,639 students
Full Tuition Scholarships? Y
Performing Arts Scholarships w/o majoring in the arts? Y
What programs caught my eye? **Web Design; Professional Writing; Museum Studies; Game Development; Esports and Gaming Management**

Wartburg College (IA) *Chapter TWENTY-NINE in this book*

https://www.wartburg.edu/
1,444 students
Full Tuition Scholarships? N
Performing Arts Scholarships w/o majoring in the arts? Y
What programs caught my eye? **Music Therapy; German; Social Work; Biology; Chemistry; Biochemistry; Business; Accounting; Health and Fitness Studies; Criminal Justice**

Webster University (MO) *Chapter TWENTY in this book*
https://www.webster.edu/
2,000 students
Full Tuition Scholarships? Y
Performing Arts Scholarships w/o majoring in the arts? N
What programs caught my eye? **Scriptwriting; Wig and Makeup Design; Human Rights; Music Direction for Musical Theatre (pit conductor); Technical Direction; Sound Recording and Engineering; Sound Design; Scene Design/Painting; Lighting Design; Games and Game Design; Film, Television and Video Production; Drama and Playwriting; Dance/Ballet/Modern; Costume Design; Biology Research and Technology**

Wesleyan College (GA)
https://www.wesleyancollege.edu/
695 students (Women)
Full Tuition Scholarships? Y
Performing Arts Scholarships w/o majoring in the arts? N
What programs caught my eye? **Equine-Assisted Therapy; Advertising and Marketing Communication; Arts Management; Nursing**

West Virginia Wesleyan College (WV)
https://www.wvwc.edu/
982 students
Full Tuition Scholarships? N
Performing Arts Scholarships w/o majoring in the arts? Y
What programs caught my eye? **The McCuskey Fellowship Program is a high-impact faculty-student research fellowship provided Students selected will design and conduct a research program over three years of study at Wesleyan. Biology, Biochemistry, Chemistry, Environmental Science, or Physics.; 5 year Masters Athletic Training; They also have Chemistry scholarships; Printmaking and drawing**

Westminster College (PA)

https://www.westminster.edu/
1,176 students
Full Tuition Scholarships? N
Performing Arts Scholarships w/o majoring in the arts? N
What programs caught my eye? **Creative Media Production; Molecular Biology; Neuroscience; Data Science; Entrepreneurship; Broadcasting and Sports Communications; Child and Family Studies; Marketing and Professional Sales**

Westminster College-Utah (UT)

https://westminstercollege.edu/
1,427 students
Full Tuition Scholarships? N
Performing Arts Scholarships w/o majoring in the arts? N
What programs caught my eye? **Outdoor Education and Leadership; Dance; Geology; Film Studies; Public Health**

Wheaton College (MA)

https://wheatoncollege.edu/
1,701 students
Full Tuition Scholarships? N
Performing Arts Scholarships w/o majoring in the arts? N
What programs caught my eye? **WheatGo Global [first semester freshman year study abroad]; Animal Behavior; Astronomy; Classics (Latin/Greek); Popular Culture, Media, and Literature; Medieval and Renaissance Studies; Ethnomusicology; Transnational Cultural Studies**

Wheaton College (IL)

https://www.wheaton.edu/
2,322 students
Full Tuition Scholarships? N
Performing Arts Scholarships w/o majoring in the arts? N

What programs caught my eye? **Wheaton in the Black Hills: Summer program astronomy, meteorology, biology, geology, and environmental science in South Dakota at WC Science Station; Wheaton in the Northwoods (WIN) at HoneyRock first few weeks of summer At the start of every summer, HoneyRock offers a variety of courses that meet the Christ at the Core requirements of Wheaton College.**

Wheeling University (WV)
https://wheeling.edu/
690 students
Full Tuition Scholarships? N
Performing Arts Scholarships w/o majoring in the arts? N
What programs caught my eye? **Nursing; Theology; Exercise Science; Criminal Justice**

Whittier College (CA)
https://www.whittier.edu/
1,325 students
Full Tuition Scholarships? N
Performing Arts Scholarships w/o majoring in the arts? Y
What programs caught my eye? **Scientific Computing Minor; Environmental Justice Studies Minor; French Cultural Studies; Latino Studies**

Whitworth University (WA)
https://www.whitworth.edu/cms/
2,368 students
Full Tuition Scholarships? N
Performing Arts Scholarships w/o majoring in the arts? N
What programs caught my eye? **U.S. Cultural Studies; Community-Based Theatre; Reading Instruction; Public History; Peace Studies; Human-Computer Interaction; Bioinformatics; Biophysics; Editing and Publishing; Front-End Design Development; Leadership in the Arts; TESOL**

Widener University (PA)

https://www.widener.edu/
2,766 students
Full Tuition Scholarships? N
Performing Arts Scholarships w/o majoring in the arts? Y
What programs caught my eye? **Robotics Engineering; International Engineering; Green Chemistry; Environmental Health & Sustainability Management; Nursing**

Wilkes University (PA)

https://www.wilkes.edu/
2,232 students
Full Tuition Scholarships? N
Performing Arts Scholarships w/o majoring in the arts? N
What programs caught my eye? **Accelerated BSN; Aerospace Studies; Bioengineering 4+1; Cannabis Production and CBD Extraction Certificate; Cannabis Chemistry; Earth and Environmental Science; Energy Studies; Environmental Engineering; Game and Emergent Technology; Hospitality Leadership; MBA 4+1; Policy Studies; Pre-Pharmacy Guaranteed Seat Program; Theatre Design and Technology**

William Carey University (MS)

https://www.wmcarey.edu/
3,264 students
Full Tuition Scholarships? Y
Performing Arts Scholarships w/o majoring in the arts? N
What programs caught my eye? **Dance (Christian focus); Cross Cultural Business Management; Supervisory Management; Christian Studies**

William Jessup University (CA)

https://jessup.edu/
1,289 students
Full Tuition Scholarships? Y
Performing Arts Scholarships w/o majoring in the arts? N
What programs caught my eye? **Aviation; Biblical Studies;
Nursing; Exercise Science; Leadership**

William Jewell College (MO)

https://www.jewell.edu/
909 students
Full Tuition Scholarships? Y
Performing Arts Scholarships w/o majoring in the arts? Y
What programs caught my eye? **Oxbridge Honors Program;
Applied Critical Thought and Inquiry; Artist Diploma in Voice;
Honors Institute in Critical Thinking; Nonprofit Leadership**

Wisconsin Lutheran College (WI)

https://www.wlc.edu/
992 students
Full Tuition Scholarships? N
Performing Arts Scholarships w/o majoring in the arts? Y
What programs caught my eye? **Diagnostic Medical Sonography;
Fermentation Science; Marine Biology; Nuclear Medicine
Technology; Nursing; Presentation and performance; Public
Health; Radiologic Technology; Respiratory Care; Script and
Storytelling; Theology**

Wittenberg University (OH)

https://www.wittenberg.edu/
1,286 students
Full Tuition Scholarships? N
Performing Arts Scholarships w/o majoring in the arts? Y

What programs caught my eye? **Neuroscience; Peace Corps Prep; Project Management; Marine Science; Technical Theatre; Forestry Co-op with Duke**

Wofford College (SC)
https://www.wofford.edu/
1765 students
Full Tuition Scholarships? N
Performing Arts Scholarships w/o majoring in the arts? N
What programs caught my eye? **Energy Studies; Middle Eastern and North African Studies; Medicine and the Liberal Arts; Arabic Studies; Music Non-Performance; Francophone Studies; Middle Eastern and North African Studies; Computational Science**

Xavier University of Louisiana (LA)
https://www.xula.edu/
2,755 students
Full Tuition Scholarships? Y
Performing Arts Scholarships w/o majoring in the arts? N
What programs caught my eye? **HBCU; The Center for Equity, Justice, and the Human Spirit; Health, Medicine, and Society; Chemistry Accelerated 3+1; Speech Pathology; African American and Diaspora Studies; Sales and Marketing**

York College of Pennsylvania (PA)
https://www.ycp.edu/
3,527 students
Full Tuition Scholarships? Y
Performing Arts Scholarships w/o majoring in the arts? N
What programs caught my eye? **Nursing; Cannabinoid Chemistry; Creative Industries and Entrepreneurship; Criminalistics; Critical Thinking and Theory; Environmental Horticulture; Esports Management; Forensic Chemistry; Hospitality**

Management/Marketing; Intelligence Analysis: Regional and Global Studies; Retailing; Spanish Business

Geographic List of the 333 Colleges

Alabama
Birmingham-Southern
Spring Hill College
University of Mobile

Arkansas
Hendrix College
John Brown University
Lyon College
Ouachita Baptist University
University of the Ozarks

California
Fresno Pacific University
La Sierra University
Menlo College
SOKA University of America
The Master's University
Thomas Aquinas College
University of La Verne
Vanguard U of Southern California
Whittier College
William Jessup University

Colorado
Regis University

Connecticut
Albertus Magnus College
University of Saint Joseph

District of Columbia
Gallaudet University
Trinity Washington University

Florida
Ave Maria University
Flagler College
Florida College
Florida Southern College

Jacksonville University
Palm Beach Atlantic University
Stetson University

Georgia
Agnes Scott College
Berry College
Brenau University
Covenant College
Oglethorpe University
Piedmont University
Thomas University
Wesleyan College

Hawaii
Brigham Young Hawaii
Chaminade University Honolulu

Idaho
Northwest Nazarene University
The College of Idaho

Illinois
Augustana College
Blackburn College
Concordia University-Chicago
Dominican University
Elmhurst University
Eureka College
Illinois College
Illinois Institute of Technology
Knox College
Lake Forest College
Lewis University
McKendree University
Millikin University
Monmouth College
Moody Bible Institute
North Central College
North Park University
Principia College
Quincy University
St. Xavier University
Trinity Christian College
University of St. Francis
Wheaton College

Indiana

DePauw University
Earlham College
Franklin College
Goshen College
Hanover College
Indiana Tech
Indiana Wesleyan University
Manchester University
Marian University
Saint Mary's College
Taylor University
Trine University
University of Evansville
University of St. Francis
Valparaiso University
Wabash College

Iowa

Buena Vista University
Central College
Clarke University
Coe College
Cornell College
Dordt University
Drake University
Graceland University
Loras College
Luther College
Morningside University
Mount Mercy University
Northwestern College
Saint Ambrose University
Simpson College
Wartburg College

Kansas

Baker University
Friends University
Kansas Wesleyan University
Newman University
University of Saint Mary

Kentucky

Bellarmine University

Berea College
Brescia University
Centre College
Georgetown College
Midway University
Spalding University
Thomas More University
Transylvania University

Louisiana
Centenary College of Louisiana
Loyola University New Orleans
University of Holy Cross
Xavier University of Louisiana

Maine
College of the Atlantic
Husson University

Maryland
Goucher College
McDaniel College
Mount St. Mary's University
St. John's College

Massachuetts
Bay Path University
Elms College
Lasell University
Springfield College
Wheaton College

Michigan
Albion College
Alma College
Andrews University
Aquinas College
Calvin University
Cleary University
Concordia University-Ann Arbor
Hope College
Kalamazoo College
Lawrence Tech University
Madonna University
Northwood University
Spring Arbor University

University of Detroit Mercy

Minnesota
Augsburg University
Bethany Lutheran College
College of St. Benedict
Concordia College-Moorhead
Concordia University-St. Paul
Dunwoody College of Technology
Gustavus Adolphus College
Hamline University
Martin Luther College
Mnpls College of Art & Design
Saint Catherine University
Saint Mary's University of Minnesota
St. John's University
The College of St. Scholastica

Mississippi
Belhaven University
Millsaps College
Mississippi College
William Carey University

Missouri
Avila University
College of the Ozarks
Cottey College
Culver-Stockton College
Drury University
Fontbonne University
Maryville University
Rockhurst University
Stephens College
U of Health Sci and Pharmacy
Webster University
William Jewell College

Montana
Carroll College
Rocky Mountain College
University of Providence

Nebraska
Clarkson College
College of Saint Mary

Concordia University -Nebraska
Doane University
Hastings College
Midland University
Nebraska Methodist College of
Nebraska Wesleyan University
Union College Nebraska

New Mexico
St. John's College

New York
Alfred University
Canisius College
Daemen University
D'Youville University
Houghton College
Iona University
Le Moyne College
Manhattan College
Nazareth College
New York Institute of Technology
Niagara University
Paul Smith's College
Siena College
St. Bonaventure University
St. John Fisher
The Cooper Union
The Culinary Institute of America
Utica University

North Carolina
Campbell University
Catawba College
Guilford College
Lees-McRae College
Mars Hill University
Meredith College
Queens University of Charlotte
Salem College

North Dakota
University of Mary

Ohio
Antioch College

Baldwin Wallace University
Capital University
College of Wooster
Franciscan U of Steubenville
Franklin University
Heidelberg University
Hiram College
John Carroll University
Marietta College
Mount Saint Joseph University
Muskingum University
Ohio Dominican University
Ohio Northern University
Ohio Wesleyan University
Otterbein University
University of Mount Union
Ursuline College
Walsh University
Wittenberg University

Oklahoma
Mid-America Christian Universi
Mid-America Christian University
Oklahoma Baptist University
Oklahoma City University
University of Tulsa

Oregon
Linfield University

Pennsylvania
Allegheny College
Cedar Crest College
Chatham University
DeSales University
Elizabethtown College
Gannon University
Gwynedd Mercy University
Holy Family University
Juniata College
King's College - Pennsylvania
La Salle University
Lebanon Valley College
Lycoming College
Marywood University
Mercyhurst University

Messiah University
Misericordia University
Moravian University
Muhlenberg College
Robert Morris U- Pennsylvania
Saint Francis University
Saint Vincent College
Seton Hill University
Susquehanna University
Ursinus College
Westminster College
Widener University
Wilkes University
York College of Pennsylvania

South Carolina
Bob Jones University
Charleston Southern University
Claflin College
Columbia International University
North Greenville University
Presbyterian College
Southern Wesleyan University
Wofford College

South Dakota
Augustana University
Dakota Wesleyan University
University of Sioux Falls

Tennessee
Christian Brothers University
Cumberland University
Fisk University
Johnson University
King University - Tennessee
Lipscomb University
Maryville College
Milligan University
Rhodes College
Southern Adventist University
Tennessee Wesleyan University
Trevecca Nazarene University
Union University

Texas

Austin College
LeTourneau University
Lubbock Christian University
McMurry University
Southwestern Adventist Univers
Southwestern University
St. Mary's University
Texas Lutheran University
Texas Wesleyan University
University of Dallas
University of St. Thomas-Texas

Utah
Westminster College - Utah

Vermont
Norwich Military University
St. Michael's College

Virginia
Eastern Mennonite University
Emory and Henry College
Hollins University
Randolph-Macon College
Roanoke College
Shenandoah University
Sweet Briar College
University of Lynchburg

Washington
Northwest University
Pacific Lutheran University
Saint Martin's University
Walla Walla University
Whitworth University

West Virginia
Davis and Elkins College
University of Charleston
West Virginia Wesleyan College
Wheeling University

Wisconsin
Alverno College
Beloit College

Carroll University
Carthage College
Concordia University-Wisconsin
Edgewood College
Lawrence University
Marian University
Milw Institute of Art & Design
Milwaukee School of Engineering
Mount Mary University
Northland College
Ripon College
Saint Norbert College
Viterbo University
Wisconsin Lutheran College

Colleges That Offer Full Tuition Scholarships*

*This list came from research of college websites during 2022 and 2023. I cannot guarantee 100% accuracy because colleges do change their financial aid and scholarship policies from time to time. In most cases, a small number of full tuition scholarships are awarded based on a combination of academic record, essays, and interviews. This will vary from college to college. The scholarships are usually full tuition (not full ride), but a few do include room and board.

Alabama
Birmingham-Southern College

Arkansas
Hendrix College
Lyon College

California
Fresno Pacific University
Menlo College
William Jessup University

Colorado
Regis University

Florida
Florida Southern College
Stetson University

Georgia
Agnes Scott College
Brenau University
Oglethorpe University
Wesleyan College

Illinois
Concordia University-Chicago
Eureka College
Illinois College
Illinois Institute of Technology
Lewis University
Millikin University

Monmouth College
Quincy University
Trinity Christian College

Indiana
Franklin College
Indiana Tech
Manchester University
Marian University
Trine University
University of Evansville
University of St. Francis
Wabash College

Iowa
Central College
Coe College
Graceland University
Mount Mercy University
Saint Ambrose University
Simpson College

Kansas
Baker University
Kansas Wesleyan University
Newman University
University of Saint Mary

Kentucky
Bellarmine University
Centre College
Georgetown College
Midway University
Thomas More University
Transylvania University

Louisiana
Centenary College of Louisiana
Loyola University New Orleans
Xavier University of Louisiana

Maryland
McDaniel College
Mount St. Mary's University
St. John's College

Massachusetts
Bay Path University

Michigan
Alma College
Aquinas College
Lawrence Tech University

Minnesota
Concordia College-Moorhead
Saint Catherine University

Mississippi
Mississippi College
William Carey University

Missouri
Cottey College
Culver-Stockton College
Drury University
Fontbonne University
Maryville University
Rockhurst University
Stephens College
Webster University
William Jewell College

Montana
University of Providence

Nebraska
Doane University
Hastings College
Nebraska Wesleyan University

New Mexico
St. John's College

New York
Daemen University
Houghton University

North Carolina
Catawba College
Lees-McRae College
Mars Hill University

Meredith College
Salem College

Ohio
Capital University
Marietta College
Mount Saint Joseph University
Muskingum University
Ohio Dominican University
Ohio Northern University
Ohio Wesleyan University
Otterbein University
University of Mount Union
Walsh University

Oklahoma
Mid-America Christian University
Oklahoma Baptist University
University of Tulsa

Pennsylvania
Cedar Crest College
Chatham University
DeSales University
Elizabethtown College
Gannon University
Gwynedd Mercy University
King's College - Pennsylvania
Lebanon Valley College
Messiah University
Misericordia University
Robert Morris U- Pennsylvania
Saint Vincent College
York College of Pennsylvania

South Carolina
North Greenville University
Presbyterian College

Tennessee
Christian Brothers University
Cumberland University
Fisk University
Lipscomb University
Maryville College
Milligan University

Southern Adventist University
Tennessee Wesleyan University
Trevecca Nazarene University

Texas
McMurry University
Southwestern Adventist University
St. Mary's University
University of St. Thomas-Texas

Virginia
Eastern Mennonite University
Hollins University
Sweet Briar College

Vermont
St. Michael's College

Washington
Northwest University
Pacific Lutheran University

Wisconsin
Alverno College
Carroll University
Carthage College
Marian University
Milwaukee Institute of Art & Design
Milwaukee School of Engineering
Mount Mary University
Viterbo University

West Virginia
University of Charleston

Colleges that Offer Some Performing Arts Scholarships* Without Having to Major or Minor in the Arts

*This list came from research of college websites during 2022 and 2023. I cannot guarantee 100% accuracy because colleges do change their financial aid and scholarship policies from time to time. Plus, the wording about eligibility in the websites can, at times, be nebulous. In most cases, these performing arts scholarships are "participation" awards. In other words the students needs to be active in the arts (e.g. choir, band, theatre, dance, art), but they do not necessarily have to major or minor in the arts. Most of these are music and/or theatre scholarships. Very few are dance or art. Some even include creative writing or other arts. Check with the colleges directly to see which areas are available to you. Most all colleges that offer programs in the Arts offer scholarships to majors and minors in their area too.

Alabama
Birmingham-Southern

Arkansas
Hendrix College
Lyon College
Ouachita Baptist University

California
Fresno Pacific University
Vanguard University
Whittier College

Connecticut
Albertus Magnus College

Florida
Florida Southern College
Stetson University

Georgia
Berry College
Oglethorpe University

Idaho
Northwest Nazarene University
The College of Idaho

Illinois
Augustana College
Concordia University-Chicago
Illinois College
Knox College
Lake Forest College
Lewis University
McKendree University
Millikin University
Monmouth College
North Central College
North Park University
Quincy University

Indiana
DePauw University
Earlham College
Franklin College
Goshen College
Hanover College
Manchester University
Marian University
Trine University
University of Evansville
University of St. Francis
Valparaiso University

Iowa
Buena Vista University
Central College
Clarke University
Coe College
Cornell College
Drake University
Graceland University
Loras College
Luther College
Morningside University
Mount Mercy University
Northwestern College
Saint Ambrose University
Simpson College

Wartburg College

Kansas
Baker University
Friends University
Kansas Wesleyan University
Newman University
University of Saint Mary

Kentucky
Bellarmine University
Brescia University
Centre College
Georgetown College
Midway University
Thomas More University
Transylvania University

Louisiana
Centenary College of Louisiana
Loyola University New Orleans

Michigan
Albion College
Alma College
Aquinas College
Concordia University-Ann Arbor
Hope College
Kalamazoo College
Madonna University
Spring Arbor University

Minnesota
College of St. Benedict
Concordia College-Moorhead
Concordia University-St. Paul
Gustavus Adolphus College
Hamline University
Saint Mary's University-Minnesota
St. John's University
The College of St. Scholastica

Mississippi
Millsaps College
Mississippi College

Missouri

Avila University
Cottey College
Culver-Stockton College
Drury University
Maryville University
Rockhurst University
William Jewell College

Montana

Carroll College
Rocky Mountain College

Nebraska

Concordia University-Nebraska
Doane University
Hastings College
Midland University
Nebraska Wesleyan University

New York

Canisius College
Daemen University
Manhattan College
Nazareth University
St. Bonaventure University

North Carolina

Catawba College
Mars Hill University

North Dakota

University of Mary

Ohio

College of Wooster
Heidelberg University
Marietta College
Mount Saint Joseph University
Muskingum University
Ohio Dominican University
Ohio Northern University
Otterbein University
University of Mount Union
Ursuline College
Walsh University

Wittenberg University

Oklahoma
Oklahoma Baptist University
University of Tulsa

Oregon
Linfield University

Pennsylvania
Allegheny College
Cedar Crest College
DeSales University
Elizabethtown College
Gannon University
Juniata College
Lycoming College
Mercyhurst University
Muhlenberg College
Saint Vincent College
Susquehanna University
Ursinus College
Widener University

South Carolina
Charleston Southern University
Presbyterian College
Southern Wesleyan University

South Dakota
Augustana University
Dakota Wesleyan University

Tennessee
King University-Tennessee
Lipscomb University
Maryville College
Rhodes College
Southern Adventist University
Tennessee Wesleyan University
Trevecca Nazarene University

Texas
Austin College
McMurry University
Southwestern Adventist University

Southwestern University
St. Mary's University
Texas Lutheran University
Texas Wesleyan University

Virginia
Emory and Henry College
Hollins University
Randolph-Macon College
Roanoke College
Shenandoah University
Sweet Briar College
University of Lynchburg

Vermont
St. Michael's College

Washington
Northwest University
Pacific Lutheran University

Wisconsin
Beloit College
Carroll University
Carthage College
Concordia University-Wisconsin
Edgewood College
Lawrence University
Ripon College
Saint Norbert College
Viterbo University
Wisconsin Lutheran College

West Virginia
Davis and Elkins College
University of Charleston
West Virginia Wesleyan College

ABOUT THE AUTHOR

V. Peter Pitts retired in 2019 from a 42 year career in college admission. Over those years, Peter had the pleasure of working with over 2,000 families as they navigated the admission and financial aid process. At various times during those 42 years Peter held these titles: Admission Counselor, Assistant Director of Admission, Director of Admission, Assistant Vice President of Admission and Financial Aid, and (for the last 27 years of his career) Regional Director of Admission for Monmouth College of Illinois (Chicago territory). Upon his retirement, Peter published his first book, *After Breakfast I Change Lives* (Amazon), which is a mix of heartwarming and humorous stories about the students he met throughout his career. His second book, *Common Sense Guide to Choosing a College: Making a Case for Small Residential Colleges* (Amazon) is a collection of essays he has written to help guide students and their parents through the college admission process. Peter actively posts articles on LinkedIn, Twitter, and on his two websites U3K4College.com and LifeChangingColleges.com. He also, on a part-time basis, does a little independent counseling with families. Peter is originally from Clinton Iowa. He has degrees from Mount Saint Clare College (IA), Wartburg College (IA), and the University of Iowa. Peter and his wife Pat live in Aurora, IL.

OTHER BOOKS BY V. PETER PITTS
(both available on Amazon)

https://www.amazon.com/After-Breakfast-I-Change-Lives-ebook/dp/B08FRPWZ3V

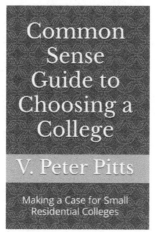

https://www.amazon.com/dp/B09T3BWFRL?ref_=pe_3052080_397514860

Made in the USA
Las Vegas, NV
04 December 2023

82058645R00216